# Effectiveness of Influencer Marketing

Jane Johne

# Effectiveness of Influencer Marketing

Jane Johne
Münster, Germany

The present work was accepted as a dissertation by the Faculty of Economics of the Westphalian Wilhelms University of Münster in the summer semester of 2022.

ISBN 978-3-658-41296-8     ISBN 978-3-658-41297-5  (eBook)
https://doi.org/10.1007/978-3-658-41297-5

© The Editor(s) (if applicable) and The Author(s), under exclusive license to Springer Fachmedien Wiesbaden GmbH, part of Springer Nature 2023
This work is subject to copyright. All rights are solely and exclusively licensed by the Publisher, whether the whole or part of the material is concerned, specifically the rights of translation, reprinting, reuse of illustrations, recitation, broadcasting, reproduction on microfilms or in any other physical way, and transmission or information storage and retrieval, electronic adaptation, computer software, or by similar or dissimilar methodology now known or hereafter developed.
The use of general descriptive names, registered names, trademarks, service marks, etc. in this publication does not imply, even in the absence of a specific statement, that such names are exempt from the relevant protective laws and regulations and therefore free for general use.
The publisher, the authors, and the editors are safe to assume that the advice and information in this book are believed to be true and accurate at the date of publication. Neither the publisher nor the authors or the editors give a warranty, expressed or implied, with respect to the material contained herein or for any errors or omissions that may have been made. The publisher remains neutral with regard to jurisdictional claims in published maps and institutional affiliations.

Planung/Lektorat: Marija Kojic
This Springer Gabler imprint is published by the registered company Springer Fachmedien Wiesbaden GmbH, part of Springer Nature.
The registered company address is: Abraham-Lincoln-Str. 46, 65189 Wiesbaden, Germany

# Foreword

Influencer marketing has become an integral part of brands' marketing strategies. Now that the first hype slowed down, it is time to examine how effective influencer marketing should be designed and how effective influencer marketing is compared to other communication measures. In her work, Jane Johne looks at precisely these questions.

To answer the questions, Jane Johne conducts two empirical studies that consider different phases of the influencer marketing management process. Jane Johne introduces the empirical studies with a systematic literature review that highlights research gaps.

In her first empirical project, Jane Johne deals with the selection of suitable influencers for a marketing campaign. She explicitly investigates the question of which influencer characteristics should be considered in the selection process in order to improve different campaign metrics along the consumer decision journey. The variables under investigation map both the personal and structural potential of an influencer. Jane Johne uses campaign data from several brands for the project and extends this data with data from a large-scale consumer survey. Jane Johne shows that influencer characteristics vary in their impact on different metrics. In general, consumer awareness, purchase interest, and engagement are increased by a high number of unique followers an influencer has. If multiple influencers are promoting the brand and the campaign aims at selling products, an overlap of followers has a positive effect on purchase interest because consumers are targeted multiple times. An overlap of followers, on the other hand, has a negative impact on consumers' attention and engagement. The expertise and fit of the influencer play a significant role in campaign success, especially at the beginning of the consumer decision journey, whereas the content itself appears more relevant for increasing purchase interest. In general, influencers with highly engaged followers can also transfer this engagement into campaigns.

In her second empirical project, Jane Johne is concerned with measuring the success of influencer marketing. She explicitly examines how influencer marketing compares with other firm and consumer activities to improve firm performance. For the project, Jane Johne uses data from one of Europe's largest specialized online retailers and analyzes it in a time series model. Jane Johne shows that influencer marketing has a substantial impact on website visits, number of orders and sales. Likewise, her findings show that other digital channels also have great effectiveness in increasing consumer engagement and firm performance. In addition, she illustrates that synergy effects of influencer marketing with other communication measures exist.

Jane Johne thus has written a thesis that makes a significant contribution to a better understanding of the effectiveness of influencer marketing. We are very pleased that this work is now being published.

In addition to shortly review Jane's dissertation, we would like to take this opportunity to thank Jane for her work at the Institute for Value-Based Marketing (IWM) at the Marketing Center Münster (MCM) at the University of Münster. Jane is the sixth doctoral student who we have both supervised. Jane, like the doctoral students before her, has helped shaping the culture of the IWM. The continued success of the IWM would not have been possible without Jane's footprint. As with all doctoral students, her time with us had its ups and downs, and we all learned a lot during that time. Jane's time at the IWM was also special as she was the first doctoral student to have a baby during the doctoral studies.

In recent years, we have developed an imagery that we would like to pass on to our doctoral students and graduates alike: Roots—in the sense of excellent academic and marketing education. Wings—in the sense of free and critical thinking in an environment that allows making mistakes and where one's own creative ideas are more than welcome.

Jane, we thank you very much for supporting us. We wish you all the best for your future.

Münster                                                                  Prof. Dr. Thorsten Wiesel
January 2023                                    apl. Prof. Dr. Sonja Gensler

# Acknowledgements

The following dissertation was developed during my time as research assistant at the Chair for Value-Based Marketing at the University of Münster. My colleagues, friends, and family all contributed to the successful completion of my dissertation and deserve a special thank you.

First of all, I would like to thank my two supervisors Prof. Dr. Sonja Gensler and Prof. Dr. Thorsten Wiesel, who continuously challenged me and pushed my development. Moreover, I am very thankful to Prof. Dr. Kristina Klein, who served as external adviser and second assessor.

My former colleagues at the institute all deserve gratitude, as they created an atmosphere that helped me gaining the needed motivation, inspiration, and support. Concerning research-specific challenges, I am grateful for valuable discussions, especially with Sophie Jansen, Christopher Stein, Lisa Richter, Karlo Oehring and Fabian Kraut. Besides the hard work, I also enjoyed the many private events that took place, to which Simon Monske, Charlotte Hufnagel, Sascha Leweling, Maris Hartmanis, Timo Dümke, Mert Onay, Petra Kestermann, Birte Geue, Gabriele Rüter, and the supporting student assistants all contributed at their best.

To master this great challenge, the support of my longtime friends Susi and Laura was especially important. Thank you for always being there for me and believing in me. You bring lightness into dark times.

However, I save my most sincere thanks for my family. Thank you for supporting me at every stage of my life and comforting me in times of doubt. Especially the love and strength of my mother, grandmother and aunt have given me the confidence and courage to overcome any challenge I face and not give up. Most of all, Andy, you have been my home base. You picked me up, built me up, and had my back. Together with Helena, you give me the energy to accomplish anything I want. Thank you for enriching my life so much.

# Contents

| | | | |
|---|---|---|---|
| **1** | **Introduction** | | 1 |
| | 1.1 Definition of Influencer Marketing | | 1 |
| | 1.2 Relevance and Management of Influencer Marketing | | 4 |
| | 1.3 Aim of Thesis | | 9 |
| | 1.4 Structure of Thesis | | 16 |
| **2** | **Literature Review** | | 19 |
| | 2.1 Literature Search Process | | 19 |
| | 2.2 Literature Review on Identification of Influencers | | 22 |
| | | 2.2.1 Social Media Advertising and Celebrity Endorsement Literature | 25 |
| | | 2.2.2 Viral Marketing Literature | 31 |
| | 2.3 Literature Review on Design of Content | | 46 |
| | | 2.3.1 Textual Elements driving Virality of Social Media Posts | 49 |
| | |     2.3.1.1 Motivational Drivers of Post Virality | 49 |
| | |     2.3.1.2 Linguistic Style | 60 |
| | |     2.3.1.3 Social Media specific Elements | 64 |
| | |     2.3.1.4 Control Variables | 69 |
| | | 2.3.2 Pictorial Elements driving Virality of Social Media Posts | 75 |
| | |     2.3.2.1 Motivational Drivers of Post Virality | 75 |
| | |     2.3.2.2 Social Media specific Elements | 79 |
| | |     2.3.2.3 Figurative Style | 80 |
| | |     2.3.2.4 Design-relevant Control Variables | 81 |
| | 2.4 Literature Review on Performance Measurement | | 83 |

|  |  | 2.4.1 | Comparing Advertising and User-generated Content | 88 |
|---|---|---|---|---|
|  |  | 2.4.2 | Comparing User-generated Content and Firm-generated Content | 95 |
|  |  | 2.4.3 | Comparing Advertising and Firm-generated Content | 96 |
|  |  | 2.4.4 | Comparing Advertising, User-generated Content and Firm-generated Content | 97 |
|  | 2.5 | Summary and Research Gaps | | 104 |
| 3 | **Predicting the Influencer Value** | | | 109 |
|  | 3.1 | Improving Influencer Selection through a Holistic Approach | | 109 |
|  | 3.2 | Positioning Study 1 within Literature | | 113 |
|  | 3.3 | Conceptual Framework and Hypotheses | | 123 |
|  |  | 3.3.1 | Impact of Personal Potential on the Consumer Decision Journey | 127 |
|  |  | 3.3.2 | Impact of Network Potential on the Consumer Decision Journey | 128 |
|  | 3.4 | Study Design | | 132 |
|  |  | 3.4.1 | Data Set | 132 |
|  |  | 3.4.2 | Operationalization of Variables | 133 |
|  |  | 3.4.2.1 Measuring Personal Potential | | 136 |
|  |  | 3.4.2.2 Measuring Network Potential | | 148 |
|  |  | 3.4.3 | Methodology | 149 |
|  | 3.5 | Results of Study 1 | | 151 |
|  |  | 3.5.1 | Awareness Phase | 152 |
|  |  | 3.5.2 | Purchase Phase | 154 |
|  |  | 3.5.3 | Engagement Phase | 156 |
|  |  | 3.5.4 | Managerial Implications of Study 1 | 158 |
|  |  | 3.5.5 | Limitations of Study 1 and Future Research | 160 |
| 4 | **Investigating the Effectiveness of Influencer Marketing** | | | 163 |
|  | 4.1 | Examine the relative Effectiveness of Influencer Marketing, Advertising, Firm-generated Messages and Consumer-generated Messages on Website Visits, Orders and Revenue | | 163 |
|  | 4.2 | Positioning Study 2 within Literature | | 166 |
|  | 4.3 | Study Design | | 169 |
|  |  | 4.3.1 | Data Set | 170 |
|  |  | 4.3.2 | Operationalization of Variables | 170 |
|  |  | 4.3.3 | Methodology | 178 |
|  | 4.4 | Results of Study 2 | | 186 |

|  |  |  |  |
|---|---|---|---|
|  | 4.4.1 | Relative Effectiveness of Channels | 186 |
|  | 4.4.2 | Interrelationships among Marketing Activities and Social Media Messages | 191 |
|  | 4.4.3 | Performance Metrics and Feedback Effects | 196 |
|  | 4.4.4 | Effects of Control Variables | 196 |
|  | 4.4.5 | Comparison with SUR Model | 205 |
|  | 4.4.6 | Managerial Implications of Study 2 | 210 |
|  | 4.4.7 | Limitations of Study 2 and Future Research | 214 |

**5 General Discussion** ............................................. 217
    5.1  Summary of Studies and Theoretical Contribution ............ 217
    5.2  Summary of Managerial Implications ....................... 220
    5.3  Outlook to the Future ................................... 223

**References** ....................................................... 227

# Abbreviations

| | |
|---|---|
| AIC | Akaike information criterion |
| al. | Aliter |
| API | application programming interface |
| b | Beta value (regression coefficient) |
| e.g. | exempli gratia (latin), for example |
| ELM | Elaboration Likelihood Model |
| eWOM | electronic word-of-mouth |
| FPE | final prediction error |
| GDPR | General Data Protection Regulation |
| HQ | Hannan-Quinn information criterion |
| i.e. | id est (latin), that is |
| KMO | Kaiser-Meyer Olkin |
| LIWC | Linguistic Inquiry and Word Count |
| LM | Lagrange Multiplier |
| LRE | Edgeworth expansion corrected likelihood ratio |
| MSA | measure of sampling adequacy |
| MVSO | Multilingual Visual Sentiment Ontology |
| OLS | ordinary least squares |
| p | P-value |
| PP | Phillip-Perron |
| SC | Schwarz information criterion |
| SEM | search engine marketing |
| SEO | search engine optimization |
| SG & A | selling, general and administrative |

| | |
|---|---|
| SUR | seemingly unrelated regression |
| TV | television |
| VAR | vector autoregression |
| VARX | vector autoregression with exogenous variables |
| WOM | word-of-mouth |

# List of Figures

| | | |
|---|---|---|
| Figure 1.1 | Central Steps of Influencer Marketing Management | 5 |
| Figure 1.2 | Structure of the Thesis | 17 |
| Figure 2.1 | Egocentric Network | 35 |
| Figure 3.1 | Impact of Message Source Characteristics on Consumer Behavior Metrics – Results of existing Studies | 118 |
| Figure 3.2 | Conceptual Framework of Study 1 | 125 |
| Figure 3.3 | Guideline of Expert Interviews | 138 |
| Figure 4.1 | Valence of Comments on Company's Instagram Profile over time | 176 |
| Figure 4.2 | Valence of Company Reviews over time | 177 |
| Figure 4.3 | Full Dynamic System of the VARX Model | 185 |
| Figure 4.4 | TV Investments over time | 192 |
| Figure 4.5 | Seasonality of Investments in SEM, Pricing and Shopping Websites, Display and Affiliate Marketing | 193 |
| Figure 4.6 | TV and Influencer Marketing Investments over time | 194 |

# List of Tables

| | | |
|---|---|---|
| Table 1.1 | Research Gaps | 9 |
| Table 2.1 | Search Protocol of Literature Review | 20 |
| Table 2.2 | Studies focusing on Source Characteristics of Influential Posts | 24 |
| Table 2.3 | Content Elements of Viral Social Media Posts | 48 |
| Table 2.4 | Effect of Post Interactivity on Post Virality | 67 |
| Table 2.5 | Studies considering more than one Type of Message | 85 |
| Table 3.1 | Studies considering the Effectiveness of Message Source Characteristics on Consumer Behavior Metrics | 116 |
| Table 3.2 | Impact of Activity of Sender and Followers on Network Structure of Sender – Results of existing Studies | 122 |
| Table 3.3 | Variable Operationalizations of Study 1 | 134 |
| Table 3.4 | Descriptive Statistics of the Variables of Study 1 | 136 |
| Table 3.5 | Overview of the Experts interviewed | 139 |
| Table 3.6 | Demographics and Social Media Usage of Sample | 140 |
| Table 3.7 | Items of Influencer Brand Fit, Influencer Image Fit and Influencer Product Category Fit | 142 |
| Table 3.8 | Data Suitability for Factor Analysis | 143 |
| Table 3.9 | Rotated Component Matrix for fixed 2-Factor Solution | 144 |
| Table 3.10 | Cronbach's Alpha of Influencer Image Fit and Influencer Product Category Fit | 145 |
| Table 3.11 | Regression Results of Factor Solution on Influencer Brand Fit | 147 |
| Table 3.12 | Regression Results of Summated Scales on Influencer Brand Fit | 147 |

| | | |
|---|---|---|
| Table 3.13 | Regression Results for Consumer Behavior Metrics along the Consumer Decision Journey | 153 |
| Table 3.14 | Summary of Results | 154 |
| Table 4.1 | Studies considering the Effects of more than one Type of Message on Consumer Behavior Metrics | 167 |
| Table 4.2 | Variable Operationalizations of Study 2 | 171 |
| Table 4.3 | Descriptive Statistics of Relevant Variables of Study 2 | 174 |
| Table 4.4 | Unit Root Test Results (PP Test) | 179 |
| Table 4.5 | Results of Granger Causality Tests | 180 |
| Table 4.6 | Lag Length Criteria | 182 |
| Table 4.7 | Results of LM-test | 183 |
| Table 4.8 | Cumulative Elasticities | 188 |
| Table 4.9 | Parameter Estimates of the VARX Model | 197 |
| Table 4.10 | SUR Model Estimates (Restricted Model with Lagged Effects) | 206 |
| Table 4.11 | Comparison of Model Fit between VARX and SUR Model | 210 |

# Introduction 1

The introduction of this thesis defines the terms influencer and influencer marketing. Further, the chapter outlines the relevance of influencer marketing for both research and practice. Subsequently, the aim of this thesis is derived and the contribution to research as well as practice is discussed. The chapter closes with the description of the structure of the thesis.

## 1.1 Definition of Influencer Marketing

Every second social media user who follows influencers has already followed the purchase recommendation of an influencer (Horizont 2019). **Influencers** are defined as opinion leaders in social media networks (Breves et al. 2019; Casaló, Flavián, and Ibáñez-Sánchez 2018; De Veirman, Cauberghe, and Hudders 2017) that "represent a new type of independent third party endorser who shape audience attitudes through blogs, tweets, and the use of other social media (Freberg et al. 2011)". Further, opinion leaders are individuals who hold an unequal amount of influence over the decisions of other people (Rogers and Cartano 1962).

The influence of social media influencers over potential buyers manifests through a large network of so-called followers (De Veirman, Cauberghe, and Hudders 2017). Followers are social media users who voluntarily choose to consume the social media influencer's content in order to interact with the influencer and his[1] content (Hughes, Swaminathan, and Brooks 2019). In viral marketing literature a user with a large network is characterized though a network size larger

---

[1] Here and in the following, the masculine form of influencer or social media user is used, although both genders are addressed equally.

© The Author(s), under exclusive license to Springer Fachmedien Wiesbaden GmbH, part of Springer Nature 2023
J. Johne, *Effectiveness of Influencer Marketing*,
https://doi.org/10.1007/978-3-658-41297-5_1

than three standard deviations above the mean (Goldenberg et al. 2009). However, there is no general consensus in research what network size an influencer must have to be perceived as influencer.

Influencers gain their popularity through creating content in one or several niches. They position themselves as experts and trusted sources of inspiration and recommendation (De Veirman, Cauberghe, and Hudders 2017). This central role as content creator differentiates social media influencers from traditional endorsers. These brand ambassadors, testimonials or celebrities gained popularity through their profession in the offline world and thus are paid to advertise products or services (Djafarova and Rushworth 2017). Consumers evaluate the recommendations from influencers more authentic and credible than from regular endorsers because they perceive influencers more similar to oneself and trustworthy (Gräve 2017).

Moreover, influencers incorporate private information within their content and foster an active dialog with their community. This makes the followers feel like they know the influencer like a good friend (Djafarova and Rushworth 2017). This kind of two-sided social interaction gives the follower the illusion of having a "real" relationship with the influencer and is called para-social relationship (Rubin and McHugh 1987). Therefore, the communication between influencer and his followers is characterized through a high level of intimacy and engagement which makes influencers more persuasive than traditional endorsers (Djafarova and Rushworth 2017).

**Engagement** describes an emotional connection. In this case, the emotional connection with the influencer. This emotional connection is the reason why followers interact with the influencer's content and communicate this to the outside world (Batra and Keller 2016). For this reason, non-transactional consumer behavior such as likes, comments and shares are also referred to as **engagement behavior** (Beckers, van Doorn, and Verhoef 2018; Hughes, Swaminathan, and Brooks 2019; Karagür et al. 2021; van Doorn et al. 2010). Brands can take advantage of the high engagement with influencer content and transfer that engagement to themselves through influencer collaborations.

**Influencer marketing** is a popular form of social media advertising that comprises the identification and cooperation with opinion leaders that hold influence over a potential target group in social media networks (Evans et al. 2017). Brands strategically leverage the unique resources of influencers to promote their products and services and increase brand performance (Leung, Gu, and Palmatier 2022). Brands recruit influencers to incorporate product recommendations within their feed. These sponsored posts are woven into the daily narratives of the influencer and are hardly to recognize as different from the other posts on the

## 1.1 Definition of Influencer Marketing

influencer's feed. Therefore, influencer marketing can be classified as native advertising. Native advertising is the creation of paid advertisement that looks like and is integrated within editorial content (Evans et al. 2017). Thus, brands indirectly promote products by utilizing the power of electronic word-of-mouth (eWOM).

Following the definition of Hennig-Thurau et al. (2004), eWOM is defined as "any positive or negative statement made by potential, actual, or former customers about a product or company, which is made available to a multitude of people and institutions via the Internet". Thus, eWOM can be classified as user-generated content, which is an overarching concept that covers any user-generated content on social media without necessarily referring to a product or company (Smith, Fischer, and Yongjian 2012). Both eWOM and user-generated content are also referred to as earned social media in the literature (Stephen and Galak 2012).

Compared to organically generated eWOM, influencers are not only motivated to share their experiences about products and brands for nonmonetary reasons. They are compensated (with either cash or free products) to generate posts on social media (Hughes, Swaminathan, and Brooks 2019). Therefore, influencers are legally bound to label sponsored posts (e.g., using "#sponsored" or "#ad"). However, even though it is known that a majority of posts is sponsored, consumers widely use this source of inspiration and seek influencers' recommendations (Boerman, Willemsen, and van der Aa 2017).

Although influencer marketing cannot be classified as earned media because of the compensation, it also cannot be classified as owned or paid media. Owned media or firm-generated content includes social media messages that are officially created by the company and over which the company has complete control. Paid media includes advertising spend on communication content, which is also completely controlled by the company (Colicev et al. 2018).

Influencer marketing can be distinguish from a purely paid advertising since consumers perceive it as credible non-purposive word-of-mouth (WOM) (De Veirman, Cauberghe, and Hudders 2017). Influencers are independent because of their status within the social media network community. Therefore, they can choose which brand they want to advocate and are in control over the message they share with their followers (Hughes, Swaminathan, and Brooks 2019). Followers know that influencers are paid to incorporate brands into their feed, but they value the influencer's recommendations as long as they perceive a prevalent intrinsic motivation of content creation (Audrezet, Kerviler, and Guidry Moulard 2018).

Thus, influencer marketing is as a special form of social media advertising that blends elements of paid and earned media (Hughes, Swaminathan, and Brooks

2019). With this feature, influencer marketing holds a high potential for companies to reach their customers in the cluttered environment of social networks. The following chapter outlines the relevance of influencer marketing in more detail and describes the management process that is necessary for successful influencer marketing.

## 1.2 Relevance and Management of Influencer Marketing

In 2021, it was expected that the worldwide number of monthly social media users exceeds three billion (eMarketer 2017). In 2019, users in North America and Europe spent on average almost two hours on social media per day (Statista 2019d). Therefore, it is important for marketers to establish a strong presence on social networking sites. The worldwide social media advertising spending was about 89.9 billion USD in 2019 and is expected to show an annual growth rate of 7%, resulting in a market volume of 125.4 billion USD by 2023 (Statista 2020).

However, simply being present on social media platforms does not provide a competitive advantage anymore (Gholston, Kuofie, and Cooper Hakin 2016; Lin, Bruning, and Swarna 2018). The general tendency of consumers to ignore and skip traditional brand driven advertisements and widely used ad-blocking systems make it more difficult for companies to reach consumers (Statista 2019a).

Furthermore, through ubiquitous use of social media networks consumers constantly create and exchange content concerning products and brands which brings additional challenges for brand management. Consumers can easily share their experiences and are pivotal authors of brand stories (Gensler et al. 2013). Therefore, brand success in the market place increasingly relies on peer-to-peer communication. For this reason, influencer marketing, which combines aspects of owned and earned media (Hughes, Swaminathan, and Brooks 2019), has become an essential part of firms' social media strategy and matured as an industry.

Brands gain influencers to market their products to leverage the power of these influencers. In 2017, 75% of national advertisers were already utilizing influencer marketing and 43% stated they had plans to increase influencer campaign spend (Association of National Advertisers 2018). Between 2017 and 2019 the investments into influencer marketing more than doubled, growing from three billion to 6.5 billion USD in the two years alone (Statista 2019b). In 2021, 38% of respondents to a global survey of marketing agencies and brands said they invest 10% to 20% of their marketing budget in influencer marketing. Even 11% of marketers said they spend more than 40% on this type of digital advertising (Statista 2022a).

## 1.2 Relevance and Management of Influencer Marketing

Nowadays, influencers are not just relevant for brands targeting teenagers. In the United States, 35% of internet users across all age groups pay attention to recommendations of social media influencers. In the age group of 23 to 38, even 54% of internet users are reached by influencers (Statista 2019c). Today, this group accounts for the largest share of annual retail spending (Business Insider 2021).

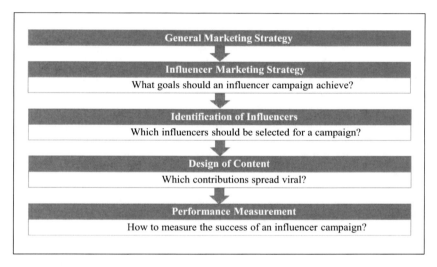

**Figure 1.1** Central Steps of Influencer Marketing Management. Source: Author's own illustration following (Kunath, Pico, and Hofstetter 2018).

To generate long-term value for the brand, marketers can only leverage the power of influencers if they gain control over the process of **influencer marketing management** (Kunath, Pico, and Hofstetter 2018; Leung, Gu, and Palmatier 2022). The process of influencer management should be integrated into the brand's general marketing strategy. Figure 1.1 illustrates the central steps of influencer marketing management.

First, brands must determine their **influencer marketing strategy** (Kunath, Pico, and Hofstetter 2018). Numerous well-known companies successfully implement influencers into their marketing strategy to achieve different goals. These goals are aligned to different touchpoints along the consumer decision journey.

In today's complex communication environment, classic hierarchical models in which the consumer follows a straight line from awareness to purchase seem rather unlikely. Consumers rather go through different phases, which do not necessarily follow one another in a linear process and are characterized by many interactions and loops. However, throughout the consumer decision journey, at some point consumers go through the phases of (1) awareness and consideration (2) development of preference and willingness to pay (3) purchase intention and purchase, and (4) engagement, loyalty and advocacy (Batra and Keller 2016).

Marketers can effectively *increase the awareness and consideration* for their brands through influencer marketing. In just ten days the Swiss chocolate manufacturer Lindt & Sprüngli could double their Instagram followers and generate about 424,000 interactions with their influencer campaign #mylindormoment (Faltl and Freese 2017). In the struggle for awareness, also well-established brands start to integrate influencers within their marketing strategy. Since Gillette lost market shares to social media specialists, like the Dollar Shave Club, they extended their endorsement strategy from the traditional star athletes to influencers. They used female influencers to wrap Gillette products for their husbands, boyfriends, or family members for Christmas on their social media channels or young fathers explaining their sons how to shave. With posts under the #GillettePartner and #MyGilletteShave they gained about 471,209 likes (Mediakix 2019).

Moreover, the relationship between influencers and their followers bears the opportunity to *build preference for the brand and develop the willingness to pay*. Influencers tell a story and describe the value of a product to the customer, which brings a high value to the firm. Gillette not only used influencers to gain awareness in social media channels, additionally though these influencers they could explain the new service to personalize your own Gillette. Moreover, influencers can motivate consumers to co-create the value of a product and therefore increase the willingness to pay for the preferred product. Dr. Oetker used this quality of influencers when working with do-it-yourself influencers under the #EisIdeen. The influencers created their own ice cream using Dr. Oetker's product and encouraged their followers to create their own flavour. In a fairly short time, this call motivated about 200 organic posts. The posts generated about 45,000 likes and 1,000 comments (Wergen 2019).

Further, the viral power of social media influencers bears the opportunity to target a large segment of consumers in a rather short period of time. Therefore, most frequently influencers are used to *generate purchase and to launch new products*. For example, the drugstore chain dm used influencer marketing to gain a rather short-term increase in sales. They commercialized limited product boxes with the favourite dm-products of famous influencers for 5 EUR. The YouTube and blogger stars Dagi Bee, Sophia Thiel, Diana zur Löwen, Paola Maria and

## 1.2 Relevance and Management of Influencer Marketing

Julia Beautx added personal notes for their fans and brought the boxes into the market under the #Schachtelglück. From Diana zur Löwen with her 641,000 followers to Dagi Bee, reaching about four million people each day, together the influencers reached about 9.5 million followers with their posts. Only after one hour the first boxes were sold out (Horizont 2016).

Finally, brands can *increase consumer engagement* through the reach of influencers at relatively low cost. Under the #bestjobever About You, one of the German leaders in influencer marketing, searched for "Germany's Next Big Influencer" to endorse their brand at low cost. The 26-year-old Melisa Dobrić from Berlin won the challenge and what's more, About You generated an overall reach of 5.4 million users and the stories created by users had an average length of ten clips and gained 1.2 million views (Horizont 2018).

Besides, a sustainable and long-term oriented strategy uses influencers to *build consumer loyalty and advocacy*. To achieve this goal, it is advantageous if the brand has a certain identification potential. If the brand shows environmental or social responsibility, 87% of customers are willing to switch from one brand to another. Influencers can shape the image of a brand and foster the consumer brand relationship. During the coronavirus outbreak P&G cooperated with Charlie D'Amelio, one of most-followed influencers on the social media platform TikTok. Together, they created a corona-related dance challenge, encouraging the audience to perform a distance dance during quarantine while keeping social distance. P&G pledged to make a donation to non-profit organizations for the first three million videos created under #DistanceDance (Mediakix 2020b). In June 2020, 16.8 billion users responded to the challenge and created videos dancing with their families, pets or alone during the quarantine (TikTok 2020). In this way, P&G ensured that consumers identify with the brand and want to show this to the outside world.

Yet, according to the Influencer Marketing Benchmarks Report 2019, the "gold rush" of influencer marketing is over. Short-sighted cooperation with influencers, only based on reach of the influencer to an unknown audience, has led to a decline of engagement. Marketers can no longer use this "spray and pray" attitude to achieve visible results (InfluencerDB 2019). If the cooperation between the brand and the influencer is meaningful, 95% of social media users indicate that they less likely skip a brand's ad (Mediakix 2020b).

Therefore, the second step of influencer marketing management builds upon these considerations. Brands must **define suitable influencers** for their specific strategy. Consequently, brands must set up a process to find and target these influencers (Kunath, Pico, and Hofstetter 2018). Which influencer is suitable, depends on the goal of the campaign, as not every influencer is suitable for every goal. Due to the large number of influencers on social networks and due to the wide range of topics that these influencers address, the selection of influencers is a major problem for brands (Forbes 2021). Not every influencer fits every brand, but often it is not clear what makes that fit.

After brands decided who is sending the message, they have to decide what message they want to communicate. The central question around this third step of influencer marketing management is **how viral messages are designed** (Kunath, Pico, and Hofstetter 2018). **Virality** is an overarching term that describes the large scale diffusion of content within social media networks, triggered by interactions of social media users with this content (Akpinar and Berger 2017). In digital marketing, virality is the major goal for activities in social media networks. Brands increasingly rely on consumer to transmit messages within the social media network and brand posts compete with other content for the attention of social media users. Accordingly, the virality of an influencer post is the valuable output that results from the attention a post attracts and the engagement it triggers.

On Instagram alone, 1,074 image posts are uploaded every second (Omnicore 2022). Within this visual cluttered world, managers of influencer campaigns need a good understanding of which posts capture consumers' attention and which content drives engagement. With this knowledge, influencer collaborations can be designed successfully.

The final phase of influencer marketing management is the **measurement of performance** (Kunath, Pico, and Hofstetter 2018). In 2018, only 34% of the marketers measured the return on investments of their social media activities (Statista 2018b). In 2022, this is still a major management issue (Leung, Gu, and Palmatier 2022). Based on the predefined goals of the campaign, marketers need to state performance indicators to justify or correct investments.

To sum up, influencer marketing is a popular form of social media advertising. If brands want to incorporate influencer marketing within their marketing strategy, they first need to define the goal they want to achieve. Second, the brand needs to know who should spread the message. They must find influencers that fit their products and their target group. Third, the brand needs to know what message is effective. To grow the viral effect, the message needs to be suited to the audience and the social media network. Finally and building upon these steps, brands need to evaluate whether influencer marketing represents an effective marketing tool at all.

## 1.3 Aim of Thesis

Along the process of influencer marketing management, relevant **research gaps** can be identified. These research gaps are illustrated in Table 1.1 and are briefly explained in the following.

**Table 1.1** Research Gaps

| Steps of Influencer Marketing Management | Research Gaps |
|---|---|
| **Influencer Marketing Strategy** | |
| What goals should an influencer campaign achieve? | 1. There is a call for research on how influencer marketing effects consumer behavior along the different stages of the consumer decision journey. |
| **Identification of Influencers** | |
| Which influencers should be selected for a campaign? | 2. Literature on source effects within social media concentrates on the perception of the communicator but ignores the source as part of a network and the influence arising from the position within the network. |
| | 3. Studies covering diffusion theory in social media focus on the structural resources of a source and nearly neglect the source characteristics. |
| | 4. Literature on influencer selection lacks a holistic approach merging the mindset of persuasion research and viral marketing literature. |
| | 5. Research lacks knowledge about the construct of influencer brand fit. |
| | 6. Besides the well-researched unitary network attributes, dyadic network attributes (e.g. follower overlap between influencers within a portfolio) should be integrated within the selection process of seeding individuals. |
| **Design of Content** | |
| Which contributions spread viral? | 7. There is a lack of research on viral influencer content. |
| | 8. Research is needed that observes the message as well as the picture of an influencer post exploring the far range of design possibilities given in visual driven social media networks. |

(continued)

**Table 1.1** (continued)

| Steps of Influencer Marketing Management | Research Gaps |
|---|---|
| **Performance Measurement** | |
| How to measure the success of an influencer campaign? | 9. Research lacks knowledge about the relative effectiveness of influencer marketing.<br>10. Channel interactions of influencer marketing are still unexplored in research. |

Source: Author's own illustration.

First, marketers have to outline their influencer marketing strategy. The effectiveness of an influencer campaign depends on the goal, which marketers have to define in step one of the influencer marketing management process. The first studies on influencers examine the impact of influencers on consumer evaluations and behavioral intention (Breves et al. 2019; Colliander and Dahlén 2011; De Vries 2019; Lee and Watkins 2016; Uribe, Buzeta, and Velásquez 2016). Moreover, Hughes, Swaminathan, and Brooks (2019) are the first to explore the impact of influencer content on actual behavior of consumers. In their study, the authors examine the factors that influence the likes and comments of sponsored blogging campaigns. However, *little is known about the effects of influencer marketing on consumer behavior along the different stages of the consumer decision journey* (Hughes, Swaminathan, and Brooks 2019).

After determining the goal of the influencer marketing campaign, the first and most relevant challenge for marketers is the choice of the most suitable influencer for their brand (Breves et al. 2019; De Veirman, Cauberghe, and Hudders 2017, 2017; Mediakix 2018). Looking at social media literature, two different streams that relate to this question can be identified.

The first stream relates to the communicator of a message and examines the source effects of personal influence. The same message can be perceived another way when different people communicate it. Source credibility is the most studied source effect and describes the positive influence of the communicator's expertise, trustworthiness, and attractiveness on communication outcomes (Ohanian 1990). The studies are mainly experiments that focus on the underlying psychological mechanisms that potentially account for these outcomes. Recent studies could show that the credibility of an influencer positively relates to source or brand evaluations and enhances the net promoter score (Breves et al. 2019; De Vries 2019). Expertise is a widely studied characteristic within the stream relating to personal influence. Source expertise relates positively with consumer evaluations and behavioral intentions for user-generated content (Hautz et al. 2014; Kunz and Seshadri 2015; Thompson and Malaviya 2013) and influencer posts (Breves et al. 2019; Uribe, Buzeta, and Velásquez 2016). Furthermore, the personal influence of an influencer increases if the physical attractiveness (Breves et al. 2019; Lee and Watkins 2016) and trustworthiness (Hautz et al. 2014; Kunz and Seshadri 2015) of the individual is high.

Overall, the *literature on source effects within social media* concentrates on the perception of the communicator but *ignores the source as part of a network and the influence arising from the position within the network*. Only a recent study by De Vries (2019) starts to combine network metrics with personal source effects. However, the study observes effects on consumer attitudes and behavioral intentions but not on real life consumer behavior.

The second stream, that is relevant for the identification of appropriate influencers, relates to the diffusion theory and examines the viral effects that are triggered by a communicator. Using the data from social media networks, viral marketing literature studies the locational resources arising from a user's local position and the impact they have on product adoption and diffusion of information (Ansari et al. 2018; Goldenberg et al. 2009). Their work is based on earlier findings concerning the seeding of viral marketing campaigns through mobile phone text messages (Hinz et al. 2011) or product adoption in the local network of physicians (Iyengar, van den Bulte, and Valente 2011).

Most of the studies find that seeding to well-connected users is beneficial for viral diffusion. More specific, studies have shown the positive relationship between the number of followers (Gong et al. 2017; Hughes, Swaminathan, and Brooks 2019) or connections within a community (Rooderkerk and Pauwels 2016) and online engagement. Moreover, the overlap of followers or followees[2] between two users can enhance the number of retweets (Peng et al. 2018). However, not only the network itself is important but also the activity of the sender (Ansari et al. 2018; Lanz et al. 2019) and the activity of followers through shares (Kupfer et al. 2018), retweets (Gong et al. 2017) or likes (Breves et al. 2019; De Vries 2019). Nevertheless, these *studies focus on the structural resources of a communicator and nearly neglect the source characteristics and the fit of the influencer with the brand or product*. Therefore, both streams concerning the influencer selection problem show considerable gaps and a *holistic approach combining both streams is needed*.

Another shortcoming of the literature concerning influencer choice is that only one communicator of the message is considered (Peng et al. 2018). However, in

---

[2] Followees are users whom the user follows (Peng et al. 2018).

practice marketers rather use a portfolio of influencers than a single influencer to reach their goals. Therefore, marketers need to *assess the potential power of a portfolio of influencers.*

Peng et al. (2018) have shown that the overlap of followers and followees between sender and receiver of a message enhances the number of retweets on Twitter. They argue that besides the well-researched unitary network attributes, these dyadic network attributes, like common connections, can be valuable input for the selection of seeding individuals. Thus, when working with more than one influencer, the influencer's overlap with other influencers within the portfolio or the unique reach (i.e., unique follower base) within a portfolio is of interest.

The relevance of network overlap and unique reach may differ depending on the goal of the campaign. Unique reach may be more relevant for the engagement stage of the consumer decision journey (e.g. liking) since consumers probably react just one time to a post. In contrast, clicking on a post or buying may require repeated exposure to the brand. Similar to the findings for cross-media campaigns, multiple viewings through network overlap of influencers used for a campaign may be beneficial for the purchase stage of the consumer decision journey (Voorveld, Neijens, and Smit 2011). Yet, neither industry nor research offer insights into what portfolio characteristics improve the effectiveness of an influencer campaign.

After finding the right influencers, the third step of the influencer marketing management process is the design of the message. There exists extensive literature on the virality of user-generated content and firm-generated content on Facebook (Meire et al. 2019; Moro, Rita, and Vala 2016; Swani and Milne 2017), Twitter (Davis et al. 2019; Jalali and Papatla 2019) or other networks, like LinkedIn (Rooderkerk and Pauwels 2016). Whereas, the literature on content on Instagram is rather scarce, only the recent studies of Li and Xie (2020) and Rietveld et al. (2020) examine firm-generated content and user-generated content on Instagram. These studies start to address the gap in literature on viral posts that *combine textual and pictorial elements.* They are the first to account for the visual modality of social media networks and they call for *more specific research on influencer posts* (Li and Xie 2020).

Because, almost no research exists that studies influencer content, the findings are limited to few variables. Hughes, Swaminathan, and Brooks (2019) observe if it is beneficial that a post is perceived as hedonic or functional, whereas Gong et al. (2017) study if a post containing more information than another post is more effective. In general, the far range of design possibilities given in visual driven social media networks is not considered within the literature on viral content on

## 1.3 Aim of Thesis

social media so far. No research exists that observes the message and the picture of an influencer post.

The last step of the influencer marketing management process is the measurement of performance. However, it is not only important to measure the short-term effects of an influencer campaign. Moreover, to leverage influencer messages marketers need to *evaluate the channel effectiveness of influencer marketing and the interactions with other channels*. To find answers to this question this thesis reflects on research that considers more than one type of message.

Previous research examined the impact of advertising, firm-generated content, and user-generated content on brand building and behavioral outcomes to measure the effectiveness of social messages (De Vries, Gensler, and Leeflang 2017). Brand building refers to the association of the brand in the minds of consumers, the evaluations and feelings towards the brand, and the loyalty that consumers feel towards the brand (Keller 2009). Studies comparing the effectiveness of advertising and user-generated content are prevalent in literature with multiple types of messages. The studies investigate the impact of different formats of user-generated content on consumer interest (Fossen and Schweidel 2019; Kim and Hanssens 2017; Pauwels, Aksehirli, and Lackman 2016), sales (Bruce, Foutz, and Kolsarici 2012; Gopinath, Chintagunta, and Venkataraman 2013; Kim and Hanssens 2017; Stephen and Galak 2012), acquisition (Villanueva, Yoo, and Hanssens 2008) or stock market performance (Tirunillai and Tellis 2012). Fewer studies compare user-generated content and firm-generated content (Goh, Heng, and Lin 2013; Kumar et al. 2013) or firm-generated content and advertising (Kumar et al. 2016; Kumar, Choi, and Greene 2017) on sales and acquisition. Studies that are more recent investigate all three types of messages to evaluate the effectiveness and interaction of channels on brand building (Colicev, Kumar, and O'Connor 2019) or firm performance (Hewett et al. 2016; Kupfer et al. 2018; Stephen and Galak 2012), or both (Colicev et al. 2018; De Vries, Gensler, and Leeflang 2017). Nevertheless, *research lacks knowledge about the effectiveness and channel interactions of influencer marketing* (Kupfer et al. 2018).

The aforementioned research gaps are diverse and the research on influencer marketing is just in a take-off phase. Even though research on effectiveness of design elements of influencers posts is scarce, there is extensive research on the design of traditional advertising offline and online. It is to be expected that the results and implications are similar since the perceptual processes should be the same. Perceiving influencer content on social media should not be different to the perception of social media messages of other sources or the perception of textual or visual elements in traditional offline advertising. Thus, the contribution to research is rather small. Apart from this, there is also a minor contribution for marketing practice since the common use of A/B-Testing[3] delivered broad results on which marketers rely on. Furthermore, influencers are rather independent in their role as content creators and know what content generates the best output for their follower community (Leung, Gu, and Palmatier 2022; Mediakix 2018). For this reason, the empirical investigations of this thesis do not focus on the design of influencer posts.

However, selecting the right influencers and measuring the return on investment of influencer campaigns are two of the biggest challenges of influencer marketing for brands (Mediakix 2018). In 2021, 78% of brands still had problems defining suitable influencers for their campaigns (Influencer Marketing Hub 2021). Therefore, the demand for data-driven evaluations of the effectiveness of influencers is constantly increasing. Marketers need to know beforehand which influencer characteristics drive campaign success along the consumer decision journey. Due to the high practical relevance, this thesis will therefore address research Gaps 1 to 6 with an empirical study on influencer selection.

In 2018, almost 70% of the marketers stated that they do not measure the return on investments of their social media activities or that they do not know about it (Statista 2018b). Furthermore, measuring the return on investment of influencer campaigns is still one of the main concerns of brands in 2021 (Linqia 2021). An empirical study investigating the channel effectiveness of influencer marketing and observing its synergies with firm-generated content, user-generated content and advertising would provide tremendous contribution for research and practice. Therefore, a second empirical study on the channel effectiveness of influencer marketing will cover for research Gaps 1, 9 and 10.

Consequently, the **overall aim of this thesis** is to *investigate the potential of influencers to influence behavioral outcomes of consumers on social media.*

**Study 1** of the thesis empirically investigates the impact of influencer characteristics on influencer campaign measures along the consumer decision journey. More precisely, Study 1 explores (i) what determines the fit of an influencer and a brand and (ii) how this influencer brand fit and the influencer's other personal characteristics as well as the influencer's network characteristics within a portfolio of influencers effect post reach (awareness phase), product link clicks within the influencer's story (purchase phase) and post likes and comments and story views (engagement phase).

---

[3] A/B testing is a method of testing two different variants of a post against each other to determine which one is more successful.

Study 2 of the thesis investigates the effectiveness of influencer marketing on consumer interest and firm performance along the consumer decision journey. More precisely, Study 2 (i) observes the relative effectiveness of influencer marketing compared to firm-generated as well as consumer-generated messages on social media and advertising on website visits, orders and revenue and (ii) explores the interaction effects among those channels.

The **theoretical contribution of Study 1 to research** is fourfold. First, the insights from Study 1 are a first step to close research Gap 1 since the study simultaneously covers effects on consumer behavior at different stages of the consumer decision journey. Second, the first study contributes to current research on seeding individuals by merging the mindset of persuasion research and viral marketing literature. The study expands the scope of previous findings on source effects and message diffusion by observing the influence of a more holistic set of influencer characteristics. The approach considers structural and personal resources of an influencer at once. In this way, research Gaps 2–4 are addressed. Third, Study 1 investigates the factors that determine the perception of influencer brand fit. Therefore, the study enriches current research on persuasion and viral marketing with insights from brand extension literature and addresses research Gap 5. Fourth, the study includes dyadic network attributes besides the well-researched unitary network attributes. To overcome research Gap 6, Study 1 considers network overlaps between a portfolio of influencers and hence contributes to viral marketing research.

Besides a theoretical contribution, **the first study of the thesis also provides insights for managers** concerning the selection of influencers. Based on the results, implications with respect to an effective implementation of selection criteria for influencers are derived. Through the comprehensive set of personal and structural influencer characteristics managers get a better understanding of which characteristics matter for what kind of performance measure. If an influencer creates value for the consumer, and therefore for the firm depends on the consumer's position within the consumer decision journey. Depending on the goals defined within their influencer marketing strategy, managers have to adapt their influencer selection to run effective campaigns. Moreover, managers receive a more detailed understanding on how consumer perceptions build influencer brand fit. Furthermore, practice lacks insights on the effectiveness of campaign posts when working with a portfolio of influencers. If managers target customers on earlier stages of the consumer decision journey and want to create awareness, they should work with influencers that have high unique follower basis and differentiate from the other influencers in the portfolio. In contrast, managers enhance purchase intention (e.g. clicking on a product link) by the selection of similar influencers. Through the follower overlap consumer are repeatedly exposed to the product, which enhances the chance of clicking.

The **theoretical contribution of Study 2 to research** is threefold. First, the study observes effects on website visits as well as orders and revenue. Therefore, the study gains insights on how influencer marketing shapes the consumer decision journey and further closes research Gap 1. Second, Study 2 simultaneously considers and compares the effectiveness of influencer marketing, other marketing investments, and firm-generated and consumer-generated messages. Third, the study investigates the interactions of the different channels and influencer marketing. Therefore, Study 2 addresses research Gaps 9 and 10.

Furthermore, **Study 2 provides insights for managers**. Since there have been no studies to date on the influence of influencer marketing costs on orders and revenue (Leung, Gu, and Palmatier 2022), this study provides the first insights into the monetary value of influencers. Moreover, the results give managers an understanding of the relative effectiveness of influencer marketing compared to other channel investments. Therefore, the study supports managers to optimize the allocation of their marketing budget across channels. Lastly, since the study covers interaction effects between the different channels, the study's insights help managers to effectively orchestrate the various channel activities.

## 1.4 Structure of Thesis

Figure 1.2 illustrates the structure of the thesis. *Chapter 1* defines the terms influencer and influencer marketing and highlights the relevance of influencer marketing. Furthermore, the aim of the thesis is outlined and the contribution to research and practice is explained. The chapter closes with the description of the thesis structure.

While research has been conducted on paid and owned media (Kupfer et al. 2018; Zhang, Moe, and Schweidel 2017) or earned media, including eWOM (Lanz et al. 2019; Wang et al. 2019), little is known about the success drivers of influencer marketing, which combines aspects of owned and earned media (Hughes, Swaminathan, and Brooks 2019; Kupfer et al. 2018). Yet, to ensure the effectiveness of influencer marketing management, managers need a good understanding of the outcome of a campaign from the onset. They must identify suitable influencers, create viral content and evaluate the effectiveness of influencer marketing.

Social media influencers are social media users with specific characteristics (e.g. Breves et al. 2019; Casaló, Flavián, and Ibáñez-Sánchez 2018; De Veirman,

## 1.4 Structure of Thesis

Cauberghe, and Hudders 2017; Djafarova and Rushworth 2017). Consequently, research findings on user-generated content should be considered when addressing the management challenges of influencer marketing. Furthermore, influencers can also be seen as human brands (Kupfer et al. 2018). For this reason, literature on firm-generated content should also be consulted to derive implications for influencer marketing. Therefore, the first concern should be to compile and process the knowledge about consumer and firm activities on social media to answer the important management questions of influencer marketing.

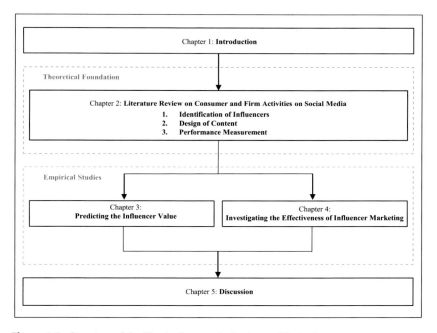

**Figure 1.2** Structure of the Thesis. Source: Author's own illustration.

Therefore, *Chapter 2* provides a comprehensive literature review about consumer and firm activities on social media, focussing on implications for influencer marketing management. Thereby, the gaps in literature are defined in different areas of this topic and provide a guideline for future research. The systematic search strategy is described in Section 2.1. Prior research is assigned to the three influencer marketing management challenges: identification of influencers (Section 2.2), design of content (Section 2.3) and performance measurement

(Section 2.4). Subsequently, the last section summarizes previous findings and gaps in literature are outlined.

Due to its high practical relevance, the first empirical study focuses on the selection of suitable influencers and seeks to predict the value of influencers for different stages of the consumer decision journey. *Chapter 3* describes the design and results of Study 1. The chapter first provides an explanatory framework that anchors an influencer's personal and structural resources in power theory (Brass and Burkhardt 1993; French and Raven 1959). Further, the study investigates the impact of the personal and structural resources of 87 influencers on campaign measures along the consumer decision journey for 13 campaigns of ten different brands. In order to measure the personal resources of an influencer, a consumer survey with 2,152 respondents is used to explore the factors building influencer brand fit. Among other network characteristics, the study focuses on the still unexplored portfolio characteristics of influencers.

Once the right influencers are selected, the managers need to know about the return on investment of influencer marketing. Therefore, the second empirical Study observes the effectiveness of influencer marketing on firm performance along the consumer decision journey. *Chapter 4* describes the design and results of Study 2. The study uses weekly data of one of the largest specialized online retailers in Europe to observe the relative effectiveness of influencer marketing compared to firm-generated as well as consumer-generated messages on social media and advertising on website visits as well as orders and revenue. Moreover, the interaction effects among those channels are observed to discover potential synergies.

Finally, *Chapter 5* provides a discussion of the key findings of the thesis and derives theoretical as well as managerial implications. Furthermore, the potential areas for future research are pointed out.

# Literature Review 2

The following chapter outlines the empirical research related to firm and consumer activities on social media, thereby positioning this thesis in the current literature. Moreover, the aim of this review is to identify relevant studies to answer the following questions regarding the management of an influencer campaign:

1. Which influencers should be selected for a campaign?
2. Which contributions spread viral?
3. How to measure the success of an influencer campaign?

The overview includes papers from three different research streams: viral marketing, social media advertising and research on user-generated content or eWOM. After describing the process of literature search, the literature concerning the selection of influencers is discussed. Thereby, findings form the different areas are gathered to gain a better understanding of the characteristics of an influential message source. Following, the review of literature identifies design elements of viral posts and debates on the effectiveness of firm and consumer activities on social media. The last chapter of the literature review summarizes the findings within these three areas and outlines the gaps for future research.

## 2.1 Literature Search Process

The literature review of Lamberton and Stephen (2016) represents one of the latest literature reviews published in an A+-ranked Journal including social media literature. The review combines the streams of digital, social media and mobile marketing to answer how new technologies have affected firms and consumers behaviors, interactions and experiences. Likewise, the thesis follows the authors' thematic approach and synthesises insights from different research streams to answer the defined research questions (Lamberton and Stephen 2016). Therefore, the procedure of selecting papers follows four-steps: general database search, focused search, additional search through references, and analysis (Webster and Watson 2002).

In *Step 1*, the search process started with a general database search, to examine keywords and citation aggregation to understand the terminology and define key authors within the various subfields within social media literature. In this thesis, searches for the literature review were conducted in *EBSCOhost* and *Google Scholar*. In order to cover a wide set of studies, papers that were potentially relevant had to contain at least one of the following search terms in the title, abstract, or key words (Briner and Denyer 2012): *online word-of-mouth, online WOM, eWOM, online reviews, blogs, user-generated content, user-generated content, social media, social media network\* sites* (De Vries 2015) as well as *influencer, opinion leader* and *influential*. The aim of this first step was the definition of a search protocol that defined the framework for the focused search (Briner and Denyer 2012). The search protocol defines the selection criteria for the literature review and is illustrated in Table 2.1.

**Table 2.1** Search Protocol of Literature Review

| Categories | Selection Criteria |
|---|---|
| Search Database | EBSCOhost, Google Scholar |
| Publication Period | 2000–2020 |
| Journals | Journal of Marketing Research<br>Journal of Marketing<br>Journal of Consumer Research<br>Marketing Science<br>International Journal of Research in Marketing<br>Journal of the Academy of Marketing Science<br>Journal of Business Research<br>Journal of Interactive Marketing<br>Marketing Letters<br>Journal of Advertising Research |

(continued)

## 2.1 Literature Search Process

**Table 2.1** (continued)

| Categories | Selection Criteria |
|---|---|
| Search Terms in Title, Abstract or Key Words | online word-of-mouth<br>online WOM<br>eWOM<br>online reviews<br>blogs<br>user-generated content<br>user-generated content<br>social media<br>social media network* sites<br>influencer<br>opinion leader<br>influential |
| Study Focus | Source characteristics of influential posts<br>Design elements of viral posts<br>Channel effectiveness and comparison |
| Types of Study | Quantitative empirical studies |
| Research Method | Research design and process are described |

Source: Author's own illustration.

In *Step 2*, a focused search was conducted in EBSCOhost and Google Scholar. The same search terms were used like in Step 1. As the search terms are broadly defined to meet the diverse terminology in different research streams, the literature search concentrates on A+, A and B Journals of Marketing. The focus on these premier journals has two reasons. First, the focus of this thesis is on marketing. Although the topics are covered in other fields (e.g., psychology, information systems or computer science), the inclusion of findings of other fields would be beyond the scope of this thesis. Second, highly cited work from lower ranked journals or journals from other fields is included through forward and backward search if it provides variables not captured by the selected literature (Lamberton and Stephen 2016). Since social media practically did not exist before 2000, only published work after 2000 was considered. The search resulted in 354 hits[1]. The abstracts and the findings were scanned and literature not related to the three research questions was excluded. The papers that were excluded from literature can be classified the following categories: (1) conceptual papers, (2) qualitative studies, (3) papers that solely provide descriptive statistics, (4) papers without

---

[1] The literature review was conducted in late 2020 and serves as the conceptual basis for the empirical projects in the thesis.

social media focus, (5) papers that focus on social media in politics, agencies, human resources, innovation management or consumer relationship management, (6) papers focusing on consumer motivations or diagnostic, (7) papers that focus on recommender systems, television (TV), website or search advertising, (8) introduction texts or editorial comments and (9) algorithm errors (e.g. table of contents). This led to the selection of 24 papers dealing with source characteristics of influential posts, 21 papers concerning design elements of influential posts and 20 papers covering channel effectiveness and comparison.

In *Step 3*, a forward and backward reference search with Google Scholar was performed (Webster and Watson 2002). Since there is extensive research in the leading marketing journals concerning the source characteristics and design elements of influential posts, studies were only included if they provide variables not captured by the selected marketing literature. For comprehensiveness, a meta-analysis on celebrity endorsement, is included for the review of effective source characteristics after the search process in Step 3. No further research needed to be included for the topic design elements of influential posts. Through the investigation of references in Step 3, three papers were included covering channel effectiveness and comparison including social media in related areas of research.

*Step 4* is the analysis of literature following the three defined research questions. Within these sections the thesis follows the conceptual approach described by Webster and Watson (2002). Hereinafter, the literature is discussed based on which characteristics of a message source increase the message effectiveness (Section 2.2), what post characteristics drive virality (Section 2.3) and which channels have higher effects on brand performance measures than others (Section 2.4).

## 2.2 Literature Review on Identification of Influencers

The literature review on identification of influencers summarizes knowledge that serves to answer the following question: Which influencers should be selected for a campaign? The literature search in leading marketing journals reveals 24 studies that focus on the effectiveness of characteristics of a message source within a social media context (see Table 2.2). The selected literature contains findings on source characteristics of user-generated content and firm-generated content since influencer marketing blends elements of user-generated content as well as firm-generated content. Furthermore, first research has been conducted on the effectiveness of source characteristics of influencer posts. The literature only contains one celebrity endorsement study since work on celebrity endorsement

## 2.2 Literature Review on Identification of Influencers

is rarely published in highly ranked journals. However, celebrity endorsement is closely related to influencer marketing, therefore, the highly cited meta-analysis from Amos, Holmes, and Strutton (2008) is included to take up the major findings of celebrity endorsement literature.

What all studies have in common is that they are theoretically based on social influence. **Social influence** is a broad term which describes the ability to change another person's beliefs, attitudes, or behavior (Myers 2009). However, the literature splits into two different streams of research studying source characteristics, each with a different perspective on social influence. The organization of Table 2.2 into two parts illustrates these two streams of literature. Furthermore, the structure of Section 2.2 also follows this structure.

The **first stream of research** describes the social influence between individuals and covers endorsement and advertising literature. Furthermore, the targeted use of this influence is called persuasion. **Persuasion** is a communication process, which is intended and motivates a change in another person's beliefs, attitudes, or behavior (Myers 2009). Influencer marketing purposefully utilises the power of influencers to change consumer preferences and buying behavior. Therefore, influencer marketing can be characterized as persuasion and relates to this stream of literature.

In this context, social influence can be seen as the **personal power** one person has over other people and describes an individual's capability to affect the decisions of others (French and Raven 1959). Within this literature, the source credibility model from Hovland, Janis, and Kelley (1953) and the attractiveness model from McGuire (1985) are prevalent in explaining personal power of a message source. Credibility with its underlying dimensions expertise, trustworthiness and attractiveness is the major focus of studies. Further, the endorser's fit is considered.

The **second stream of research** investigates the influence between individuals under the influence of a powerful third party and is the theoretical underpinning of viral marketing literature. The research sheds light on the function of a message source as intermediary between the media and people. The two-step flow model by Katz and Lazarsfeld (1955) is predominant in this stream and explains the power of the media through so-called "influentials". The flow of information occurs in two steps. Media reaches for opinion leaders, who pass on the message to a broader audience. This audience is characterized as a rather passive crowd of followers searching for guidance and social confirmation. The opinion leaders are characterized through a central position and act as multiplicators.

This view raised the interest in personal networks as channels for information diffusion and broad up a series of studies mainly focussing on the centrality of

**Table 2.2** Studies focusing on Source Characteristics of Influential Posts

| Study | Credibility | Expertise | Trustworthiness | Attractiveness | Endorser Fit | Network Structure Sender | Activity of Sender | Activity of Followers | Source-related Controls |
|---|---|---|---|---|---|---|---|---|---|
| **Social Media Advertising and Celebrity Endorsement Literature** | | | | | | | | | |
| Amos, Holmes and Strutton 2008 | x | x | x | x | x | | | | |
| Breves et al. 2019 | | x[a] | x[a] | x[a] | x | | | | x |
| Colliander and Dalhén 2011 | x | | | x | | | | | x |
| De Vries, 2019 | x | | | | | | | x | |
| Hautz et al. 2014 | | x[a] | x[a] | | | | | | x |
| Kunz and Seshadri 2015 | | x[a] | x[a] | x[a] | | | | | x |
| Lee and Watkins 2016 | | | | x | | | | | x |
| Thompson and Malaviya 2013 | | x[a] | x[a] | x[a] | | | | | |
| Uribe, Buzeta, and Velásquez 2016 | x | x | | | | | | | |
| Yuan, Kim, and Kim 2016 | | x[a] | x[a] | x[a] | | | | | x |
| **Viral Marketing Literature** | | | | | | | | | |
| Ansari, et al. 2018 | | | | | | x | x | x | x |
| Chen et al. 2019 | | | | | | x | | | x |
| Goldenberg et al. 2009 | | | | | | x | | | x |
| Gong et al. 2017 | | | | | | x | x | x | |
| Hughes et al. 2019 | | x | | | | x | x | | x |
| Katona, Zubcsek, and Sarvary 2011 | | | | | | x | | | x |
| Kupfer et al. 2018 | | | | | x | x | x | x | x |
| Lanz et al. 2019 | | | | | | x | x | | |
| Namkoong, Ro, and Henderson 2019 | | | | | | x | | | |
| Peng et al. 2018 | | | | | | x | x | x | x |
| Rooderkerk and Pauwels 2016 | | x | | | | x | | | x |
| Trusov, Bodapati, and Bucklin 2010 | | | | | | x | x | x | x |
| Valsesia, Proserpio, Nunes 2020 | | | | | | x | x | | x |
| Wang et al. 2019 | | | | | | x | x | x | x |
| Zhang, Moe, and Schweidel 2017 | | | | | | x | x | x | |

Source: Author's own illustration. Notes: [a] Variable is dimension of source credibility.

## 2.2 Literature Review on Identification of Influencers

individuals (e.g. Ansari et al. 2018; Goldenberg et al. 2009; Hinz et al. 2011; Lanz et al. 2019). The social influence of an influencer is similar. Influencers hold an unequal amount of social influence on followers in social media networks. Brands leverage the power of influencers and therefore indirectly shape consumer preferences and buying behavior. Therefore, findings from this research can be used to draw conclusions about the potential of an influencer's network. Constructs that describe the personal network of the source, such as the network structure of the source and the activity of the source and its followers, are predominant in viral marketing literature.

In the following, the analysis of literature separates through the two streams of endorsement as well as advertising literature and viral marketing literature. According to these views, different constructs play an important role in the different streams.

The constructs form the columns of Table 2.2. As proposed by Webster and Watson (2002) a conceptual approach is applied. Thereby, the literature review synthesizes findings concerning the impact and the interactions of each construct.

### 2.2.1 Social Media Advertising and Celebrity Endorsement Literature

The subsequent chapter summarizes the source effects described by social media advertising and celebrity endorsement literature. The review of literature will be based on the first section of Table 2.2 and starts with a short introduction into the methodology of the papers. In the following, the **superordinate constructs** are marked bold and will be discussed from left to right. If a further subdivision is structurally necessary, this is expressed with an italicized and boldly marked layer in this chapter.

Studies that have their origins in social media advertising and celebrity endorsement employ survey data from online advertising experiments. The experiments work with stimulus from Instagram, YouTube, Facebook, Blogs or smaller online communities to investigate the source effects. In contrast to viral marketing literature that captures the effectiveness of a message source though impact on consumer behavior, social media advertising and celebrity endorsement literature considers effectiveness on attitude or behavioral intention. The impact of the source effects is measured through a change in ad, product or brand evaluations (Breves et al. 2019; Colliander and Dahlén 2011; Thompson and Malaviya 2013; Yuan, Kim, and Kim 2016), purchase intension (Colliander and Dahlén 2011; Hautz et al. 2014; Lee and Watkins 2016; Uribe, Buzeta, and Velásquez 2016), intention to recommend the brand or product (Breves et al. 2019; Uribe, Buzeta, and Velásquez 2016) and customer equity drivers and therefore customer lifetime value (Yuan, Kim, and Kim 2016). Further, a few studies also focus on source effects on the evaluation of the source itself (De Vries 2019) and the willingness to interact with the source or recommend it (De Vries 2019; Kunz and Seshadri 2015). Beyond the social media context, the meta-analysis of Amos, Holmes, and Strutton (2008) summarizes the results of advertising experiments that analyze the influence of celebrity characteristics on consumer attitudes towards an ad and the associated brand, consumers' purchase intention, as well as other measures of effectiveness.

Credibility

One of the most prominent constructs in advertising and celebrity endorsement literature is **source credibility**. The source credibility is broadly defined as a communicator's positive characteristics that effect the receiver's acceptance of a message (Ohanian 1990). Within the studies under analysis the construct is used and measured differently. Breves et al. (2019) and Yuan, Kim, and Kim (2016) describe credibility as the positive attributes of a message source, including three factors defining source credibility: expertise, trustworthiness and attractiveness. Thompson and Malaviya (2013) and Kunz and Seshadri (2015) also use these three dimensions without directly labelling them as dimensions of source credibility. Therefore, these authors follow the scale development of Ohanian (1990), based on the source credibility model (Hovland, Janis, and Kelley 1953) and the attractiveness model (McGuire 1985). Hautz et al. (2014) also follow this understanding but focus on expertise and trustworthiness as the two major dimensions. If the studies measure the overarching construct of source credibility through distinct dimensions, the dimensions were marked within Table 2.2 and not credibility.

Besides this dimensional view, credibility can be seen as an autonomous characteristic. A message source is then perceived as credible if he is convincing, believable and unbiased (Colliander and Dahlén 2011). Eline De Vries (2019) includes trust in her general measurement of account credibility but treats source expertise and source attractiveness (here the dimension familiarity) as separate constructs. Uribe, Buzeta, and Velásquez (2016) use six items instead of three, but they share the understanding by De Vries (2019).

The studies confirm a positive influence of source credibility on adverting effectiveness. Transferring earlier findings from celebrity endorsement research (Amos, Holmes, and Strutton 2008), recent research finds that the source credibility of Instagram influencers positively influences the intention to recommend

## 2.2 Literature Review on Identification of Influencers

a brand mediated by the liking of the brand (Breves et al. 2019). Furthermore, Yuan, Kim, and Kim (2016) find that the perceived credibility of the basketball star Lebron James increases the customer lifetime value of young adults for the brand Nike since it influences the customer equity drivers.

Furthermore, research shows that source credibility is even more important for social media than for traditional media. The source of a social media message is perceived as an integral part of the message since social media is a place to share rather personal content (Colliander and Dahlén 2011). Hautz et al. (2014) investigate the effectiveness of user-generated and agency-generated video ads to promote the destination Tirol. They also find that the source acts as an integral part of the message. Moreover, their findings indicate that the source credibility has a positive effect on the intention to visit the destination and the willingness to share the ad with others. They also show that the credibility of the source is higher when the same video ad is marked as user-generated as when it is marked as agency-generated.

However, Thompson and Malaviya (2013) find that the disclosure of a consumer as the source of a message can have opposing effects on different dimensions of source credibility and thus diverging impacts on ad and brand evaluations. On the one hand, background information on the consumer that created the ad enhances identification with the source and therefore source attractiveness. On the other hand, cognitive elaboration on the consumer who created the advertising can raise scepticism about the expertise and trustworthiness of the source.

Besides the effects of source credibility on attitudes and behavioral intensions towards the brand or product, the credibility of a source also effects attitudes and behavioral intensions towards the sender of a message. Eline De Vries (2019) demonstrates that the perceived credibility of an influencer's account positively influences the profile's evaluation and the likelihood to follow the account and recommend it to others. Moreover, Kunz and Seshadri (2015) show that, if a person's CouchSurfing profile is perceived highly credible, it increases the likelihood of an offline interaction.

The hypothesized interdependencies between source credibility and related constructs are divers. Colliander and Dahlén (2011) state that blog articles generate more positive brand attitudes and higher purchase intention than articles in online magazines since bloggers create higher para-social interaction with users. In mass communication, **para-social interaction** is defined as the illusion of a face-to-face relationship with a media performer (Horton and Wohl 1956). Furthermore, they argue that the writer's credibility is more important on blogs than in online magazines and that this is due to para-social interaction. However, they do not specify the relationship of this two variables. Yuan, Kim, and Kim (2016) hypothesize that the relationship of source credibility on customer equity drivers and the related increase in customer lifetime value is mediated by a para-social relationship and they find significant results. However, Breves et al. (2019) claim that the perceived fit between an influencer and a brand is used as a heuristic cue to determine the influencer's credibility, but this effect diminishes if the level of para-social relationship is high. The authors assume, if the para-social relationship is high, credibility depends on the assessment on former experiences with the influencer and other factors decrease in their importance. This explanation implies that the effect of para-social relationship on attitudes and behavioral intensions is mediated by source credibility. Taking this into account, literature agrees on the strong connection of para-social relationship and source credibility, but the direction of this impact remains rather unclear and more empirical work is needed.

Besides that, other studies examine factors affecting the assessment of source credibility. The message sidedness, the advertising intent and the communicator's expertise influence the perception of source credibility. The results show that two-sided messages, an expert source and implicit advertising intent are beneficial for the perception of source credibility (Uribe, Buzeta, and Velásquez 2016). Other work investigates peripheral cues like the ratio of likes to followers (De Vries 2019) or the quality of a video ad (Hautz et al. 2014) and their impact on source credibility.

Eline De Vries (2019) describes an inverted U-shaped relationship between the like follower ratio of a profile's posts and the credibility of the account. Users perceive a source as less credible if the account gets disproportionally high as well as low numbers of likes given the accounts follower size. The negative impact of a disproportionally high like follower ratio can be prevented by the use of additional hashtags since hashtags increase the likely audience and it is believable that posts get a higher proportion of likes.

Hautz et al. (2014) claim that users perceive video ads of low quality as more credible since the associate this kind of content rather with user-generated content than professional content from agencies. Since social media profiles usually provide many personal information, they provide a rich environment for peripheral perception of a source. Long-time membership, considerable experiences or many friends and references can enhance the credibility of a source. Furthermore, through information provided on age, gender, hobbies and interest, users can identify similarities between them and other users, which increases the perceived credibility of the message source. Furthermore, the communication behavior can be used as valuable cue. High response rates and speed as well as a structured and

## 2.2 Literature Review on Identification of Influencers

clear communication style lead to higher source credibility (Kunz and Seshadri 2015).

Overall, the credibility of a source is an important characteristic for a persuasive source. A message send by a credible source can increase positive attitudes and evaluation towards the message itself, the product and the brand. Because of the nature of social media messages, users perceive the credibility of the source as integral part of the message. However, the credibility of the source can depend on the context of endorsement.

### Expertise

In literature, **source expertise** is also considered as autonomous characteristic of a message source. Source expertise is the extent to which a communicator is perceived to be a source of valid information and knowledge and should predict the endorsers effectiveness (Ohanian 1990). Within the social media context the expertise of a source can be defined as the audience's perception of an influencer's "skills, competency, and knowledge (Uribe, Buzeta, and Velásquez 2016, p. 4404)" concerning the subject of a blog or other social media formats.

Reflecting on celebrity endorsement literature, source expertise is one of the most impactful characteristics of an endorser (Amos, Holmes, and Strutton 2008). Findings on social media confirm those from celebrity endorsement research and indicate that blogger expertise increases the credibility of the blogger and the behavioral intensions towards the product recommended (Uribe, Buzeta, and Velásquez 2016).

Taken together, the expertise contributes to the social influence of a source in two ways. First, it indirectly influences the attitudes and behavioral intensions through an increase of source credibility. Secondly, it has positive direct impact on attitude change and evaluation formation.

### Trustworthiness

Besides expertise, the **trustworthiness** of a source is often treated as a separate quality of a source. Besides negative information, the trustworthiness of a source is found to be the second most influence on celebrity endorsement effectiveness (Amos, Holmes, and Strutton 2008). Consumers perceive a source as trustworthy if they have confidence in the source's intention to share the most valid information (Ohanian 1990). In the advertising context, consumers perceive celebrities as trustworthy if they rate their honesty, integrity and believability as high (Erdogan 1999). However, within the social media context trustworthiness was only considered as dimension of credibility and not as separate construct.

Prior research shows that source trustworthiness and expertise make independent more contributions to the effectiveness of a source but constantly contribute to source credibility (Amos, Holmes, and Strutton 2008). However, more research is needed on the trustworthiness as separate construct within the social media context.

Attractiveness
Similar findings exists for **source attractiveness** (Amos, Holmes, and Strutton 2008). The attractiveness of the source is multi-dimensional in nature and encompasses physical attractiveness as well as familiarity and likability (Erdogan 1999). In some studies, source attractiveness is measured through separate dimensions (Kunz and Seshadri 2015; Thompson and Malaviya 2013), which can reduce the impact of source attractiveness.

Lee and Watkins (2016) focus on the effects of the attractiveness of video bloggers on consumer perceptions of luxury brands. They categorize source attractiveness in social attractiveness originated form attitude homophily and perceived similarity and physical attractiveness. Both dimensions have a positive significant influence on the purchase intension of luxury brands. This is due to the increase of para-social interaction and a resulting increase in positive perceptions of the brands through upwards social comparison with attractive video bloggers. Therefore, Lee and Watkins (2016) contribute to endorsement literature by confirming first, the multi-dimensional nature of attractiveness, and second, an impact of both dimensions on advertising effectiveness within the social media context.

Taken together, attractiveness can be separated in a psychological and a physical dimension. Both contribute to persuasion of the message source.

Endorser Fit
Only a few studies consider the impact of **endorser fit** on brand evaluations and behavior intentions (Breves et al. 2019; Colliander and Dahlén 2011). Early research captured the influence of writer brand relationship of blog post and magazine authors on brand attitude and purchase intention. For this purpose, authors with a high writer brand relationship were compared with authors with a low writer brand relationship. The classification into these groups was based on an index reflecting whether the writer likes, uses, and finds the brand to be good (Colliander and Dahlén 2011).

Recent research observes the impact of influencer brand fit on brand evaluations and behavior intentions (Breves et al. 2019). The authors base their proposition on the match-up hypothesis, which has its origins in social adaption

## 2.2 Literature Review on Identification of Influencers

theory (Kahle and Homer 1985) and the Elaboration Likelihood Model (ELM) (Petty and Cacioppo 1986). In line with both theories, visual cues affect the effectiveness of persuasion, especially in a low-involvement context. The attractiveness of a source, for instance, can function as informational cue to convince consumer to use a specific beauty product. Therefore, a source is more effective if the source's image is congruent with the image of the brand (Kahle and Homer 1985).

Research shows that the endorser's brand fit positively influences brand evaluation and purchase intention (Breves et al. 2019; Colliander and Dahlén 2011). Especially in the context of blogging, the relationship between bloggers and the brand is important for ad effectiveness (Colliander and Dahlén 2011). Moreover, the effectiveness of an Instagram ad is positively influenced by the influencer brand fit mediated through the credibility of the influencer. If the para-social relationship between the followers and the influencer is high, the impact of influencer brand fit decreases since former experiences with the influencer rather shape attitudes and behavior (Breves et al. 2019). The fit between the celebrity and the product plays an important role within celebrity endorsement literature. However, no consensus exists which dimensions of a celebrity and a product should be matched (Amos, Holmes, and Strutton 2008).

Overall, endorser brand fit has a positive direct and indirect effect on consumer attitudes and behavior. However, the impact depends on the context. In the context of social media influencers, the influencer brand fit of a message source seems to be more important if the consumer has no other information to rely on.

All in all, it can be summarized that social media advertising and celebrity endorsement literature explain the social influence on an individual. However, this perspective usually neglects the structural potential. This potential, which results from structural resources, is particularly important for determining social influence within a network and selecting suitable influencers. For this reason, the following chapter explains the results from the field of viral marketing and will discuss the structural resources of an information source in detail.

### 2.2.2 Viral Marketing Literature

Apart from the personal resources of a message source discussed in advertising and endorsement literature, viral marketing focuses on the resources arising from the network of the message source. The following section relates to the second part of Table 2.2. It starts with a short theoretical and methodical classification in the field and then analyzes the constructs from left to right. The same meaning of highlighting is applied.

Theoretical foundation of this stream lies in the two-step flow model by Katz and Lazarsfeld (1955) describing the influence of a third party (mass media) through so called "influentials". This theory is also applicable for brands since they also reach for a greater audience on social media through social media influencers. Research on this phenomenon is based on field data from different social media networks and on one field experiment within a social media network. Some work combines real-world data with controlled lab experiments. Most of the studies investigate individual networks within Facebook (Hughes, Swaminathan, and Brooks 2019; Kupfer et al. 2018; Trusov, Bodapati, and Bucklin 2010), Twitter (Namkoong, Ro, and Henderson 2019; Peng et al. 2018; Valsesia, Proserpio, and Nunes 2020; Zhang, Moe, and Schweidel 2017) and Weibo, a Chinese microblog website similar to Twitter (Gong et al. 2017; Wang et al. 2019). Other work focuses on the impact of an individual's network on the diffusion of a message in the Chinese online community Qiushi-Baike (Chen et al. 2019) or on the adoption of virtual products within the Korean network Cyworld (Goldenberg et al. 2009). Some studies observe the activities of a source to shape its own network (Ansari et al. 2018) or the responsiveness of targeted seeding individuals (Lanz et al. 2019) on a music-sharing platform. Furthermore, a study observes the effect of connections on the responsiveness of users on LinkedIn (Rooderkerk and Pauwels 2016).

The stream can be further divided in two areas. The first area of interest is the effectiveness of seeding individuals in viral marketing campaigns. It identifies seeding individuals through data on the diffusion of information within a network. Therefore, the effectiveness of a message source is measured through the number of retweets and reposts (Chen et al. 2019; Namkoong, Ro, and Henderson 2019; Peng et al. 2018; Valsesia, Proserpio, and Nunes 2020; Wang et al. 2019; Zhang, Moe, and Schweidel 2017), likes or favorites (Hughes, Swaminathan, and Brooks 2019; Namkoong, Ro, and Henderson 2019; Peng et al. 2018) and comments (Hughes, Swaminathan, and Brooks 2019; Rooderkerk and Pauwels 2016; Valsesia, Proserpio, and Nunes 2020). In the context of a music-sharing platform, diffusion was measured through songs played (Ansari et al. 2018; Lanz et al. 2019). Research in this area verifies findings which characterize effective seeding individuals apart from the social media context (Hinz et al. 2011).

The second area predicts the adoption probability of connected consumers within a social network. Goldenberg et al. (2009) study the adoption of virtual products to decorate the personal home page within the Cyworld community and Katona, Zubcsek, and Sarvary (2011) study the adoption of the network service

## 2.2 Literature Review on Identification of Influencers

itself. Gong et al. (2017) measure the virality of broadcasting information via Weibo posts through adoption of show viewing and channel follower increase. Furthermore, Kupfer et al. (2018) can show the influence of an actor's structural resources on sales for the movie industry. These authors apply social network analysis to predict adoption within the context of social media and contribute to findings from the offline context, like the adoption of prescription drugs by physicians (Iyengar, van den Bulte, and Valente 2011; van den Bulte and Joshi 2007), the adoption of commercial kits to perform a specific molecular biology method by co-authors in life science (Hu and van den Bulte 2014) or the adoption of new consumer packaged goods (Du and Kamakura 2011).

Source Expertise

Recent studies within the stream of viral marketing have started to address a more holistic view of the influence of a message source (Hughes, Swaminathan, and Brooks 2019; Kupfer et al. 2018; Rooderkerk and Pauwels 2016). They include findings from persuasion research and combine personal and structural resources to predict the effectiveness of the message source. Since persuasion research found that with a social media setting **source expertise** positively influences purchase intention and recommendation (Uribe, Buzeta, and Velásquez 2016), this finding should be replicable for real-life consumer behavior.

Research on LinkedIn finds that not the number of connections, but the expert status of the message source have a significant influence on online discussions (Rooderkerk and Pauwels 2016). Other research differentiates these findings and proves blogger expertise only influential for awareness campaigns and only on blog comments not on Facebook likes. Without the interaction effect of campaign intent and blogger expertise, the study finds a significant positive effect on blog post comments but a significant negative effect on Facebook likes. However, blogger expertise is measured through profile information like higher educational degree (e.g. Bachelor of Arts) or blogger credentials (e.g. "social media consultant"). Source expertise is usually defined as being knowledgeable, experienced and skilled within a specific area (Ohanian 1990). Since the data came from 57 different campaigns, expertise could be perceived different if it is not captured over general attributes like educational background. To elaborate further on this, the authors use an experiment to replicate these findings and performed a manipulation check with the scale by Ohanian (1990). They find a significant negative effect of source expertise on purchase likelihood but an even larger positive significant effect for the interaction of source expertise and campaign intent when interactions were included.

Findings suggest that the influence of source expertise depends on the targeted output of the campaign. The results suggest that expertise of the message source is more likely to contribute to community communication and exchange through comments, but it reduces likes. However, it remains to be clarified whether the results will hold for different contexts and measurements of expertise.

Endorser Fit
Moreover, the results of Kupfer et al. (2018) also show that **endorser fit** is particularly important for the effectiveness of the message source. The authors investigate the association of fit between the celebrity endorser and the endorsed product with composite movie ticket sales. They measure this characteristic with a binary dummy variable. The endorser fit is one when the movie actor is "most known" for the focal movie's genre.

Kupfer et al. (2018) find positive significant influence of endorser fit and composite movie ticket sales and stress the importance of fit between a brand and an endorser for the formation of brand alliances. Moreover, they call for more specific research in the context of influencer marketing.

Network Structure Sender
Social network analysis relies on graph theory to visualize a social network. Graphs illustrate **network structures of the sender** by using nodes to represent individuals and ties or edges to represent the relationship between them. In particular, viral marketing literature within the social media context mainly focuses on ego networks (see Figure 2.1), which uses ego network measures to describe the structural and locational properties of a central actor (the "ego"). The network captures the friends or followers and followees the ego is connected to and the connections among them (Wasserman and Faust 1999). In social media literature three prominent measures of the network structure of the ego are discussed: degree centrality, betweenness centrality and ego network density.

The most researched measure is the ***degree centrality*** of an actor. The number of ties is often termed as "degree of a node". Within undirected networks degree centrality can be measured though number of real-life friends (Katona, Zubcsek, and Sarvary 2011), friends on Facebook (Trusov, Bodapati, and Bucklin 2010), friends on a music-sharing platform (Ansari et al. 2018) or connections on LinkedIn (Rooderkerk and Pauwels 2016). Within directed networks the centrality of an actor can be measured though in-degree and out-degree centrality (Goldenberg et al. 2009).

The number of followers on Facebook² (Hughes, Swaminathan, and Brooks 2019; Kupfer et al. 2018), on Weibo (Gong et al. 2017; Wang et al. 2019), or on Twitter (Hughes, Swaminathan, and Brooks 2019; Namkoong, Ro, and Henderson 2019; Peng et al. 2018) are measures of the in-degree of a message source in social media networks. The number of followers or the in-degree represents the status of an actor within a network (Lanz et al. 2019) or the prestige of an actor within directed networks (Wasserman and Faust 1999). Whereas the out-degree is measured through number of followees, e.g. on Twitter (Peng et al. 2018).

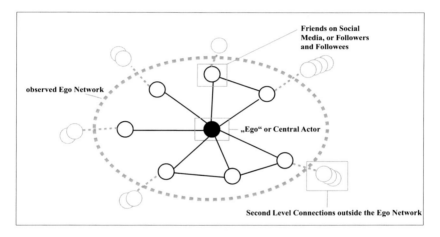

**Figure 2.1** Egocentric Network. Source: Author's own illustration, adapted from Ansari et al. (2018).

Moreover, these measures are also used to define specific user types. Therefore, a user with a high degree centrality is defined as social hub (Goldenberg et al. 2009). Or the ratio of followers to followees is used to determine if a user is an information disseminator or diffuser. The user is considered an information disseminator if the ratio is greater than one since more followers are interested about his content than the other way around. Whereas a ratio smaller than one indicates that the user is rather seeking for information from others. Whereby, it

---

² If the relationships between normal users are considered, Facebook can be seen as a unidirectional network since friendships that are formed are always reciprocal (Trusov, Bodapati, and Bucklin 2010). However, professional profiles, such as those of brands, actors or influencers, can also be followed in one direction (Hughes, Swaminathan, and Brooks 2019; Kupfer et al. 2018).

lies in the nature of hub-users to be rather information disseminators than non-hub users (Wang et al. 2019; Zhang, Moe, and Schweidel 2017). Which user type the sender of the message is, more specifically, how central the position of the message source within the network is, determines the impact on message effectiveness.

The number of followers of a source is positively related with the number of likes or comments on blog, Facebook or Twitter posts (Hughes, Swaminathan, and Brooks 2019; Namkoong, Ro, and Henderson 2019). However, research on LinkedIn finds no significant effect of the total number of connections on the number of comments on the user's posts. In the context of professional groups on LinkedIn, rather the expert status of a message source seems to drive post comments (Rooderkerk and Pauwels 2016).

In their work on tweets about events that capture the public's attention, Namkoong, Ro, and Henderson (2019) show that a message source with a high in-degree centrality receives 5.98% more retweets than a message source with an average number of followers. Studies on Twitter and Weibo confirm that tweets from information disseminators, users who have more followers than followees, can increase retweets (Wang et al. 2019; Zhang, Moe, and Schweidel 2017). In the context of micro influencers, recent research has specified that the number of followers increases the number of retweets and likes. However, the number of people the influencer follows reduces the number of retweets and likes, as it makes the influencer appear less autonomous (Valsesia, Proserpio, and Nunes 2020). Online success on music-sharing platforms, captured by the total number of songs played, is also positively influenced by the degree centrality of an artist (Ansari et al. 2018).

However, recent research finds that targeting central users can be risky for viral campaigns (Lanz et al. 2019). The authors introduce the concept of risk to the context of viral messaging and show that the responsiveness of those central users is low if the artist has a rather low status (low number of followers) compared to the seeding target. Nevertheless, these findings relate to a context of seeding under the absence of incentives.

Comparing company tweets with tweets from incentivized influential users with many followers, influentials are found to be more effective in bringing followers to the company's profile. Through this increase in company's followers, influentials indirectly raise TV show viewing, which adds to their direct effect on TV show viewing (Gong et al. 2017).

Apart from the diffusion process of information, the centrality of a source affects the adoption process of products or services. Research shows that users with high degree centrality are early adopters within the adoption process and

## 2.2 Literature Review on Identification of Influencers

increase the growth process and the overall adoption within the market. Furthermore, about 38% of the hubs are innovative hubs. Not only do these innovative hubs adopt earlier because they gather more information through their social connections, they are innovators and by definition adopt before all their friends. While market size can be predicted by the adoption of hubs in general, the adoption speed of virtual products in social networks is driven by innovative hubs (Goldenberg et al. 2009).

Katona, Zubcsek, and Sarvary (2011) examine adoption but from a different perspective. The authors concentrate on the likelihood of an actor's adoption of a social network service, depending on his already adopted friends. On the one hand, they confirm that the adoption likelihood of an actor increases with the number of friends already using the service. On the other hand, they show that the social influence on adoption proportionally weakens, with the total number of an actor's friends. These findings reflect the understanding, that a hub user is not necessarily an opinion leader or influential (Goldenberg et al. 2009).

While structural resources play an important role for the effectiveness of message diffusion and product adoption, it is likely that they interact with the personal resources of an individual. These interactions must be further studied in future research. A too strong focus on structural resources could have the consequence that although many users are reached, attitudes and behavior remain unaffected. One study that starts to address this challenge and observes the impact of the structural potential and the exertion of persuasion of a message source on product sales is Kupfer et al. (2018). They show that the number of Facebook followers of an actor is positively related to the revenues of the composite movie starring the actor. However, this impact interacts with the exertion of persuasion.

In summary, a sender of a message with a high degree centrality is beneficial both for the diffusion of information and for the adoption of products or services. Moreover, the number of connections within social media network increases likes and comments on the content of the sender. Nevertheless, hub user can be less responsive for the diffusion of information if they do not receive a compensation. Moreover, the central position of an actor interacts with other sources of persuasion. Therefore, degree centrality is a conducive, but not always sufficient basis for social influence.

The second measure of the centrality of an ego network is ***betweenness centrality***. The interaction of two social media actors can depend on other actors of the network. For example, if the shortest path between actor $a_1$ and $a_2$ is $a_1 a_3 a_2$, it can be assumed that actor $a_3$ in the middle has certain amount of influence on the other two actors. The influence of this actor in the middle or between the others is captured through betweenness centrality (Wasserman and Faust 1999).

However, Ansari et al. (2018) could not detect a significant effect of the betweenness centrality of an artist on online success on a music-sharing platform, but they argue that the betweenness centrality may be of greater importance for economic transaction where the intermediary may have more influence.

Furthermore, Katona, Zubcsek, and Sarvary (2011) only find partial support for a positive effect of local betweenness for the adoption of a social network service between friends. This could be due to the assumption that the connection on a social media networking platform replicates people's real-life friendships. It may be that some connections are missing since some people do not become members of the social media network.

So far, social media research finds only little proof for the positive effect of betweenness centrality. Future work on the impact of centrality within social media networks should take up this topic since research outside the social media context found that high-betweenness seeding holds comparable positive impact on the likelihood to react to a viral marketing campaign as high-degree seeding (Hinz et al. 2011).

The third measure of the centrality of an ego network is ***ego network density***. The concept of network density sets the number of ties or the degree in proportion to the maximum possible number of ties within the network (Wasserman and Faust 1999). The clustering coefficient is measured as proxy for the network density and reflects this proportion (Katona, Zubcsek, and Sarvary 2011). Therefore, the ego network density describes the cohesiveness of an ego network (Ansari et al. 2018). The relationship of network density and social influence lies in social capital theory (Coleman 1988). Proceeding from this theory, the social influence of two actors on an individual is greater if the two actors are connected to each other.

Diffusion research shows that the density of an artist's ego network positively impacts songs played on a music-sharing platform (Ansari et al. 2018). Moreover, a recent study by Chen et al. (2019) specifies implications for seeding of information within dense networks. Within a dense network the information redundancy increases through the increased likelihood of repeated exposure to the same information from multiple friends. The authors differentiate between creators and diffusers within a network. Other than Wang et al. (2019) and Zhang, Moe, and Schweidel (2017), they do not define diffusors through the ratio of followers to followees. In their study a diffusor is a user that never created new content within the last three months. The results show that within dense networks diffusors have a higher propensity to repost than creators since they have a lower need for uniqueness in the context of information redundancy. If a brand wants

## 2.2 Literature Review on Identification of Influencers

to approach a creator within a dense network, they must provide new information for the creator or incentivize the diffusion.

Research on adoption confirms a positive effect of network density (Katona, Zubcsek, and Sarvary 2011). The authors proof that the density of a network of consumers that already adopted a social network service has a strong positive influence on the adoption decision of their real-life friends. Taken together, sending a message through a source with a dense network increases information dissemination and adoption.

Besides these ego network measures, only a few studies focus on dyadic networks within the social media context (Peng et al. 2018; Wang et al. 2019). They include the number of mutual followers or reciprocal ties, which means that the connection is both sided and hence indicates the *tie strength* between two individuals. Since hub users have more followers than followees, consequently they have less reciprocal ties with their followers than non-hub users do (Wang et al. 2019).

Several studies have shown that the adoption of hub users increases diffusion of information and adoption of products (Goldenberg et al. 2009; Namkoong, Ro, and Henderson 2019; Zhang, Moe, and Schweidel 2017). At first it might be counter intuitive that the diffusion increases with weak ties, as strong ties like within dense networks predict social influence (Ansari et al. 2018; Coleman 1988). At the second glance, weak ties have a significant advantage for the diffusion process of information because they act as "bridges" and connect distant individuals or link different groups with strong ties with each other. Therefore, they increase the access or spread of new information within large networks (Granovetter 1973).

Research on Weibo confirms this view by showing the significant negative influence of the percentage of mutual followers on the number of reposts (Wang et al. 2019). Therefore, these findings on tie strength through reciprocal ties confirm that hub-user process much influence within social media networks. Although tie strength reflects the social impact, as evidenced by the positive impact of dense networks, hub users are particularly important in large networks to connect these small units.

Peng et al. (2018) are the only authors capturing the overlap of network structure between sender and receiver of a message. They consider the dyadic network attributes common followers, common followees and common mutuals. The authors find that the sharing propensity of a message receiver increases if the network structure of the receiver and the sender overlap. Furthermore, they illustrate differences of impact depending on the type of network overlap. They show that the effect of common followers is higher than the effect of common mutual followers. Moreover, they show the moderating influence of content popularity on these effects. Similar to Chen et al. (2019) in the context of network density, the authors explain the diminishing or even negative impact of overlap with the increase of content popularity through the need for uniqueness in social consumption.

In summary, this means that users are more likely to share content if their network overlaps with that of the message source. However, this also increases the probability that they have already received the information from another source. The likelihood that they will share the content depends on whether they consume and share content or rather create it themselves.

Activity of Sender
Besides the local position of an actor within the network, the activity of the network matters for the effectiveness of a message source (Kupfer et al. 2018; Trusov, Bodapati, and Bucklin 2010). Some research argues that the influence of an actor depends less on his number friends but rather on his activity which in turn effects the activity level of his followers. Even though the number of friends highly correlates with the influence predicted on the basis of log-in activities, only a small number of friends has an impact on the activities of users within social media. The results show that the 5% to 10% of highly influential individuals within a network can be identified using the activity of their network (Trusov, Bodapati, and Bucklin 2010).

Proving this relationship between locational resources of the message source and the activity level of the source, research shows that the interaction of product-related posts and social media network size on Facebook is significant and positive associated with sales. This positive interaction effect holds also true for product-related posts and follower activity (Kupfer et al. 2018). Similar findings on Weibo approve that the activity level of followers determines the influence of a message source. The study demonstrates that the comparative advantage of hub users to non-hub users even increases if their followers are active while the post is forwarded (Wang et al. 2019).

The activity of the network can be separated into the activity of the message source and the activity of the receivers or followers. The **activity of a sender** within social media networks includes posting activities (Ansari et al. 2018; Gong et al. 2017; Hughes, Swaminathan, and Brooks 2019; Kupfer et al. 2018; Zhang, Moe, and Schweidel 2017), messaging, liking and commenting or friend requests (Ansari et al. 2018; Lanz et al. 2019). The posting behavior of a message source is the most observed activity.

## 2.2 Literature Review on Identification of Influencers

The ***number of posts*** of an endorser increases Facebook likes (Hughes, Swaminathan, and Brooks 2019). Moreover, Gong et al. (2017) show that a company can increase their follower base and boost TV show viewing through retweets of influentials, which are characterized through a high posting activity. Nevertheless, the authors find that unrelated posting activities of the influential have an insignificant but negative effect on show viewing. Moreover, the impact on follower gain of the company is significantly negative and thus also indirectly reduces show viewing.

Research capturing the posting frequency prior to the focal tweet shows a negative significant influence of unrelated posts on likes and retweeting on Twitter (Valsesia, Proserpio, and Nunes 2020; Zhang, Moe, and Schweidel 2017). These effects could indicate that content receives less attention if the sender has a high posting activity that is not related to brand content. If posting activity remains high after the campaign post, new content could displace old content and thus reduce attention. This explanation is supported by results on social media post location (De Vries, Gensler, and Leeflang 2012).

In the context of a music-sharing platform new song uploads have a significant but negligible impact on online success of an artist. However, song uploads are different from other posts on social media because they need to be developed in a long-lasting creative process. Therefore, they are not such a flexible tool like friend requests or comments send. Moreover, the friends of the artist were not automatically updated on new song uploads, like it is the common way in frequently used networks (Ansari et al. 2018).

However, Kupfer et al. (2018) find positive effects of posting activity of the sender for the adoption of products. The authors show a strong overall impact of product-related posts from movie actors on composite movie ticket sales. Moreover, the authors differentiate the type of posts and elaborate on the diverse findings. They find a strong positive relationship between authentic, exclusive and persuasive product-related posts, whereby persuasive posts had the strongest effect followed by exclusive and authentic posts. However, the number of non-product-related posts has a negative impact on sales. They argue that posts that are not related to the campaign intent could distract followers or take attention away from the campaign post.

In general, it can be assumed that users with a high posting activity in social networks also have a high influence. Accordingly, this also reflects in higher information diffusion and product adoption. However, when it comes to advertisement or diffusion of brand content, the posting activity of the endorser should be related to brand, so that unrelated content does not cannibalize the effects.

Besides the creation of content, the purpose of an actor's activities can be to build relationships with other users through e.g. friend requests or the follow-for-follow strategy, liking the content of others or messaging others. These activities of the sender can be summarized under the term ***outbound activities*** (Ansari et al. 2018; Lanz et al. 2019).

On the one hand, the number of friend requests of a user has a positive influence on the long-term online success of artists since it increases the network size of the artist on a music-sharing platform. On the other hand, it decreases the network density of the artist's ego network, which, like network size, relates positively to songs played online. In the long run this negative effect of ego network density diminishes since friends integrate into the network, but actors should avoid randomly sending out friend requests (Ansari et al. 2018).

Moreover, Lanz et al. (2019) find that follows and likes applied by and artist have an effect on the attention the artist's profile is getting, but the direction of this effect changes within the different models, which leaves room for further research. Private messages directed to other artists within the network were the least effective activities to attract awareness. In their study, the authors observe the effects of outbound activities aimed at other artists on a vocal artist's online success, rather than looking at activities aimed at followers. The effects could be bounded to the specific context of targeting influentials for unpaid endorsements. Resent research on micro influencer shows that the users likes on others content increase his own likes and retweets (Valsesia, Proserpio, and Nunes 2020).

Generally, the impact of outbound activities with an unpaid endorsement setting decreases the higher the status difference from sender and receiver is. However, the potential return is higher for high status (in-degree) individuals. Considering the risk of no reply and budget restraints of outbound activities, actors should invest a fraction of their outbound activities to high status individuals with a high risk for low returns and a fraction to low status individuals with low risk to slowly grow (Lanz et al. 2019). In a more general context, research shows that a senders liking activity is positively related to virality (Valsesia, Proserpio, and Nunes 2020).

Besides, the activities of a social media actor can be directed at the interaction with other users' content. The outgoing comments of an artist on his followers' profile posts result in an increase of songs played in the same period. In the long run the positive influence on online success is caused by an indirect change of network structure (Ansari et al. 2018). Lanz et al. (2019) find similar effects for the writing of comments on songs. Their results show that comments are the most effective way to draw attention of a high-status user to an artist's profile. However, in the context of movie revenues the number of responsive comments,

## 2.2 Literature Review on Identification of Influencers

acknowledging or promotional comments of an actor have no significant effect on sales (Kupfer et al. 2018).

Overall, comments on other users' profiles have a higher short- and long-term impact than friend requests since friend requests can have bilateral effects. Therefore, social media users should prioritize their activities to shape their network structure and online success (Ansari et al. 2018).

Activity of Followers

Caused by the activity of the message source, the **activities of the followers** mainly shape the actor's network activity. In other words, the impact of an influential user is characterized by a high level of sharing or reposting behavior of his followers (Gong et al. 2017; Kupfer et al. 2018). The activity of followers comprises log-in activity (Trusov, Bodapati, and Bucklin 2010; Wang et al. 2019), posting activity (Gong et al. 2017; Kupfer et al. 2018; Peng et al. 2018; Zhang, Moe, and Schweidel 2017), liking activity (Peng et al. 2018) or incoming friend requests (Ansari et al. 2018).

Zhang, Moe, and Schweidel (2017) show that the posting frequency of users following a company significantly increases the number of retweets. Moreover, Wang et al. (2019) find that the number of synchronic followers positively moderates the positive effect of posting activity of the sender on the number of reposts on Weibo.

The number of incoming friend requests positively influenced the online success of musicians. Furthermore, the number of incoming friend requests enhances the degree centrality of an actor and the density of his ego network. Both variables have a positive influence on online success, whereby the number of incoming friend requests has an indirect influence on the diffusion of songs (Ansari et al. 2018). Findings on adoption confirm these findings. Results show a strong positive association between an actor's follower network activity on Facebook and composite product sales (Kupfer et al. 2018).

In summary, this means that the activity of the followers significantly determines the influence of an actor within social networks. However, studies have not yet compared the effectiveness of different activities.

Control Variables

In addition to these essential characteristics of a message source, the studies also include demographic **control variables** of the message source. Research controls for gender and age (Chen et al. 2019; Colliander and Dahlén 2011; Goldenberg et al. 2009; Katona, Zubcsek, and Sarvary 2011; Kunz and Seshadri 2015; Lee and Watkins 2016; Rooderkerk and Pauwels 2016; Trusov, Bodapati, and Bucklin 2010; Wang et al. 2019), ethnicity (Trusov, Bodapati, and Bucklin 2010) or endorser type (Hughes, Swaminathan, and Brooks 2019; Kupfer et al. 2018).

Some of the studies include the gender or age of message source as fixed effect (Chen et al. 2019) or covariate (Colliander and Dahlén 2011) but do not specify results. Others use gender and age to define their sample structure (Kunz and Seshadri 2015; Lee and Watkins 2016; Wang et al. 2019). However, Trusov, Bodapati, and Bucklin (2010) find that female users influence the log-in behavior on Facebook of male friends more than other gender combinations. Similar to that, Katona, Zubcsek, and Sarvary (2011) find that female users are more influential, whereas Goldenberg et al. (2009) find that hub-user are rather male. Rooderkerk and Pauwels (2016) find no significant difference between female or male post author on number of post comments for professional groups on LinkedIn. However, authors of posts with zero comments were more often female. Therefore, the influence of source gender seems to depend on context or platform type.

Considering the age of social media users, all studies show that the average social media user is in his mid-twenties. Moreover, influential users are rather young (Goldenberg et al. 2009; Katona, Zubcsek, and Sarvary 2011) and older friends of user have less influence on them (Trusov, Bodapati, and Bucklin 2010).

Furthermore, is the influence between similar individuals greater than between dissimilar individuals (Katona, Zubcsek, and Sarvary 2011). For example, a user is more influenced by a user with the same ethnicity (Trusov, Bodapati, and Bucklin 2010).

Kupfer et al. (2018) additionally control for the brand and promotion strength of the message source outside the social media context. Both the success of the actor's last films and his recent appearance on TV or in magazines has a positive significant influence on movie ticket sales. To control for a selection bias of bloggers, Hughes, Swaminathan, and Brooks (2019) implement a selection model that incorporates information from the bloggers' profile. The bloggers that were selected for a campaign were rather similar and were foodie or travel blogger. However, the included inverse Mills ratio has no significant influence on blog posts comments or Facebook likes.

Furthermore, research controls for account characteristics of the user. Studies include the time since account registration (Ansari et al. 2018; Chen et al. 2019; Goldenberg et al. 2009; Peng et al. 2018; Valsesia, Proserpio, and Nunes 2020) and information on the account's verification status (Peng et al. 2018; Valsesia, Proserpio, and Nunes 2020; Wang et al. 2019). Valsesia, Proserpio, and Nunes (2020) find that users who have been active on the platform for a long time and

## 2.2 Literature Review on Identification of Influencers

verified users gain more likes and retweets. Further the authors control for length of the user's bio, if the bio contains a link and whether the user has kept the default profile and default profile image. The results show that it is beneficial for likes and retweets if users have a profile picture posted and have not implemented a link in the bio. The other studies do not find any significant effects or do not further specify the effects.

Moreover, the studies include moderating or mediating effects of para-social interaction (Breves et al. 2019; Colliander and Dahlén 2011; Lee and Watkins 2016; Yuan, Kim, and Kim 2016) and type of source (agency-generated vs. user-generated) (Hautz et al. 2014) and are discussed in the chapters above.

Besides those characteristics directly related to the source, research controls for characteristics of the receiver (e.g. former purchase behavior, motivation to use social media or brand loyalty) (Ansari et al. 2018; Breves et al. 2019; Chen et al. 2019; Colliander and Dahlén 2011; De Vries 2019; Thompson and Malaviya 2013; Trusov, Bodapati, and Bucklin 2010; Yuan, Kim, and Kim 2016) or context-related variables (e.g. awareness vs. trial campaign or product and industry type) (Amos, Holmes, and Strutton 2008; Colliander and Dahlén 2011; Goldenberg et al. 2009; Hughes, Swaminathan, and Brooks 2019; Katona, Zubcsek, and Sarvary 2011; Kupfer et al. 2018; Lee and Watkins 2016; Namkoong, Ro, and Henderson 2019; Peng et al. 2018; Rooderkerk and Pauwels 2016; Thompson and Malaviya 2013; Trusov, Bodapati, and Bucklin 2010). If those effects were relevant for the interpretation of the effectiveness of a message source, they were discussed in the chapters above.

Many studies address content-related variables (Ansari et al. 2018; Chen et al. 2019; Colliander and Dahlén 2011; De Vries 2019; Gong et al. 2017; Hautz et al. 2014; Hughes, Swaminathan, and Brooks 2019; Kupfer et al. 2018; Lanz et al. 2019; Namkoong, Ro, and Henderson 2019; Peng et al. 2018; Rooderkerk and Pauwels 2016; Uribe, Buzeta, and Velásquez 2016; Wang et al. 2019; Zhang, Moe, and Schweidel 2017). However, the analysis of these content-related effects is outside the scope of this literature review on source effects within social media. In the following chapter on the design of viral posts, though, the relevant literature is discussed in detail.

The analysis of the last two chapters has shown that a holistic approach is needed. In order to measure the effectiveness of a message source in social media networks, the influence of both structural and personal resources must be considered.

## 2.3 Literature Review on Design of Content

Within the last chapter, the structural resources of a message source on the diffusion of this message were discussed. Besides these source effects, the design of content matters for a post to go viral (Rietveld et al. 2020). The literature review on content design summarizes knowledge that serves to answer the following question: Which contributions spread viral?

The literature search in leading marketing journals reveals 21 studies that focus on design elements of viral posts (see Table 2.3). Only one study deals specifically with influencer posts (Hughes, Swaminathan, and Brooks 2019). However, the findings on the design of user-generated and firm-generated content on social media offer extensive insights for the design of influencer posts. The forward and backward search of references led to no further inclusion of literature since studies from lower ranked journals or journals from related areas provided more empirical evidence but raised no new constructs.

In digital marketing, virality is the major goal for activities in social media networks. Brands increasingly rely on consumer to transmit messages within the social media network and brand posts compete with other content for the attention of social media users. Virality is the large scale diffusion of content within social media networks triggered by interactions of social media users with this content (Akpinar and Berger 2017). Therefore, the studies that observe virality define effectiveness by its impact on consumer behavior metrics such as views, likes, comments, clicks and shares. To derive managerial implication on the design of viral content for influencer marketing campaigns, this chapter reviews literature on message characteristics driving such consumer behavior metrics within social media networks.

Table 2.3 reveals that research predominantly focuses on textual modalities of social media posts. That seems reasonable since the text of the post is the central element within social media networks, like Twitter, Facebook or Weibo. Referring to persuasion theory, rational appeals can lead to higher elaboration and persistent change (Petty and Cacioppo 1986). The textual elements of a social media post provide the opportunity of reasonable argumentation and hence should increase the persuasion or virality of a message.

However, through the development of social media networks the importance of visual elements of social media posts increased rapidly. Social media networks like Instagram or TikTok increase in popularity and are based on visual experiences (Li and Xie 2020; Rietveld et al. 2020). The visual elements of posts draw

## 2.3 Literature Review on Design of Content

the attention of social media users to the message. Therefore, they can act as peripheral cue, induce persuasion and motivate further elaboration and cognitive processing (Petty and Cacioppo 1986). Recent research has started to address the impacts of visual design elements on virality (Akpinar and Berger 2017; Li and Xie 2020; Rietveld et al. 2020; Tellis et al. 2019).

The structure of Table 2.3 follows this classification in text and image. Drawing on the different types of processing (cognitive vs. peripheral) (Petty and Cacioppo 1986), the analysis of literature is also structured according to the type of content under research and the important constructs, given the specific modality. In that way, the structure of this chapter reflects the development of the research area over time, from text to pictorial elements of social media posts.

The columns of Table 2.3 capture the relevant design elements of viral social media posts. Core constructs like emotionality, informativeness, product or brand centrality and reference to events are observed for post text as well as for pictures and videos. Furthermore, for the text of social media posts the novelty of the text is examined. Moreover, the linguistic style of the post texts is analyzed. Thereby, the readability, the sidedness, as well as the personalization of the text and the rhetorical type is observed. More recent studies start to include social media specific elements like hashtags, mentions or emojis and estimate their value for virality. Further, the interactivity of text and picture posts is examined.

Through the visual driven nature of social media networks latest research extends the literature on post virality by peripheral perception. They shed light on the impact of colorfulness of posts or image quality on virality. Besides, the viral effectiveness of human face or text within pictures and videos is explored. Moreover, research investigates the image text fit of social media posts. Design-relevant control variables from both areas are general content type, post position, posting time and post text and video length.

As for Section 2.2 a conceptual approach is applied (Webster and Watson 2002). Thereby, the thesis synthesizes findings concerning the impact and the interactions of each construct.

**Table 2.3** Content Elements of Viral Social Media Posts

| Study | Emotionality | Informativeness | Novelty | Brand/Product Centrality | Events | Readability | Sidedness | Personalization | Rhetoric Type | Interactivity | # | @ | Emojis | Colorfulness | Image Quality | Human Face | Text within Image | Image Text Fit | Content Type | Position | Time | Length |
|---|---|---|---|---|---|---|---|---|---|---|---|---|---|---|---|---|---|---|---|---|---|---|
| **Textual Elements driving Virality of Social Media Posts** | | | | | | | | | | | | | | | | | | | | | | |
| Araujo, Neijens, and Vliegenthart 2015 | x | x | | | | | | | | x | x | | | | | | | | | | | |
| Borah et al. 2020 | x | | x | | | | | | x | | | | | | | | | | | | | |
| Davis et al. 2019 | x | | | | | x | | | | | | | | | | | | | x | | x | x |
| De Vries et al. 2012 | x | x | | | | x | | | | | x | x | x | | | | | | x | x | x | x |
| Heimbach and Hinz 2016 | x | x | | | | | | | | x | | | | | | | | | x | x | x | x |
| Hughes et al. 2019 | x | x | | | | | | | | x | | | | | | | | | | | | |
| Jalali and Papatla 2019 | x | | | x | x | | | | | x | | | | | | | | | | x | x | x |
| Kanuri et al. 2018 | x | x | | | | | | x | | | x | x | x | | | | | | | x | x | x |
| Li and Xie 2020 | x | | | | | x | | | x | | | | | | | | | | x | | | |
| Meire et al. 2019 | x | x | | | | | | | | | x | x | x | | | | | | | | x | x |
| Moro, Rita, and Vala 2016 | | | | x | | | | | | x | | | | | | | | | x | x | x | x |
| Namkoong, Ro, and Henderson 2019 | x | x | x | | | | | | x | | | | | | | | | | | | | |
| Ordenes et al. 2019 | x | x | | | | | x | | x | x | x | | | | | | | | x | x | x | x |
| Rietveld et al. 2020 | x | | | x | | | x | | x | x | x | | | | | | | | | | x | x |
| Rooderkerk and Pauwels 2016 | x | x | | | | x | x | | | | | | | | | | | | | | | |
| Swani and Milne 2017 | x | x | | x | | | | | | | | | | | | | | | x | x | | |
| Tucker 2014 | | | | | | | | x | | | | | | | | | | | | | x | |
| Wang et al. 2019 | x | x | | | | | | | | | | | | | | | | | | x | x | |
| Zhang, Moe, and Schweidel 2017 | | | | | | | | x | | | | | | | | | | | | x | | |
| **Pictorial Elements driving Virality of Social Media Posts** | | | | | | | | | | | | | | | | | | | | | | |
| Akpinar and Berger 2017 | x | x | | x | | | | | | | | | | | | | | | | | | |
| Li and Xie 2020 | x | | | | | | | | | | | | | x | x | x | | x | x | | | x |
| Ordenes et al. 2019 | | | | | | | | | | | | | | | | | | | x | | | |
| Rietveld et al. 2020 | x | x | | x | | | | | | | | | | | | | x | | | | | |
| Tellis et al. 2019 | x | x | | x | x | | | | | | | | | | | | | | | | | x |

Source: Author's own illustration.

## 2.3.1 Textual Elements driving Virality of Social Media Posts

In the following, drivers of virality of social media posts are derived from the literature, focusing on the textual design of a post. The review of literature will be based on Table 2.3 and the constructs will be discussed from left to right. As in Section 2.2, the **superordinate constructs** are marked bold.

Since the analysis focuses on actual behavior of users within social media, most of the studies employ real-life observational data. Two studies conduct a field experiment (Tucker 2014; Wang et al. 2019) and some studies confirm their findings from the field with further experiments (Akpinar and Berger 2017; Borah et al. 2020; Hughes, Swaminathan, and Brooks 2019; Jalali and Papatla 2019; Meire et al. 2019; Namkoong, Ro, and Henderson 2019). The field data is primarily from Facebook, Twitter and Weibo. Besides, Rooderkerk and Pauwels (2016) specialize on consumer reactions to online posts in professional groups on LinkedIn and more recent studies observe likes and comments on Instagram posts (Li and Xie 2020; Rietveld et al. 2020).

The impact of textual elements is observed on various consumer behavior metrics. It reaches from consumer awareness through impressions (Tucker 2014), over consumer interaction with the content through likes and comments (De Vries, Gensler, and Leeflang 2012; Heimbach and Hinz 2016; Hughes, Swaminathan, and Brooks 2019; Rietveld et al. 2020; Rooderkerk and Pauwels 2016; Swani and Milne 2017) and carries on to sharing behavior (Heimbach and Hinz 2016; Li and Xie 2020; Ordenes et al. 2019; Zhang, Moe, and Schweidel 2017) and post clicks (Kanuri, Chen, and Sridhar 2018; Moro, Rita, and Vala 2016; Tucker 2014).

### 2.3.1.1 Motivational Drivers of Post Virality
This consumer behavior can be motivated by design elements of social media posts. Such motivational drivers of post virality include emotionality, informativeness, novelty, brand or product centrality and reference to events.

Emotionality
Enjoyment is a major motivation for social media users to be a member of a network or participate in a virtual community (Cheung, Chiu, and Lee 2011; Dholakia, Bagozzi, and Pearo 2004; Lin and Lu 2011). Therefore, it is not surprising that the **emotionality of a message** is one of the most discussed constructs. In a broad understanding, a message is categorized as emotional if it contains emotion or high arousal, evokes sensory emotions, includes entertaining content, uses

speech to build a community, calls to action or mobilization or includes promotions (Meire et al. 2019). A rather basic definition is the presence or absence of emotional cues (Heimbach and Hinz 2016; Rooderkerk and Pauwels 2016; Swani and Milne 2017).

Other studies focus on rather concrete characteristics, like if the posts is entertaining or not (De Vries, Gensler, and Leeflang 2012). The emotionality of a message is mainly measured through manual coding of post text on scales (Hughes, Swaminathan, and Brooks 2019) or through dummy coding (De Vries, Gensler, and Leeflang 2012; Meire et al. 2019; Swani and Milne 2017; Wang et al. 2019). For example, Hughes, Swaminathan, and Brooks (2019) measure the hedonic value of a posts through a factor resulting out of manual coding process with a 20-item seven-point emotion scale, indicating if the content is for example attention grabbing, creative, emotional energetic, warmhearted or humorous. Other studies determined the sentiment of post text with the Linguistic Inquiry and Word Count (LIWC) software (Borah et al. 2020; Davis et al. 2019; Heimbach and Hinz 2016; Kanuri, Chen, and Sridhar 2018; Li and Xie 2020; Rooderkerk and Pauwels 2016) or the emotional polarity with TextBlob for Phython (Namkoong, Ro, and Henderson 2019). Ordenes et al. (2019) use their own trained automated text classification for the measurement of message intention for 12,374 Facebook posts and 29,413 tweets from Twitter. According with speech act theory they define emotional messages as expressive speech that works with affection, appreciation or evocation of desires.

Analyzing the literature on emotionality of post text on post virality, there is a positive association between an emotional brand or influencer message and blog post comments (Hughes, Swaminathan, and Brooks 2019), Facebook comments (Swani and Milne 2017) and the sentiment of Facebook comments (Meire et al. 2019). Furthermore, this effect also occurs for Facebook and Twitter likes (Hughes, Swaminathan, and Brooks 2019; Li and Xie 2020; Swani and Milne 2017). More specific, Heimbach and Hinz (2016) also find that emotionality enhances likes and that this effect is driven through positive as well as negative emotions like awe and anger. However, Li and Xie (2020) show in one of their data sets on Twitter that likes are positively related with positive emotions but negative related with negative emotions. However, these findings can be explained since a large amount of content is user-generated content. Therefore, there exist different motivations for the diverse consumer behavior metrics. While the sharing of negative content, like negative product experiences, can be helpful and increase further sharing, liking such user-generated content seems to be insensitive. Furthermore, they show that likes were not driven by emotionality within post text on Instagram. This shows that in the context of visual social

## 2.3 Literature Review on Design of Content

networks post text only plays a minor role. Nevertheless, these effects should be separately tested for brand and influencer content.

Further studies show that the context matters for these effects on comments and likes. On Facebook, De Vries, Gensler, and Leeflang (2012) find no effect for entertaining posts on comments and even a marginal negative (p-value < .10) effect on likes for brand posts. These effects can be explained by the definition of entertaining posts. Entertaining posts are described as entertaining content that is not brand-related. Therefore, they are not emotional posts per se but can include emotional appeals. In the context of brand communities on Facebook, content that entertains but is rather unrelated to the brand can have a negative association with post likes since brand fans are interested in the brand. Rooderkerk and Pauwels (2016) find no impact of post sentiment, neither for positive nor negative posts, on commenting on LinkedIn. However, their work focuses on content in professional groups, thus it is reasonable that users rather rely on informational content.

Besides the effects on likes and comments, high emotional content can increase the number of tweets on Twitter and Weibo (Heimbach and Hinz 2016; Li and Xie 2020; Wang et al. 2019). Nevertheless, Li and Xie (2020) find differentiating results on their two data sets on Twitter mainly focusing on user-generated content. For airline tweets positive and negative emotions triggered retweets, but for tweets on specific car models only negative emotions are related to retweets. These results can be explained by the different behavior of brand communities for the two categories. Negative and positive airline post content described the bad or good experience with the focal service. Therefore, positive as well as negative content is helpful and increases sharing but not liking for the later one. Negative posts on car models rather explained why new models are worse than the focal car model. These posts increase sharing and liking. Moreover, Namkoong, Ro, and Henderson (2019) find varying effects of emotional messages on post likes depending on the uncertain event. Hence, the product type or context could moderate the effect of emotionality on virality of user-generated content.

However, research on Facebook brand posts finds no difference for the positive impact of emotional content on comments and likes for products and services (Swani and Milne 2017). Research on Facebook and Twitter shares confirms the effectiveness of emotion through affective speech (expressive acts) in social media brand posts, compared with directive messages (Ordenes et al. 2019). Even though some studies find no significant direct effect on retweeting on Twitter, they show that emotion or humor can enhance the direct effects of information and hashtags (Araujo, Neijens, and Vliegenthart 2015) as well as improvised brand messages (Borah et al. 2020) on virality. Therefore, it could be that Twitter compared to Facebook is rather informational driven, even though emotion boost post retweets.

These conclusion are also drawn by Ordenes et al. (2019) since Facebook is rather a network connecting friends and therefore more emotional driven than Twitter. They base their assumption on a positive significant effect of the control variable positivity of message on sharing of Facebook posts. However, they find no such significant effect for sharing on Twitter. These findings for emotional text messages stay robust in the subsample for image and video posts. Davis et al. (2019) also finds no significant effects of positivity on Twitter, which speaks for this understanding. Moreover, Heimbach and Hinz (2016) confirm this view based on their findings on various platforms. They show that emotions like awe and anger enhance Facebook likes, but engagement on Twitter is rather driven by interest. Nevertheless, they find a significant negative relationship of the quadratic term of positivity and Facebook likes as well as sharing on Twitter, which implies an inverted U-shaped relationship. Therefore, content should include a rather moderate number of positive words, whereas exaggeration should have negative effects.

Focusing on consumer behavior at a later stage of the consumer decision journey, Kanuri, Chen, and Sridhar (2018) show the interdependencies of emotional content, post clicks and consequential gross profits. They find that high-arousal positive post content relates positively with post clicks, whereas they find no such relationship for high-arousal negative post content. However, they find interesting interaction effects between posting time and emotional posts. Facebook posts with rather negative emotions gained more post clicks in the morning than in the afternoon or at night. This effect does not appear for positive content. Moreover, they show that the adaption of posting time of negative emotional content based on these findings leads to an increase of 1.6% post clicks and translates into gross profits. However, their findings are special since their data comes from the news industry.

Nevertheless, they show that brands must account for the interaction effects of emotional posts. According to Ordenes et al. (2019) the rhetorical element of word repetition has a significant effect on Facebook shares, but this effect significantly weakens if used within emotional messages compared with direct messages. Whereas on Twitter repetition within emotional messages is significantly more positive than in directive messages. However, for a subsample with image and video posts the negative effect becomes insignificant for posts on Facebook. The positive results for Twitter stay the same. The interaction of alliteration and emotional messages is significant positive compared with directive messages

## 2.3 Literature Review on Design of Content

for sharing on both platforms, but for the image subsample it is significant negative on both platforms. Whereby, the direction and significance of the direct effect of alliterations on sharing differ in the various models. Therefore, more research is needed on the interactions of the emotionality of a message and the rhetoric style of a message. Moreover, Hughes, Swaminathan, and Brooks (2019) make the counterintuitive finding that the interaction effect of awareness campaign and high hedonic content is highly significant and negative on Facebook likes. They argue that the perceived risk and persuasion knowledge is higher for trial campaigns as for awareness campaigns. High hedonic posts alleviate feelings of distrust towards an ad and therefore foster cognitive processing and liking for trial campaigns on Facebook. However, research should further elaborate on these interaction effects to give clear implications for marketers.

Overall, the effects of emotionality on post virality are rather strong and positive, especially for brand content. Furthermore, emotional posts drive engagement on different platforms. This impact of emotion on post virality exists for goods as well as for services (Swani and Milne 2017). Meire et al. (2019) even show that brand fans positive engage with emotional content, independent from the offline performance of the brand. Moreover, Wang et al. (2019) show that the weaker source impact of non-hub users to hub-users on Weibo reposts decreases if non-hub users' content has high emotional valence. Even though content with emotional valence also increases hub-users' reposts, the elasticities are much higher for non-hub users. However, marketers need to pay attention what platforms they consider relevant for their target group since this influences the effectiveness of emotional content. For example, it is still unknown if emotional text of brand posts enhances engagement within visual driven networks like Instagram. Moreover, the campaign intent and the type of emotion determine the impact on post virality on different platforms.

Informativeness
The usefulness through information is a further reason for the use of social media networking sites or virtual communities (Cheung, Chiu, and Lee 2011; Dholakia, Bagozzi, and Pearo 2004; Lin and Lu 2011). Therefore, extensive research exists on the **informativeness** of posts text content on post virality. Within the basic definition, informational posts contain information on the product, the service, the brand, the company or events (Araujo, Neijens, and Vliegenthart 2015; De Vries, Gensler, and Leeflang 2012; Meire et al. 2019; Swani and Milne 2017).

The variable is measured with manual coding of dummy variables. Informative content can also be described by the distinction of emotional content.

Ordenes et al. (2019) define informational content as assertive act, which comprises information that contain neither emotion nor valence and can be true or wrong. Hughes, Swaminathan, and Brooks (2019) capture the factor functional through manual coding with a 20-item seven-point emotion scale. The post is defined as functional if it is perceived as sincere, informative, and understandable or considers using the product. However, informativeness is an overarching concept that unites several related more specific constructs. Jalali and Papatla (2019) study promotional tweets on Twitter and define informational tweets as content that includes promotion-related words. The informativeness of a tweet is captured by the share and position of promotional words within a Twitter message. Namkoong, Ro, and Henderson (2019) focus the abstraction level of an informational message on likes and shares on Twitter and distinct between abstract versus concrete information. Wang et al. (2019) concentrate on personal relevant content as informational message with high personal relevance. Kanuri, Chen, and Sridhar (2018) capture informal language through insights and causality through the LIWC. In research on post virality in professional groups on LinkedIn, the informativeness of a post was captured by coders who rated the practical usefulness, self-centeredness, and topical ambiguity of posts on a seven-point Likert scale. Therefore, informative posts should be high in practical utility and low in self-centeredness and topic ambiguity (Rooderkerk and Pauwels 2016). Similar Li and Xie (2020) describe informative content through content that has useful information and is rather not self-enhancing.

Although previous studies apart from the social media context have shown that informative content promotes virality (Berger and Milkman 2012), these findings do not translate to consumer engagement through likes and comments on social media networking sites (Heimbach and Hinz 2016). The informativeness of brand posts on Facebook had no influence on likes or comments (De Vries, Gensler, and Leeflang 2012; Heimbach and Hinz 2016; Swani and Milne 2017) or comment sentiment (Meire et al. 2019). Similar to these results, Hughes, Swaminathan, and Brooks (2019) find no significant effect of functional influencer posts on blog post comments or Facebook likes. Again when concentrating on user-generated content the findings differ. Rooderkerk and Pauwels (2016) show that the practical utility increases comments in professional groups on LinkedIn. However, self-centeredness and topic ambiguity have no influence on comments. For the airline industry, Li and Xie (2020) find that useful information have a significant negative effect on liking and sharing, while post text that should let the sender "look good" is positively related to both. Whereas in posts on cars useful information have no effects on liking but significant positive effects on sharing and for self-enhancing

## 2.3 Literature Review on Design of Content

posts it is the other way around. For the Instagram context both variables have no effect on likes, confirming the secondary role of text for Instagram.

When trying to replicate the results of Berger and Milkman (2012), Heimbach and Hinz (2016) could not show that practical utility influences the number of tweets on Twitter or One-ups on Google+. However, Araujo, Neijens, and Vliegenthart (2015) find that informational cues, like product details, predict high levels of retweeting on Twitter. Ordenes et al. (2019) confirm a significant positive association of informational brand content with sharing on Twitter but find that no significant association of informational content exists with sharing on Facebook. Like stated in the discussion on emotionality, they assume that Facebook is rather emotional driven, whereas Twitter is informational driven. This view is further proved through other research. For promotional tweets, Jalali and Papatla (2019) find that informational posts increase sharing on Twitter. The impact is rather driven through an early location of topic-related words, than through the share of topic-relevant words. Moreover, the authors also find a positive significant influence of the symbol $ and shares. Since the study focuses on promotional messages, a $ symbol can be seen as informational cue. Wang et al. (2019) replicate this findings for Weibo and user-generated content. They show that informational messages with high personal relevance increase sharing on Weibo. When focusing on user-generated tweets on events with causal uncertainty abstract messages increase the number Twitter likes and shares since they reduce the causal uncertainty and enhance cognitive processing (Namkoong, Ro, and Henderson 2019).

Kanuri, Chen, and Sridhar (2018) find no direct effects of informational content on post clicks. However, they specify that the impact varies over time of day. Informational content gains larger numbers of post clicks in the afternoon and evening than in the morning since it requires cognitive processing which depends on working memory. They explain their findings by the higher concentration of working memory on focal information to that time of day since during the day it inhibits irrelevant information and distracting tasks at the increased deprivation. Therefore, the authors emphasize the importance of research on interaction effects.

Similar with the findings on emotionality and rhetorical elements, the positive effect of word repetition on Facebook shares weakens if used within informational messages compared with direct messages. Whereas on Twitter neither the direct effect of repetition on shares nor the interaction effect with informational message gets significant. Nevertheless, for a subsample with image and video posts effects change. The interaction of alliteration and informational messages is significantly positive compared with directive messages for sharing on Twitter, but no effect occurs on Facebook. For the image subsample, the interaction effect is insignificant on both platforms. However, the direction and significance of the direct effect of alliterations on sharing differ in the various models (Ordenes et al. 2019). Therefore, given these results and the results on emotional posts, the interdependencies between rhetorical styles and message intention are far from clear.

Apart from the context condition of different platforms, research needs more insights on situations in which information matters for virality. For example, Meire et al. (2019) find a significant and strong impact of informational content on comment sentiment on Facebook when the brand performed weak (loss of game). Wang et al. (2019) find that non-hub users can gain influence compared to hub-users if they post informational content on topics with high personal relevance.

Taken together, it does not seem like informative brand content can induce like and commenting. However, useful information can induce sharing and the spread of this information within the consumer network. This holds true especially for networks where consumers are motivated through information seeking and sharing. Still, it is not completely clear in which context informativeness of text boost virality and in which it has no effect or even lowers virality.

<u>Novelty</u>
A recent study by Borah et al. (2020) observes the "unanticipation" of brand messages responding to an external event. Moreover, Ordenes et al. (2019) study the message intent categories emotional (expressive), informational (assertive) and directive but also observe the consistency of message intent. The authors assume that in a sequence of messages it is advantageous to change the message intentions. The novelty of the message breaks the monotony and makes it more interesting for the receiver. This motivates the receiver to share the message. In this respect, novelty is the opposite of consistency.

Like described in the last sections on emotionality and informativeness of message, Ordenes et al. (2019) dummy coded their brand message intent with automated text classification according to the presence and absence of emotional, informational and directive speech. The 22.8% of Facebook posts and the 13.2% of the Twitter posts containing more than one message intent were classified based on a classification rule following the weighting of speech act theory (assertive < expressive < directive). Thereafter, they use the Herfindahl-Hirschman index over the last three subsequent messages to operationalize the consistency of a focal brand massage as follows:

## 2.3 Literature Review on Design of Content

$$Consistency_i = \left(\frac{\sum_{i=-2}^{1} Assertive_i}{3}\right)^2 + \left(\frac{\sum_{i=-2}^{1} Expressive_i}{3}\right)^2 + \left(\frac{\sum_{i=-2}^{1} Directive_i}{3}\right)^2$$

where $Assertive_i$, $Expressive_i$, and $Directive_i$ are the dummy variables indicating whether a message was classified as each type (1) or not (0). Then the sum of the squared relative frequency per message type was computed. Whereby the consistency was highest for three subsequent brand messages with the same intent and a constancy measure of one.

Both studies find that novelty has a positive association with sharing (Borah et al. 2020; Ordenes et al. 2019). Considering the whole message, unanticipated improvised brand messages on external events increase the virality on Twitter (Borah et al. 2020). If multiple sequences of a message are observed, the novelty of message intent draws the consumer's attention towards the message and therefore the virality of the focal message increases on Facebook and Twitter. This argumentation is verified through the manual coding of the level of originality, unconventionality and newness across messages for an additional sub sample. However, when message intent through picture is included, a positive significant influence for message consistency on Twitter is found (Ordenes et al. 2019). Therefore, it remains unclear how the consistency or novelty over picture and text impacts post virality.

<u>Brand/Product Centrality</u>
A further motivation for consumer to participate in social media networks is the self-enhancement (Hennig-Thurau et al. 2004), which motivates them to create their own brand stories (Gensler et al. 2013). Moreover, through the engagement with brand messages, consumers can express their identity and attachment with the brand (Swani and Milne 2017). Therefore, consumer need to be aware of the brand or product through the post design, to activate this kind of behavior.

Almost all studies with multiple brands control for the brand itself or product category, but a few studies actually focus on the brand or product being part of the post text of social media messages (Jalali and Papatla 2019; Moro, Rita, and Vala 2016; Rietveld et al. 2020; Swani and Milne 2017). **Brand or product centrality** could also be handled as informative textual appeal. However, the results reviewed for the construct informativeness deal with broader concepts and this section analyzes rather concrete mentioning of product or brand-related information. Moreover, due to the importance of brands and products for consumer identity and self-enhancement it is observed as separate factor (Swani and Milne 2017).

Brand and product centrality is observed for posts on Instagram, Twitter and Facebook. Rietveld et al. (2020) concentrate on textual brand and product mention of 46,900 Instagram posts from 59 brands. Furthermore, they analyze the mention of special deals and product price and location. They focus on brands form the producing industry (e.g. Health and Beauty, Food, Apparel and Accessories) that have a high digital competence. Moro, Rita, and Vala (2016) focus on the Facebook brand page of one cosmetic company and categorize posts according to action posts, product posts (containing product and brand-related content) and inspirational posts (containing non-brand-related content). However, Swani and Milne (2017) and Jalali and Papatla (2019) include products as well as services. Swani and Milne (2017) observe 1,467 Facebook wall posts of 213 brands of the Fortune 500 companies and Jalali and Papatla (2019) investigate 14,148 tweets of 62 brands with the most Twitter followers in the sectors Automotive and Food and Beverage as well as Airlines and Dining. While Swani and Milne (2017) and Moro, Rita, and Vala (2016) used human coders to detect the presence or absence of brand or product within text, others used approaches of automated text classification (Jalali and Papatla 2019; Rietveld et al. 2020). Jalali and Papatla (2019) not only include the mention of brand but also the share of brand-related words and the location of brand-related words.

Rietveld et al. (2020) find that brand mentions within post text have a positive association with likes and comments on Instagram. On the contrary, product mentions are negatively associated with likes and comments. The authors find no significant effects for the mention of special deals or product price and location on post virality. Swani and Milne (2017) also find a positive but non-significant impact of brand mention on post likes. Moreover, they find a negative effect on Facebook comments and no significant effects for product mentions. However, the authors argue that interaction effects of brand and product centrality and product category determine impact on post virality. Product and services differ within their branding strategy and hence should design their post text differently. Since services are less tangible than products, they are more difficult to assess. Therefore, the corporate brand name becomes more important for services since it represents a certain service promise and image. Swani and Milne (2017) confirm this view through a significant positive interaction effect of brand mention and service on Facebook likes and comments. Besides, they find a significant negative interaction effect between service and product brand name on likes and comments. These results support their hypothesis that products rather rely on a product-based branding strategy and thus product name will generate more likes and comments on brand messages for products than for services.

Jalali and Papatla (2019) also find a strong and positive significant effect of brand mention on Twitter retweets for products and services. Moreover, they find a positive association between share of brand-related words and retweets. Furthermore, an early position of these words within the text has a positive but not significant effect on retweets. However, the authors specialize on promotional tweets, which may be subject to other motivations than self-enhancement. In this case it could be that the informational value that enhances engagement behavior.

Moro, Rita, and Vala (2016) find that the impact of content category on brand post clicks on Facebook, including product and inspirational posts, is 10%. Product post and inspirational posts increase are positively related with clicking, though they have less influence than action posts. However, this may depend on the strategy of the one cosmetic company observed. Moreover, the authors do not differentiate between promotion, product or brand information.

Taken together, the inclusion of brand or product name within post text should have a positive effect on consumer engagement on brand posts. However, the effect can be influenced through branding strategy or rather the product type. Moreover, the impact may depend on the platform and aim of brand post. Even though, Jalali and Papatla (2019) find a positive relationship between share of brand-related words, research still lacks knowledge on how central the brand or product should be within post text. Furthermore, the varying effects between brand and product mention within text of Instagram posts could indicate that in this context brand image fosters self-enhancement. However, mentioning the product is perceived as to intrusive. Given the context of influencer marketing, research should shed light on the effects of brand and product centrality of influencer posts.

Events

Apart from the brand or product centrality of a post, the mention of special **events** can influence the engagement on social media posts. Jalali and Papatla (2019) include the mentioning of events, like St. Patrick's Day or Valentine's Day, into their analysis of promotional tweets, since the events often coincide with promotions. Similar to their measurement of brand centrality, they measure the presence, share and location of event-related words.

These findings suggest that the presence of event-related words is significant and negatively related with brand retweets. However, the share of event-related words has the second highest influence on retweets. The authors argue that even a small increase in the share of event-related words in brand posts can compensate the negative main effect and raise the number of brand retweets. The location of event-related words has no significant effect on retweets (Jalali and Papatla 2019).

### 2.3.1.2 Linguistic Style

Besides these overarching constructs found within social media messages, research analyzes linguistic elements such as readability, sidedness, personalization or rhetoric type of social media posts.

<u>Readability</u>
An important linguistic element of social media posts is **readability** of the post (Kanuri, Chen, and Sridhar 2018; Rooderkerk and Pauwels 2016). Kanuri, Chen, and Sridhar (2018) measure readability with the FOG index. The index reflects how many years of education the understanding of text requires. This means, if the index is high the effort increases to understand the message. Borah et al. (2020) consider word length and sentence length within their own readability index. Rooderkerk and Pauwels (2016) use human raters to rate readability on a seven-point Likert scale. Therefore, a higher readability reduces the effort to understand the message and increases the likelihood of commenting on posts within professional groups, whereas post and sentence length should require higher effort to understand the message. Moreover, they include the variable sentence length. Heimbach and Hinz (2016) use writing complexity to describe the comprehensiveness of the message. They measured the author's writing complexity with automated analysis applying the Flesch Reading Ease test. Within a preliminary study, Davis et al. (2019) find that the tweet length (i.e., number of words per tweet), the average word length (i.e., characters per word), the frequency of non-words (i.e., number of words not found in the lexicon), the noun-to-verb ratio, the average parse tree depth (i.e., syntactic measures reflecting sentence complexity) and Twitter-specific cues (i.e. hashtags, at-mentions and emojis) relate negatively to readability of text. However, the results of text length and social media-specific characters can be found in the sections provided for these specific variables.

Within professional groups on LinkedIn Rooderkerk and Pauwels (2016) show that readability has the highest elasticity on number of comments. The increase of readability by 1% results in an increase of comments by 2.62%. Moreover, Davis et al. (2019) also find a positive effect of readability on Twitter likes since non-words and a high noun-to-verb ration significantly decrease liking. However, sentence length (Rooderkerk and Pauwels 2016) or word length (Davis et al. 2019) have no effect on engagement.

Furthermore, non-words, high noun-to-word ratio and sentence complexity have a negative effect on shares. Therefore, high readability of Twitter posts increases sharing. The findings of Kanuri, Chen, and Sridhar (2018) confirm a positive effect on post clicks. Even though Heimbach and Hinz (2016) find no effects of writing complexity on Facebook likes, retweets and Google One-ups, their findings have to be interpreted with caution since they relate to the writing complexity of news article posts and are therefore special. Borah et al. (2020) also find no impact of readability on retweets.

Davis et al. (2019) find that the effects of readability interact with brand hedonism. Hedonic brand positively moderates the negative influence of non-words and sentence complexity. However, the interaction with average word length becomes negative. Therefore, hedonic brands should use shorter words, but in general the readability of post text is less important than for functional brands.

All in all, readability increases post virality. Considering the processing fluency, the virality of posts should increase if they are rather short and easy to understand. Nevertheless, the impact varies depending on the context and for hedonic brands readability of posts plays a less important role.

Sidedness

Persuasion groundwork found that opposing arguments can be beneficial for the persuasiveness of a message (Hovland, Lumsdaine, and Sheffield 1949; Williams, Bourgeois, and Croyle 1993). Rooderkerk and Pauwels (2016) argue that in the context of professional groups on LinkedIn the **sidedness** of arguments delivers benefits for other users and fosters post virality. They base their findings on Festingers theory of cognitive dissonance (Festinger 1957), which proposes that people seek for reduction of dissonance. With the engagement through comments users can reduce the perceived dissonance emerging from message content. Rooderkerk and Pauwels (2016) measure the sidedness of a message through manual coders that rate the controversy of message on a seven-point Likert scale.

The controversy of message results in more comments on LinkedIn. It has the second highest elasticity on post comments in professional groups. It seems like the sidedness of arguments within social media networks drives at least specific forms of post virality. Since the study of Rooderkerk and Pauwels (2016) is one of the first to address the impact of sidedness on post virality, it seem questionable if this results depend on the context of profession groups or the platform LinkedIn. It is assumed that professionals have more knowledge on the topic and are more involved with the topic. Therefore, they rather engage in cognitive processing, which is needed for the impact of reasonable arguments (Petty and Cacioppo 1986). Nevertheless, De Vries, Gensler, and Leeflang (2012) find similar results for positive and negative user-generated comments that drive comments on brand posts. They argue that brand fans engage in this behavior since they want to differentiate their opinion from others. Therefore, the controversy of the discussion boosts further discussion. However, De Vries, Gensler, and Leeflang (2012) find no effects of both-sided comments on likes which suggests that controversy only drives comments and likes are rather driven by consensus.

Personalization

Another design element of viral posts is the **personalization** of messages. Within a Facebook field experiment Tucker (2014) manipulates the personalization of a social media ad through the presence and absence of personal information within text that was gathered through the user's profile page. The text was personalized by mentioning the user's home university or by referring to a celebrity with whom the user shows an affinity. Furthermore, the authors analysis if target posts increase engagement. Since the data is provided by a non-profit organization which offers education for girls in East Africa, the organization approaches users that have a connection with a university or a celebrity that is committed to the education of women within the targeted condition. Kanuri, Chen, and Sridhar (2018) also observe if the posts was targeted or not. Therefore, targeted posts indirectly create a better fit between post content and a specific audience. Rietveld et al. (2020) also measure how targeted the post is through the actual mention of target audience within an Instagram brand post. Furthermore, Zhang, Moe, and Schweidel (2017) specialize on the individual level and analyze the message user fit for Twitter messages. The fit of the message to the user is high if the message content is similar to the typical content shared by the user. The authors pre-specified six different topics related with university matters and used latent Dirichlet allocation to calculate the similarity between topic of the university's tweet and an individual's topic preference based on historical tweeting behavior.

Rietveld et al. (2020) show that a rather direct approach of targeting is ineffective for the enhancement of post virality. The mention of target audience within brand post text has a negative significant impact on likes and comments on Instagram. It could be that post virality within visual driven social networks is more driven through implicit approaches of personalization. Moreover, Zhang, Moe, and Schweidel (2017) find a positive association between the message user fit and retweeting of universities' posts. Since the brand content is adjusted to the user's typical content, the user feels implicit related to this content. Moreover, it is a more individualistic method of targeting than mentioning the audience in general.

In support for this, Kanuri, Chen, and Sridhar (2018) find that targeted posts increase post clicks. However, there was no variation in the target filters, thus the authors could not specify their results with respect to targeting effectiveness. Surprisingly, Tucker (2014) found that personalized ads could not increase post virality. In fact, personalized content got less clicks than content without personalized information. The authors explain these findings with the privacy concerns of users. However, during the experiment the privacy settings of Facebook changed which enabled the authors to observe the interaction of personalized messages and privacy concerns. Even though users gained more control over their personal information through this new privacy settings, the targeting process remained the same since it is based on anonymized data. After the users perceived to have more control over their private information personalized targeted content significantly increased clicks on content. Moreover, they show that personalization of content is more effective if the content is targeted at a smaller audience.

All in all, personalization of social media messages provides the opportunity to increase post virality if users perceive to have control over their personal information. Furthermore, brands should use an implicit targeting strategy, such as fitting brand content to the user's content or broadcast according to specific criteria, rather than direct targeting. Personalization on an individual level is especially impactful.

Rhetoric Type
Just as the personalization of the message is important for the virality of content, so is the **rhetoric type** of the message. Ordenes et al. (2019) argue that rhetorical style elements, as alliteration and repetition, are often used in brand messages. For example, "deal of the day" is an alliteration. It evokes a rhythmic effect if two successive or closely spaced words start with the same letter. A similar effect occurs for repetition of the same word for one time or multiple times (e.g. "We really really really really really like potatoes"). However, rhetoric can also be the usage of specific language or persuasive words to reach an audience. For example, Rooderkerk and Pauwels (2016) analyze the degree of jargon used in post within professional groups on LinkedIn. Furthermore, Li and Xie (2020) include five linguistic content categories to measure the rhetoric style of Twitter and Instagram posts. They measure these categories with the LIWC dictionary and determine the percentage of affect words, social words, cognitive words, perceptual words, and words for drive and need. Borah et al. (2020) use the LIWC dictionary to capture authentic, informal and powerful language style.

Rooderkerk and Pauwels (2016) find a positive but not significant effect of degree of jargon within LinkedIn posts on comments. However, this type of rhetoric style highly correlates with practical utility of the message and expert status of the sender which both have a significant positive impact on comments. Therefore, more information is needed on the interrelations of these influence factors. Li and Xie (2020) find no impact of the five linguistic content categories on likes neither for Twitter nor for Instagram.

The use of alliteration shows no significant effect on Facebook but a significant negative effect on retweets. The negative effect weakens if used in assertive or expressive posts compared with directive posts. For the extended study with image content variables the effect of alliterations on Facebook shares gets significant and negative. The negative effect gets stronger when used with expressive speech. The significant effect on retweets disappears. Furthermore, repetitions are not significantly related with retweets in the main study but significant negative related for the image subsample. This negative effect is less important if repetition is used within expressive speech. In the main study repetitions have a positive association with shares on Facebook. The positive effect weakens if used in assertive or expressive posts compared with directive posts. The positive effect on Facebook gets non-significant for the subsample, but the interaction effect of repetition and assertive speech become significant and positive. Moreover, Li and Xie (2020) also find no significant relationship of linguistic content categories and sharing on Twitter. Borah et al. (2020) find no influence of authentic, informal and powerful language style on Twitter retweets.

All in all, alliterations seem to be not effective for the virality of posts. Moreover, it is also not clear if repetition drives post virality. In a professional context degree of jargon should have a positive impact on post virality. However, in another context of social media networks it may reduce the readability and have negative effects. The non-existing effects of linguistic content categories both on Twitter and Instagram suggest that rhetorical style elements have less influence within social media posts than in traditional contexts. It could be that social media users pay less attention to text within social media and rather concentrate on social media network specific cues (e.g. images or hashtags). However, not many studies analyze the usage of rhetorical style elements on post virality within social media and further research is needed.

### 2.3.1.3 Social Media specific Elements

Social media networks open up new forms of communication, which can have a major impact on the virality of social media posts. The interactivity of social

## 2.3 Literature Review on Design of Content

media posts plays a major role in this context. Further, posts include social media specific elements like hashtags, mentions or emojis to drive post virality.

<u>Interactivity</u>
Another advantage of social media networks is that the users can interact with each other and with the message itself. Within their theoretical framework Liu and Shrum (2002) define **interactivity** within an online environment as "the degree to which two or more communication parties can act on each other, on the communication medium, and on the messages and the degree to which such influences are synchronized" (Liu and Shrum 2002, p. 54). Post text characteristics vary according to their level of interactivity and can differ in their effect on post virality (De Vries, Gensler, and Leeflang 2012). Social media messages deliver different design opportunities for the users to control and customize the interaction with the message. Moreover, message characteristics define if the post fosters reciprocal communication and synchronicity. Therefore, different degrees of a posts interactivity exist (Liu and Shrum 2002). De Vries, Gensler, and Leeflang (2012) operationalize low interactivity through link and voting within brand post text, a medium interactivity post through call to act and contest and high interactivity through question. The authors observe the different levels of interactivity. However, most of the studies rather control for individual variables. They control for links and question within text on comments (Rooderkerk and Pauwels 2016) or shares (Jalali and Papatla 2019; Ordenes et al. 2019). Jalali and Papatla (2019) extent the insights for call to act with position and share of words that call to action within promotional posts, the timeline for call to act within text as well as exclamation mark and number of exclamation on Twitter shares. Moreover, studies control for the encouragement to reply to a post through comment (Rooderkerk and Pauwels 2016) or the use of the acronym for "retweet if ..." (RT_if) and blank spaces that motivate the reader to complete (Jalali and Papatla 2019). Hughes, Swaminathan, and Brooks (2019) measure the presence or absence of giveaways since they encourage customers to engage with social media content in order to get the incentive. For the prediction model of Moro, Rita, and Vala (2016) posts were categorized as action posts if the content included different interactive design elements. The brand manager manually coded the post category depending on the type of campaign intent.

Rooderkerk and Pauwels (2016) find a significant negative association between links within post text and number of comments on posts within professional groups on LinkedIn and De Vries, Gensler, and Leeflang (2012) at least confirm a marginal negative effect on Facebook comments. Moreover, De Vries, Gensler, and Leeflang (2012) find no further impact of low and medium interactivity on comments and likes, only contest increases likes. However, they show that high interactivity through question positively influences comments but is negatively associated with likes on Facebook brand posts. Rooderkerk and Pauwels (2016) confirm the positive association of questions on comments within LinkedIn professional groups and add prove for the positive effect of encouragement to reply on comments. Hughes, Swaminathan, and Brooks (2019) show similar cannibalizing effects for giveaways as De Vries, Gensler, and Leeflang (2012) show for question within social media posts. Giveaways significantly increased comments on posts, however they significantly decrease Facebook likes.

Ordenes et al. (2019) show that a link within a post is positively associated with Facebook shares but negatively with Twitter shares. When they extended their data by the implication of image acts, the variables lost their influence. However, Jalali and Papatla (2019) find that links within promotional posts are positively related to shares on Twitter. Araujo, Neijens, and Vliegenthart (2015) find no significant direct effect of the different type of links on Twitter shares. Nevertheless, they show a positive interaction effect with hashtags. For promotional tweets, Jalali and Papatla (2019) prove that medium interactivity through call to action and timeline for this action have the largest impact on the number of retweets. However, they find that the share of call to action is negatively related with shares and should therefore be used purposefully and not inflationary. This is confirmed by the negative effect of number of exclamations on shares. The encouragement of retweets (RT_if) is positively related to shares of promotional posts and blanks and questions are negatively related with shares. Yet, Ordenes et al. (2019) can only confirm the negative effect of question for Twitter shares within their subsample including message intent through image. Other than that, they find that question drives Facebook and Twitter shares.

With their prediction model Moro, Rita, and Vala (2016) show that the post category, including action posts, accounts for 10% of the clicks a brand post gains on Facebook. Moreover, the influence of a posts categorized as action post on consumer clicks is significantly higher than the influence of product or inspiration posts. However, the results are based on a single Facebook brand page of a cosmetic firm and do not differentiate between the various types of interaction elements. Moreover, the authors acknowledge that the impact may depend on the company's strategy.

All in all, the question remains how interactivity shapes post virality since only few studies consider the interactivity of post in a broad understanding (De Vries, Gensler, and Leeflang 2012). Table 2.4 summarizes the operationalization of post interactivity and the impact on post virality. The categorization of interactivity follows the level approach of De Vries, Gensler, and Leeflang (2012).

## 2.3 Literature Review on Design of Content

**Table 2.4** Effect of Post Interactivity on Post Virality

| Level of Post Interactivity | Operationalization | Likes | Comments | Shares |
|---|---|---|---|---|
| Low | Link | n.s.[a] | $(-)^a/-^c$ | $+^a/-^b/+^b/$ n.s.[b] |
|  | Voting | n.s.[a] | n.s.[a] |  |
| Medium | Call to act | n.s.[a] | n.s.[a] | $+^b$ |
|  | Contest | $+^a$ | n.s.[a] |  |
|  | Exclamation |  |  | n.s.[b] |
|  | Number of exclamations |  |  | $-^b$ |
| High | Question | $-^a$ | $+^a/+^c$ | $(+)^a/+^b/-^b$ |
|  | Blanks |  |  | $-^b$ |
|  | Encouragement |  | $+^c$ | $+^b$ |
|  | Giveaway | $-^a$ | $+^d$ |  |

Source: Author's own illustration. Notes: [a] Facebook, [b] Twitter, [c] LinkedIn, [d] blog, $+/- =$ positive/negative effects, n.s. = not signficant effects. Empty cells represent effects that have not been studied.

No study considers likes, comments and shares simultaneous and compares the effects with each other. However, research including comments and likes shows cannibalizing effects between the different measures of engagement (De Vries, Gensler, and Leeflang 2012; Hughes, Swaminathan, and Brooks 2019). Therefore, the interactivity of a post should always be tailored to the campaign objective. Relying on the studies reviewed, likes can be increased through contest and are decreased through questions, whereas comments are increased through questions and encouragement to reply and rather decreased through links within text. Shares can be increased through call to action and encouragement to retweet. Blanks that motivate the user to fill in reduce sharing, maybe because they foster engagement through comments. Other effects of interactivity are rather unclear due to different results.

### Hashtags (#), Mentions (@) and Emojis

Within the last two years, social media research has paid more attention to social media specific cues. The impact of **hashtags (#)**, **mentions (@)** or **emojis** is measured on Twitter (Araujo, Neijens, and Vliegenthart 2015; Davis et al. 2019; Jalali and Papatla 2019; Li and Xie 2020; Ordenes et al. 2019), Facebook (Ordenes et al. 2019) and Instagram (Li and Xie 2020; Rietveld et al. 2020). The studies measure the number of hashtags, mentions and emojis through key word detection. The underlying assumption is that these social media specific cues increase the potential exposure.

Li and Xie (2020) find no effect of the number of hashtags within Twitter posts on likes for posts on airlines, but they find significant negative effects for hashtags on likes for posts on cars. However, Davis et al. (2019) find a significant positive association of hashtag use in brand tweets on Twitter likes over different product categories. Since Li and Xie (2020) include user-generated content, it could be that on Twitter the positive effect rather occurs for brand content. On Instagram, hashtags have either no effect (Li and Xie 2020) or even a negative effect (Rietveld et al. 2020). Since popularity on Instagram is more driven through visual elements than text, consumers may not pay attention to the post text or find a variety of hashtags too intrusive. This is also underlined by the non-significant effects of emojis on Instagram likes. However, the number of mentions had a positive effect on likes on Instagram (Li and Xie 2020) and Twitter (Davis et al. 2019).

For airline posts, Li and Xie (2020) and Davis et al. (2019) find a significant and positive influence of the number of hashtags and mentions on retweets. Other studies confirm the positive effect of hashtags on retweets for brand posts over different product categories (Araujo, Neijens, and Vliegenthart 2015; Jalali and Papatla 2019). The authors conclude that the use of hashtags before topic-related content draws attention to the topic of the post. On the contrary, Ordenes et al. (2019) find significant negative effects of hashtags on Facebook and Twitter shares. However, for the image subsample the effect gets positive significant for Facebook posts if image act is included. Li and Xie (2020) find a negative effect of emoji usage on retweeting for both samples.

Taken together, most of the studies find proof for the effectiveness of hashtags and mentions on sharing. Although the effects of using hashtags on comments and likes are mixed on different platforms, the use of hashtags on textual driven platforms should not hurt post virality. Moreover, the effects for mentions should be positive on different platforms. However, the only study considering emojis finds no effect or negative effects on post virality. Since these design elements are heavily used within social media, research should gain more insights on the effectiveness on post virality on different platforms. For example, could the usage of emojis within influencer messages be positively associated with post virality because they share a closer relationship with their followers than brands. Moreover, could the use of hashtags, mentions and emojis within an image have different effects on post virality (e.g. on Instagram).

## 2.3 Literature Review on Design of Content

### 2.3.1.4 Control Variables

Besides these content variables, most papers control for contextual variables. Some of these are relevant to design, such as content type, position, time, and length and are discussed in more detail below.

Content Type

Since the discussed research mainly focuses on textual analysis, many of the studies control additionally for **content type**. Typically, the authors control for image and video (Borah et al. 2020; Davis et al. 2019; De Vries, Gensler, and Leeflang 2012; Li and Xie 2020; Moro, Rita, and Vala 2016; Ordenes et al. 2019; Swani and Milne 2017). However, Moro, Rita, and Vala (2016) further differentiate between the content type status update and posts that only consist out of a link[3]. Moreover, Li and Xie (2020) distinguish between direct images and images that are connected through a higher link.

Swani and Milne (2017) and De Vries, Gensler, and Leeflang (2012) find no effects for images within brand posts on Facebook likes. Additionally, both studies find a negative effect of images on Facebook comments, but only Swani and Milne (2017) find a significant effect. Nevertheless, their findings differ with regard to videos. First, De Vries, Gensler, and Leeflang (2012) find a positive and significant effects of brand posts with videos on Facebook likes and Swani and Milne (2017) find a negative but non-significant effect. Second, Swani and Milne (2017) show a significant and negative effect of videos on Facebook comments, but De Vries, Gensler, and Leeflang (2012) find no significant effects. De Vries, Gensler, and Leeflang (2012) explain the positive effect of video on likes through the higher level of vividness. Since multiple senses are addressed, videos increase the preference for the brand posts. However, research explains the negative or non-significant effects on image and video on comments or likes through attention constraints. Consumers are less likely to engage in commenting and liking when they decode the content of image or video (De Vries, Gensler, and Leeflang 2012; Swani and Milne 2017). Where this might be true for commenting, Li and Xie (2020) find that direct images increase likes on Twitter. Like for the positive results of De Vries, Gensler, and Leeflang (2012) for video, this effects may occur through the preference of vivid content. Davis et al. (2019) confirm this since they find significant positive effects of rich content (i.e. image or video) on Twitter likes. However, linked images have a significant and negative effect on

---

[3] Since the authors define a link as content type and do not analyze it as part of a post's text, it is discussed within the section of controls and not within the section referring to interactivity.

Twitter likes (Li and Xie 2020). Therefore, it is suggested that social media users do not have the motivation to open the link.

Moreover, rich content also increases shares on Facebook (Ordenes et al. 2019) and Twitter (Davis et al. 2019). In contrast to Davis et al. (2019), Ordenes et al. (2019) measure image and video as separate variables and specify the effects for Twitter. Even though images also increase sharing on twitter, videos are negatively associated with Twitter shares. Li and Xie (2020) confirm the positive effect of direct images on Twitter shares but find negative results for linked image. Borah et al. (2020) find no significant effect on tweet an retweets.

Within the prediction model of Moro, Rita, and Vala (2016) content type accounts for 36% of clicks on brand posts. However, the do not further elaborate on the differences of content type on clicking except on the primary influence of status update. When the brand publishes status updates on Facebook, it receives about twice as many clicks as for video, image or link.

Taken together, the impact of content type differs across consumer behavior metrics. Vivid content drives post clicks and sharing. Equally, brands can increase clicks through regular status updates since they outperform other content. While images or videos can drive likes on Facebook or Twitter, they are negatively related with comments. It could be that commenting requires cognitive processing and that this type of processing is rather induced through text than vivid content. Furthermore, it could be that the decoding of images or videos requires processing capacity and therefore reduces the likelihood of commenting on content. However, research calls for more detailed analysis of vivid content (Li and Xie 2020; Rietveld et al. 2020).

Position

As for banner advertising, **position** of content also matters for social media posts (De Vries, Gensler, and Leeflang 2012). Most of the studies measure the position of social media posts indirect through the frequency of posting (Jalali and Papatla 2019; Kanuri, Chen, and Sridhar 2018; Ordenes et al. 2019; Zhang, Moe, and Schweidel 2017). A high posting frequency on brand page indicates that posts spend less time on the top position since older posts shift down when new content is posted. Some of the studies measure top position directly through number of days the post has a top position on the brand page (De Vries, Gensler, and Leeflang 2012; Heimbach and Hinz 2016) and others control for the time the post is online (Jalali and Papatla 2019; Swani and Milne 2017). Wang et al. (2019) include position fixed effects.

A top position on brand page had a positive significant influence on Facebook likes (De Vries, Gensler, and Leeflang 2012; Heimbach and Hinz 2016) and

## 2.3 Literature Review on Design of Content

comments (De Vries, Gensler, and Leeflang 2012). In favor of recent content, it is recommended to not post too frequently since the replaced content gets fewer attention at a lower position. Besides, Swani and Milne (2017) control for the number of days online and find positive and significant effects on likes and comments on Facebook. If the brand posts frequently, this would mean that the top position is less relevant for post virality. However, Swani and Milne (2017) do not include posting frequency and it could be assumed that number of days online positively correlates with number of days a post spends on top position if the brand posts not to frequently.

Following this thought, Jalali and Papatla (2019) find that posting frequency is negatively associated with retweets and number of days the post is online has a negative but non-significant effect. Zhang, Moe, and Schweidel (2017) confirm the negative effects of posting frequency on retweeting and Heimbach and Hinz (2016) associate top posting on brand page with a higher number of Twitter shares. Therefore, top position of social media content also drives post virality through sharing. Nevertheless, research fails to show a significant effect of time difference between post in a sequence and Facebook and Twitter shares (Ordenes et al. 2019) and posts clicks (Kanuri, Chen, and Sridhar 2018).

In summary, all significant effects show that a top position is favorable to enhance post virality. However, the measures that captures the top position could deliver different results in a different on the context. For example, could a high posting frequency over time increase the number of brand or influencer followers and thus virality since consumers are constantly searching for new content.

Time
Next to the position, the **time of posting** impacts the virality of social media content. Some of the studies include time fixed effects (Davis et al. 2019; Kanuri, Chen, and Sridhar 2018; Li and Xie 2020; Rietveld et al. 2020; Tucker 2014; Wang et al. 2019). Moreover, research controls for postings on holidays (Borah et al. 2020), weekends (Hughes, Swaminathan, and Brooks 2019; Ordenes et al. 2019; Rooderkerk and Pauwels 2016) and weekdays (De Vries, Gensler, and Leeflang 2012; Jalali and Papatla 2019; Moro, Rita, and Vala 2016). Furthermore, most of the studies analyze if the hour of posting (Moro, Rita, and Vala 2016; Ordenes et al. 2019) or the time of day (Heimbach and Hinz 2016; Jalali and Papatla 2019; Kanuri, Chen, and Sridhar 2018; Rietveld et al. 2020) impacts the effectiveness of social media content. If studies observe data over a longer time period, they control for month (Moro, Rita, and Vala 2016) or year (Rietveld et al. 2020). Some authors specialize on posts about events and analyze the

time elapsed after the event occurred (Borah et al. 2020; Namkoong, Ro, and Henderson 2019).

Weekend blogger posts generate higher Facebook likes, however they had no influence on the number of comments (Hughes, Swaminathan, and Brooks 2019). For brand content, De Vries, Gensler, and Leeflang (2012) find no significant but negative effects of weekday posts on Facebook likes and comments. Rooderkerk and Pauwels (2016) find significant negative effects of weekend posts on LinkedIn comments. However, the study analyzes comments within professional groups and it is more likely that users engage with that kind of content on working days. With regard to time of day of posting, Heimbach and Hinz (2016) show that brand content released between 6:00 at night and 6:00 in the morning had a positive association with Facebook likes and Google one-ups. Moreover, Namkoong, Ro, and Henderson (2019) show that the minutes elapsed after an uncertain event occurred negatively influence Twitter likes.

Nevertheless, posts on weekends received less shares on Facebook and Twitter (Ordenes et al. 2019). Jalali and Papatla (2019) confirm that apart from Saturday all other weekday posts generate higher retweets than posts on Fridays. Regarding post timing, posting at a later hour drives Facebook shares but decreases Twitter shares (Ordenes et al. 2019). However, Jalali and Papatla (2019) find no effects of time of day on retweeting (Jalali and Papatla 2019). Again, time elapsed after an event occurred negatively influences Twitter shares (Borah et al. 2020; Namkoong, Ro, and Henderson 2019). Holidays have no significant effect on virality on Twitter (Borah et al. 2020).

Within their prediction model, Moro, Rita, and Vala (2016) find that month accounts for 15%, hour for 8% and weekday for 7% of consumer clicks on brand content. The authors observe a certain seasonality for posts since between April and June, and November and February the posts receive more clicks. These seasonal effects could be specific for the cosmetic industry and differ depending on the context. Moreover, they observe a slight decrease of clicking behavior from Monday to Thursday, however the clicks were the highest on Friday. Moro, Rita, and Vala (2016) find no significant differences between the different hours of posting. However, Kanuri, Chen, and Sridhar (2018) find that in general afternoon and evening posts receive less clicks than morning posts. Especially, negative emotional content should be posted in the morning, where it is not that important for positive emotional content. However, targeted content has positive effects in the afternoon and cognitive content gains also more clicks in the afternoon and evening.

Taken together, posts that are not related to the work context should receive more likes and comments when posted on weekends. However, sharing of content

## 2.3 Literature Review on Design of Content

and clicking on content seems to be higher during the week. Since Moro, Rita, and Vala (2016) find that engagement was the highest on Fridays, it would be interesting if the results would differ if Fridays would be classified as weekend posts. The assumption behind that classification is that consumer interact more with social media content if they have spare time. This would also explain why the interaction with social media posts is generally higher in the evening or at night than in the morning. Only for news content containing high arousal was publication in the morning more effective. Moreover, when a post refers to a special event, the time of the post should be as close as possible to the time of the event.

### Length

Most of the studies include the **length** of text message within their studies on engagement with social media posts (Borah et al. 2020; Davis et al. 2019; De Vries, Gensler, and Leeflang 2012; Heimbach and Hinz 2016; Jalali and Papatla 2019; Kanuri, Chen, and Sridhar 2018; Li and Xie 2020; Namkoong, Ro, and Henderson 2019; Rooderkerk and Pauwels 2016). The authors usually assume a negative relationship of post length and post virality.

For Facebook brand posts, De Vries, Gensler, and Leeflang (2012) find a negative but marginal ($p < .1$) effect of brand post length on likes. Li and Xie (2020) can confirm this effect for user-generated content within the sector Automotive, for the sector Airline no effect occurs on likes. Similar to these results, Heimbach and Hinz (2016) find mixed significant effects of text length depending on the variables included within the model. However, they measure the text length of the original article, which is not directly related to the post length promoting this article. On Instagram, Li and Xie (2020) find no effects on the number of words on Instagram likes, conforming the secondary role of post text within visual driven networks.

Within professional groups on LinkedIn Rooderkerk and Pauwels (2016) show that post length decreased the number of comments, but sentence length had no effect. They argue post length could have a positive effect in other settings since it indicates higher quality of content. However, De Vries, Gensler, and Leeflang (2012) find no effects of brand posts length on Facebook comments.

The effects of post length are unstable (Heimbach and Hinz 2016; Jalali and Papatla 2019) or non-significant (Borah et al. 2020; Li and Xie 2020) on consumer sharing. Moreover, Kanuri, Chen, and Sridhar (2018) find a negative association between message length on post clicks. However, even though Davis et al. (2019) find positive effects of tweet length on retweets, the impact seems to depend on the context. For hedonic brand, shorter messages increased retweets.

In addition, Namkoong, Ro, and Henderson (2019) show positive effects of the text length of tweets about uncertain events on retweeting. Therefore, it can be assumed that longer messages contain more information and increase virality in case of uncertainty.

All in all, length of post text decreases post virality. However, following the argumentation of Rooderkerk and Pauwels (2016) the impact of text length could vary in different environments. In the context of influencer recommendations, posts length could have a positive effect on post virality since it shows the effort and quality of argumentation. Moreover, it could be that messages with few words are missing important content or meaning and therefore an optimum level needs to be found. The findings of Davis et al. (2019) and Namkoong, Ro, and Henderson (2019) underline this assumption since they show that longer posts with more information can increase post virality.

Additional Control Variables

After the design-relevant control variables have been explained, the following section gives a short list of **additional control variables**. They are not part of Table 2.3 since they are not directly related to the design of content. However, they are outlined for the comprehensiveness of the review.

As described within the Section 2.2, studies include characteristics of the source. The studies include followers of the posting source (Borah et al. 2020; Hughes, Swaminathan, and Brooks 2019; Jalali and Papatla 2019; Kanuri, Chen, and Sridhar 2018; Li and Xie 2020; Moro, Rita, and Vala 2016; Namkoong, Ro, and Henderson 2019; Rietveld et al. 2020; Rooderkerk and Pauwels 2016; Swani and Milne 2017; Wang et al. 2019), followees (Jalali and Papatla 2019; Namkoong, Ro, and Henderson 2019; Wang et al. 2019) and posting activity (Davis et al. 2019; Hughes, Swaminathan, and Brooks 2019; Zhang, Moe, and Schweidel 2017). Moreover, Wang et al. (2019) and Zhang, Moe, and Schweidel (2017) also analyze the network size or activity of the target users. Further, Borah et al. (2020) control for the brands reputation, friends, and social media influence score. Meire et al. (2019) and De Vries, Gensler, and Leeflang (2012) control for the valence or volume of content-related user-generated content.

Furthermore, the studies control for context specific source type (e.g. gender, food blogger or brand is on Interbrand-100-list) (Heimbach and Hinz 2016; Hughes, Swaminathan, and Brooks 2019; Jalali and Papatla 2019; Li and Xie 2020; Rooderkerk and Pauwels 2016), name of the brand (Li and Xie 2020; Ordenes et al. 2019), expertise (Hughes, Swaminathan, and Brooks 2019; Namkoong, Ro, and Henderson 2019; Rooderkerk and Pauwels 2016) or brand evaluations (Rietveld et al. 2020). Other studies control for industry or product

## 2.3 Literature Review on Design of Content

type (Davis et al. 2019; De Vries, Gensler, and Leeflang 2012; Jalali and Papatla 2019; Rietveld et al. 2020; Swani and Milne 2017) and campaign goal (Hughes, Swaminathan, and Brooks 2019). If the variables interacted with other variables, this was explained in the analysis above.

Since the papers focus on the content characteristics of viral posts, they also include further controls for context specific topic (e.g. September 11 for airline posts) (Kanuri, Chen, and Sridhar 2018; Li and Xie 2020; Zhang, Moe, and Schweidel 2017), multiple intentions or content origin (share of others) (Ordenes et al. 2019). Moro, Rita, and Vala (2016) and Heimbach and Hinz (2016) analyze if the contend was further advertised. Furthermore, Meire et al. (2019) control for characteristics of offline brand-related events. As described on the section on personalization, Tucker (2014) discuss the change of platform privacy settings and relevance of privacy. Moreover, they include target group fixed effects.

### 2.3.2 Pictorial Elements driving Virality of Social Media Posts

After the textual elements of viral social media posts were discussed, the following analysis of literature concentrates on the visual elements of posts driving post virality on social media. Three of the summarized studies in Section 2.3.1 examine text and image of social media posts and are therefore taken up again. The studies analyze mainly field data, however Akpinar and Berger (2017) additionally conduct three experimental studies. Three studies analyze image content on Instagram (Li and Xie 2020; Rietveld et al. 2020), Twitter (Li and Xie 2020; Ordenes et al. 2019) and Facebook (Ordenes et al. 2019). They observe post virality through shares (Li and Xie 2020; Ordenes et al. 2019) and comments or likes (Li and Xie 2020; Rietveld et al. 2020). Akpinar and Berger (2017) and Tellis et al. (2019) investigate the content of social media ads obtained from YouTube and the ad-tracking platform Unruly. They observe shares on various social media platforms.

#### 2.3.2.1 Motivational Drivers of Post Virality
Motivational drives also play an important role in the analysis of image content of viral posts. Studies observe emotionality, informativeness, brand or product centrality and reference to events within image posts.

Emotionality

Users have various motivations to engage with emotional content on social media (Berger 2014). Therefore, it is not surprising that the first papers analyzing visual content integrate **emotionality** of visual content. For example, Akpinar and Berger (2017) classify video content on a seven-point Likert scale indicating if the content is rather emotional or informational (1 = "informative," and 7 = "emotional"). Tellis et al. (2019) use manual coding of discrete emotions (e.g. love, pride, joy, sadness, shame, anger or fear) on a six-point Likert scale to capture how emotionally focused video content is. A factor analysis on those emotions reveals four positive emotional dimensions "inspiration," "warmth," "amusement," and "excitement," as well as the negative dimensions of "fear" and "shame". Li and Xie (2020) measure emotionality of image through the presence of happy face, whereby this feature is detected by the application programming interface (API) of Google Cloud Vision. Rietveld et al. (2020) define emotion posts through two dimensions.

The first dimension is the valence, which can be positive or negative. Therefore, the valence measures if the visual cues of the image transfer positive or negative feelings. The second dimension is the level of arousal. Whereby, visual arousal is defined as the activation through the encoding of image information. The authors use the Multilingual Visual Sentiment Ontology (MVSO) model that relates emotion keywords with images. Rietveld et al. (2020) calculate one total score for the four different valence-arousal-combination.

Rietveld et al. (2020) show that positive high-arousal images increase likes and comments on Instagram. Furthermore, positive low-arousal images also increase likes but negatively affect comments. Negative high-arousal content decreases likes and has no effect on comments. However, negative low-arousal content is positively associated with likes and comments. Surprisingly, negative high-arousal content has even the highest elasticity on likes (.52%) and comments (.43%). The positive effect of pensiveness mainly drives this positive impact. Content is tagged as pensive if the image is "expressing or revealing thoughtfulness". Images with a high pensiveness score have a higher correlation with presence of human face than any other emotion. Therefore, the presence of human face partially drives the positive effect low-arousal. Additionally, Li and Xie (2020) find similar relationships of human face on Twitter likes, however, happy human face has a positive but non-significant effect on Twitter likes.

Moreover, the authors find that the presence of happy face has a negative significant effect on retweets of airline and car model posts. A possible explanation is that most of the pictures are selfies. As described in Section 2.3.1, useful information can increase sharing, especially on information-driven social media

## 2.3 Literature Review on Design of Content

platforms like Twitter. Selfies contain information for the vocal user's own follower base, but do not motive to share this information with a broader audience not related to the vocal user (Li and Xie 2020). Their non-significant effects on Instagram underline this explanation. Apart from human face, Tellis et al. (2019) confirm the positive impact of positive emotion on likes for shares. The dimensions inspiration, warmth, amusement and excitement enhance sharing of video ads. The negative emotions had no significant effect on sharing. Akpinar and Berger (2017) not only find that emotional video ads have higher shares on social media than informational content, moreover, they show with three experimental studies that the willingness to share was always higher for emotional video ads than for informative video ads.

Additionally, Tellis et al. (2019) hypothesize that specific drama elements and drama-supporting elements within a visual narrative positively affects engagement through the increase of positive emotion. The authors use manual coders to rate the use of seven different drama elements and regress each of the positive emotional dimensions over these drama elements. Dramatization is positively associated with inspiration, warmth and amusement. A surprising outcome of the narrative also increases the amusement of the video ad. Furthermore, if a celebrity is part of the video ad of a brand, the inspiration and excitement triggered by the content increases. Moreover, the use of babies and animals has a positive impact on inspiration, warmth and amusement. Therefore, the authors confirm findings from traditional advertising for the social media context.

Overall, emotionality of visual content drives post virality. However, the valence of emotion can have different effects depending on the context and platform. Especially for the in combinations with human face, research needs more insights to derive clear implications.

Informativeness
Akpinar and Berger (2017) define the informative content as counterpart of emotional content, and measure the **informativeness** of video ads on a Likert scale (1 = "informative," and 7 = "emotional"). Tellis et al. (2019) specify informative content through three criteria. First, the video contains reasonable argumentation, why a brand outperforms others. Second, the video contains information on the product. Third, the ad outlines the benefits of the product. According to this definition coders rated informativeness of video as on a six-point scale (0 = "very weak," and 5 = "very strong").

As described above, Akpinar and Berger (2017) find that informative video ads are shared less often than emotional video ads. Tellis et al. (2019) confirm this negative and significant effect of informative video ads on social media shares.

However, this effect varies by platform and context. Since LinkedIn is a platform connecting professionals, informational ads have no negative effect on sharing. On Facebook and Twitter, sharing of video ads is rather driven through amusement. Nevertheless, informative content has a positive interaction effect with new product and moderate as well as high price product. Therefore, if the video ad contains novel information on new products, it can enhance shares on social media. Moreover, the informational content enhances sharing for moderate and high-priced products since the risk of purchase is higher with increasing price and information can reduce that risk.

Therefore, the informativeness of video ads has rather negative effects on post virality on social media. However, in settings where information is novel and valuable it can enhance sharing. Moreover, research lacks knowledge on different types of information within visual content.

Brand/Product Centrality

Especially the visual **brand or product centrality** within social media posts can be a relevant cue for consumers. Akpinar and Berger (2017) measure brand centrality through the integralness of brand within the video ad (1 = "not integral at all," and 7 = "very integral"), indicating if the brand is clearly part of the narrative content of the video. Furthermore, the authors control for brand presence and measure it through size of brand in video and duration of that presence. Within their analysis, they show that these constructs are indeed separate from each other. Brand prominence is also included by Tellis et al. (2019) and measured through frequency and duration of placement. The only work considering the brand appearance within image is the study by Rietveld et al. (2020). The authors measure visual brand centrality with the API of Google Vision and define it as the percentage of the surface area of brand element in the image in relation to the whole image size. Product centrality is measured through a combined approach including object-detection of Google Vision and manual allocation of objects to product category. The sum of objects relevant to product category builds the product centrality on a scale from zero to ten (0 = no product-specific object; 10 = 10 product-specific objects).

Rietveld et al. (2020) find that the centrality of brand within an image on Instagram has no significant influence on likes but increases comments. However, likes and comments are significantly negative related with visual product centrality. Similar with the findings for textual brand and product mention, the authors conclude that the brand centrality of an Instagram posts can increase post virality whereas product centrality can be perceived as persuasive and hurt post virality.

## 2.3 Literature Review on Design of Content

Akpinar and Berger (2017) find that brand centrality is higher for informational ads than for emotional ads. Moreover, informational videos with high brand centrality increase sharing. However, it is found that emotional videos are rather shared than informational video. The brand is used less frequently in the narrative of emotional video ads but has no negative impact on shares. Within three experiments, Akpinar and Berger (2017) can show that integrating the brand as part of the narrative does not hurt the sharing of emotional ads. Moreover, emotional integral ads outperform informal ads. They increased the brand evaluations, purchase likelihood and sharing intentions.

As expected, the brand presence has a negative effect on shares for informational content, however this effect is non-significant for emotional ads. Tellis et al. (2019) show that placing the brand on the end of the video ad increases sharing compared to placing it early or recurrently. However, they find no significant effects for brand duration.

Taken together, brand elements within the image of social media posts may serve as recognition cue and increase post virality because of their relevance for self-enhancement or identity-signaling. However, the centrality of product decreases post virality since it can induce the feeling of traditional advertising and lead to avoidance. To prevent these negative effects, brands should be placed within emotional videos or at the end of video.

Events
Since consumers also relate to contemporary **events** through social media, the connection of visual content and events (e.g. Super Bowl, Olympics or Thanksgiving) can be important for post virality within social media. Still, Tellis et al. (2019) are the only ones that consider the relationship between visual content and events. Manual coders rated the presence (1) and absence (0) of eight contemporary events within social media ads.

Even though the authors find positive significant effects in different models, they find no significant association of video ads including event-specific elements on sharing within their final model. However, research would need more insights on that since seasonality and event specific information within text have positive significant effects on post virality (Jalali and Papatla 2019; Moro, Rita, and Vala 2016).

### 2.3.2.2 Social Media specific Elements

Since there is little research on the visual design elements of viral posts, the results on social media specific elements are limited to the interactivity of the image.

Interactivity

Social media offer different ways to interact with the message and with others (Liu and Shrum 2002). The level of interactivity of a post text can be measured directly, e.g. by link or question, whereas the **interactivity** of an image must be measured indirectly. Ordenes et al. (2019) published the first study that used manual coders to measure the interactivity of images of social media posts. Images were rated on a seven-point scale, which indicates whether the images "require a response from the viewer" (p. 1,000) (e.g. a person is waving hand to the viewer).

Surprisingly, Ordenes et al. (2019) find that posts with interactive images are less shared on Facebook and Twitter than posts containing non-interactive content (e.g. image showing a landscape or passive person). However, interactive images highly interact with message intention through text. An interactive image within a Facebook or Twitter posts has positive effect on consumer sharing when combined with an emotional or informational text message rather than directive speech. Therefore, interactive images should be used cautiously so as not to be too intrusive.

### 2.3.2.3 Figurative Style

Besides the motivational drivers to share social media posts, research identifies further properties of visual content: Colorfulness and Image Quality. Both characterize the figurative style of the image and can trigger post virality.

Colorfulness

First, Li and Xie (2020) measure the **colorfulness** through the Google Clout Vision API, which identifies the dominant colors of an image. The authors calculate the sum of top three colors' pixel percentage. If the image is colorful, the pixel percentage of the top three colors is low.

As described within Section 2.3.1, Instagram likes are rather driven through image content than through text since Instagram is a visual driven network. Colorful images increase likes on Instagram. However, the authors find mixed results for the effectiveness of colorful images on Twitter shares. Whereas posts within the airline community are shared more if they are colorful, posts on car models are shared more if the colors are monotonous. Therefore, the impact of color is dependent on platform type or product category. Moreover, Li and Xie (2020) focus on predominantly user-generated posts about airline services, through brand posts about products are common on Instagram. Future research on brand or influencer post could prove the effectiveness of colorfulness on post virality over different product categories.

Image Quality
Second, Li and Xie (2020) measure the **image quality** through three different categegory measures: screenshot, amateur photo and high-quality picture. The coders indicated if the image content was a screenshot or amateur photo. Both variables represent a rather low quality of image in contrast with the category high-quality picture, which was also binary coded (presence = 1, absence = 0).

Li and Xie (2020) find that high-quality picture increase liking on Twitter and on Instagram. Furthermore, screenshots or amateur pictures decrease linking on both platforms. Moreover, screenshots and amateur pictures receive less retweets than professional content, even though the effects become only significant in one of the two samples. Images that are rated as high-quality content increase retweets. The authors explain this finding though the higher informativeness of professional content. Additionally, it is more appropriate to share professional than amateur content since amateur pictures often contain personal information.

### 2.3.2.4 Design-relevant Control Variables

The papers under review also include design-relevant control variables which specifically relate to the image of the social media post. These include human face, text within image and image text fit. As for post text, the studies consider content type and message length as control variable.

Human Face
Li and Xie (2020) control for the presence of **human face** within images of Twitter and Instagram posts. They measure presence of human face with the face detection function of Google Clout Vision. The authors find a positive significant increase on Twitter shares (80.4%) and likes (38.76%) for posts with human faces. As mentioned within the section on emotionality, this positive effect slightly decreases if the human face expresses happy feelings. However, Li and Xie (2020) cannot replicate this positive effect for Instagram.

Text within Image
Furthermore, not only the presence of human face can be relevant for post virality of social media posts. As well as the text of the post itself, can **text within the image** influence behavior. Therefore, Ordenes et al. (2019) include the occurrence of any text with the image of a social media post as control variable (1 = includes readable text; 0 = does not include readable text). The authors find that text within the image text increases sharing on Facebook and Twitter. One reason for this positive effect could be that the text within image is high relevant for the image intent.

Image Text Fit

For that reason, Li and Xie (2020) controls for **image text fit**. The image text fit or image relevancy indicates if the picture contributes to the understanding of the post text or if it distracts the user from the original message intent. The image text fit is measured through a binary dummy variable and manually coded. The results of Li and Xie (2020) show a positive association between image text fit and Twitter likes. However, this effect does not occur for Instagram posts. One reason for the diminishing effect could be that users only pay little attention to Instagram post text.

Content Type

Apart from the controls considering text, Ordenes et al. (2019) further control for **content type** within their image sample. They distinguish between images that are part of an album (=1) or not (= 0) and between real images (= 1) or screenshot a video (= 0). If images are part of an album, it reduces Facebook shares. Moreover, image content increased sharing on Facebook and twitter compared with video content.

Length

Research controls for **the length of video ad** in seconds (Akpinar and Berger 2017; Tellis et al. 2019). Moreover, Tellis et al. (2019) include linear as well curvilinear effects. Whereas Akpinar and Berger (2017) find no significant effects, Tellis et al. (2019) find an inverted U-shaped relationship between ad length and shares on social media platforms. Shares are the highest for videos that last around 1.2 minutes. The authors assume that longer videos are shared more often, as the plot and characters can be better developed within longer videos. Moreover, the authors find that after the peak the impact decreases much faster for informational videos than for emotional video ads.

Additional Control Variables

For comprehensiveness, the **additional controls** are outlined. The controls of Ordenes et al. (2019), Rietveld et al. (2020) and Li and Xie (2020) that are not design-relevant were specified in Section 2.3.1.4. Moreover, Akpinar and Berger (2017) control for video language, type of product, product involvement and brand equity for their field observations. Tellis et al. (2019) also control for product type and brand subscribers. Furthermore, they include a variable, which indicates if the video has a timeline.

In summary, there is a large amount of literature that deals with the influence of content design on post virality in social media. However, research is only just beginning to include the analysis of visual content in its investigations, even though it is ubiquitous in social media. Moreover, only a few studies deal with influencer content and none include visual elements of influencer posts. However, since most influencer marketing takes place on visual social networks, these findings would be particularly important for the design of brand-sponsored influencer posts.

## 2.4 Literature Review on Performance Measurement

The last two chapters show that extensive literature exists capturing the effectiveness of one single source or one single message. Research shows that influencers positively influence brand evaluations (Breves et al. 2019) and purchase intention (Lee and Watkins 2016; Uribe, Buzeta, and Velásquez 2016). Moreover, Hughes, Swaminathan, and Brooks (2019) find that influencers encourage consumers to engage with brand-sponsored content and thus increase brand awareness and sales.

After brands have identified suitable influencers and the message has been crafted, the final phase of the influencer marketing management process occurs. In the performance management phase, the following question arises: How to measure the success of an influencer campaign?

To measure the success of influencer campaigns, brands need to understand the effectiveness of influencer marketing along the consumer decision journey. Therefore, the effectiveness of a channel can be assessed by its impact on brand building and consumer behavior (De Vries, Gensler, and Leeflang 2017).

Brand building describes the process from the visibility of the brand in the minds of customers, through the image that consumers form of the brand, resulting in the evaluations, feelings and loyalty that consumers associate with the brand (Keller 2009). Within the literature on channel effectiveness, brand building along the consumer decision journey is measured through awareness, consideration, preference, purchase intent and satisfaction (Colicev et al. 2018; Colicev, Kumar, and O'Connor 2019; De Vries, Gensler, and Leeflang 2017).

Moreover, to measure the effectiveness of marketing activities, consumer behavior, such as website visits, can be used as proxy for the different stages of the consumer decision journey (Wiesel, Pauwels, and Arts 2011). For example, research captures consumer interest through website traffic on retailers' websites (Fossen and Schweidel 2019), offline and online store visits (Pauwels, Aksehirli, and Lackman 2016) or online search volume (Kim and Hanssens 2017).

Further, studies that observe channel impact on consumer behavior, relate the effectiveness of channels to their ability to acquire consumers (Corstjens and Umblijs 2012; De Vries, Gensler, and Leeflang 2017; Kumar et al. 2013; Trusov, Bucklin, and Pauwels 2009; Villanueva, Yoo, and Hanssens 2008) and increase sales (Fossen and Schweidel 2019; Kumar et al. 2016; Kumar, Choi, and Greene 2017; Kupfer et al. 2018; Stephen and Galak 2012; You, Vadakkepatt, and Joshi 2015). Furthermore these effects can translate into a brand's stock market performance (Colicev et al. 2018; Nam and Kannan 2014; Tirunillai and Tellis 2012).

If brands want to know how effective influencer marketing is for building their brand and influencing consumer behavior, they need to compare this channel to other channel investments. However and first of all, no knowledge on the effectiveness of influencer marketing compared to brand-owned activities in social media networks and advertising exists. And secondly, there is no research on the effects of influencer marketing on sales.

To address this problem, the literature review synthesizes research that considers user-generated messages and firm-generated messages since influencer marketing blends elements of user-generated content and firm-generated content. Moreover, studies are only included in the analysis if they consider social media messages and advertising simultaneously. Therefore, interdependencies between channels can be observed.

Taking these criteria into account, the literature search revealed 20 articles. Additionally, two articles from the Management Science (Gopinath, Chintagunta, and Venkataraman 2013) and Information Systems Research (Goh, Heng, and Lin 2013) were included by forward and backward search. For the purpose of completeness, the meta-analysis by You, Vadakkepatt, and Joshi (2015) on the eWOM elasticity is added to the literature, which contains the findings from management and marketing science as well as from information systems research. The relevant research is illustrated in Table 2.5.

Table 2.5 shows that the literature can be classified according to the channels, which are compared in terms of their effectiveness. One branch of research compares the impact of advertising and user-generated content on consumer interest behavior (Fossen and Schweidel 2019; Pauwels, Aksehirli, and Lackman 2016), customer acquisition (Corstjens and Umblijs 2012; Trusov, Bucklin, and Pauwels 2009; Villanueva, Yoo, and Hanssens 2008) and sales (Bruce, Foutz, and Kolsarici 2012; Corstjens and Umblijs 2012; Fossen and Schweidel 2019; Gopinath, Chintagunta, and Venkataraman 2013; Gopinath, Thomas, and Krishnamurthi 2014; Kim and Hanssens 2017; Onishi and Manchanda 2012; You, Vadakkepatt, and

**Table 2.5** Studies considering more than one Type of Message

| Study | Communication Channels | | | Metrics along the Consumer Decision Journey | | | | | |
|---|---|---|---|---|---|---|---|---|---|
| | Advertising | UGC | FGC | Brand Building | Consumer Interest | Acquisition | Sales | Stock Market Performance |
| *Comparing Advertising and UGC* | | | | | | | | |
| Bruce, Foutz, and Kolsarici 2012 | x | Consumer ratings | | | | | x | |
| Corstjens and Umblijs 2012 | x | Twitter, Facebook | | | | x | x | |
| Fossen and Schweidel 2019 | x | Twitter | | | $x^a$ | | x | |
| Gopinath, Chintagunta, and Venkataraman 2013 | x | Blog, Consumer ratings | | | | | x | |
| Gopinath, Thomas, and Krishnamurthi 2014 | x | Forum | | | | | x | |
| Kim and Hanssens 2017 | x | Blog | | | $x^b$ | | x | |
| Nam and Kannan 2014 | x | Blog | | | | | | x |
| Onishi and Manchanda 2012 | x | Blog | | | | | x | |

(continued)

**Table 2.5** (continued)

| Study | Communication Channels | | | Metrics along the Consumer Decision Journey | | | | |
|---|---|---|---|---|---|---|---|---|
| | Advertising | UGC | FGC | Brand Building | Consumer Interest | Acquisition | Sales | Stock Market Performance |
| Pauwels, Aksehirli, and Lackman 2016 | x | Forum, blog, Twitter, Facebook | | | $x^a$ | | | |
| Tirunillai and Tellis 2012 | x | Ratings, online reviews | | | | | | x |
| Trusov, Bucklin, and Pauwels 2009 | x | WOM refferals | | | | x | | |
| Villanueva, Yoo, and Hanssens 2008 | x | WOM refferals | | | | x | | |
| You, Vadakkepatt, and Joshi 2015 | x | WOM | | | | | x | |
| *Comparing UGC and FGC* | | | | | | | | |
| Goh, Heng, and Lin 2013 | | Facebook community | x | | | | x | |
| Kumar et al. 2013 | | Facebook, Twitter | x | | | x | x | |

(continued)

## 2.4 Literature Review on Performance Measurement

**Table 2.5** (continued)

| Study | Communication Channels | | | Metrics along the Consumer Decision Journey | | | | |
|---|---|---|---|---|---|---|---|---|
| | Advertising | UGC | FGC | Brand Building | Consumer Interest | Acquisition | Sales | Stock Market Performance |
| *Comparing Advertising and FGC* | | | | | | | | |
| Kumar et al. 2016 | x | | x | | | | x | |
| Kumar, Choi, and Greene 2017 | x | | x | | | | x | |
| *Comparing Advertising, UGC and FGC* | | | | | | | | |
| Colicev et al. 2018 | x | Facebook, Twitter, YouTube | x | x | | | | x |
| Colicev, Kumar, and O'Connor 2019 | x | Facebook | x | x | | | | |
| De Vries, Gensler, and Leeflang 2017 | x | Twitter, Forum | x | x | | x | | |
| Hewett et al. 2016 | x | Twitter | x | | | | x$^c$ | |
| Kupfer et al. 2017 | x | Consumer ratings | x | | | | x | |
| Stephen and Galak 2012 | x | Blog, community | x | | | | x | |

Source: Author's own illustration. Notes: UGC = user-generated content, FGC = firm-generated content, $^a$online and offline store traffic, $^b$online search, $^c$customer deposit.

Joshi 2015) or stock market performance (Nam and Kannan 2014; Tirunillai and Tellis 2012).

At about the same time, other researchers are studying the interactions and influences of user-generated content and firm-generated content on customer acquisition and sales (Goh, Heng, and Lin 2013; Kumar et al. 2013). Later studies of Kumar et al. (2016) and Kumar, Choi, and Greene (2017) focus on the comparison of elasticities of firm-generated content and advertising.

Furthermore, latest research compares the effects of traditional advertising and different social messages on brand building metrics (Colicev et al. 2018; Colicev, Kumar, and O'Connor 2019; de Vries, Gensler, and Leeflang 2017), acquisition (de Vries, Gensler, and Leeflang 2017), sales (Hewett et al. 2016; Kupfer et al. 2018) and stock market performance (Colicev et al. 2018).

The structure of Table 2.5 and the structure of the following chapter follow this classification of research. Starting from left to right, the columns of the table represent the relevant constructs, i.e., the relevant communication channels, as well as the target metrics along the consumer decision journey. Research comparing the channel effectiveness of different channels includes advertising, firm-generated content, and consumer-generated content on social networks. Effectiveness is measured in terms of brand building, consumer interest, acquisition, sales and stock market performance.

The further analysis of literature follows a conceptual approach (Webster and Watson 2002). Thereby, the chapters summarize the findings on the effects and the interactions of the individual communication channels, which are compared in the respective branch of research.

### 2.4.1 Comparing Advertising and User-generated Content

The following chapter summarizes the results of research dealing with the effects and interactions of traditional marketing channels and consumer-generated social media messages. The review of literature will be based on the first section of Table 2.5. The **superordinate constructs** are marked bold and will be discussed from left to right. However, since the focus of the present analysis is on the comparison of effects, the constructs are explained first, followed by a discussion of the results across all observed channels according to the different effectiveness metrics.

The term **advertising** covers all offline and online marketing activities of a company or brand that are not related to social media networks. Some of the earlier studies focus on media appearance and sponsored events (Trusov, Bucklin,

## 2.4 Literature Review on Performance Measurement

and Pauwels 2009) or TV advertising (Onishi and Manchanda 2012; Tirunillai and Tellis 2012).

However, most of the studies use an accumulated measure of expenditures on marketing channel including spending on TV, newspaper, online ad banner or emails (Bruce, Foutz, and Kolsarici 2012; Gopinath, Chintagunta, and Venkataraman 2013; Kim and Hanssens 2017; You, Vadakkepatt, and Joshi 2015) or the cumulated number of advertisements in those channels (Gopinath, Thomas, and Krishnamurthi 2014). Since Nam and Kannan (2014) observe channel effectiveness on stock market performance, they measure advertising with "selling, general and administrative" (SG & A) expenditures from brands' financial reports.

Corstjens and Umblijs (2012) specify the individual spending for retail, internet, print, TV, radio and outdoor for advertising of flat screen TVs or broadband services. Next to those channels, Pauwels, Aksehirli, and Lackman (2016) add the spending for paid online search of an apparel retailer. Fossen and Schweidel (2019) expand the knowledge on online marketing activities by comparing TV, online display spend, online search spend and online video spend.

In general, **user-generated content** is defined as content, which is brand-related but created by users of the social media network (Tirunillai and Tellis 2012). Since the goal is to summarize the findings on the effectiveness of social media messages, this definition will also apply in the following analysis.

According to this definition, user-generated content is a specific form of WOM or specific eWOM. For the purpose of completeness, papers that do not specify WOM or eWOM in more detail, but are often cited in this research stream, will also be included: Trusov, Bucklin, and Pauwels (2009), Villanueva, Yoo, and Hanssens (2008), You, Vadakkepatt, and Joshi (2015).

For example, Trusov, Bucklin, and Pauwels (2009) investigate the impact of direct WOM referral acquiring customers for an anonymous social network, though the authors do not specify type of referral. Furthermore, Villanueva, Yoo, and Hanssens (2008) compare the value of customers acquired through WOM referral and traditional marketing activities. However, the broadly define WOM referral as recommendation from other consumers and institutions not necessarily related to online communication. Within their meta-analysis on eWOM volume and valence elasticity, You, Vadakkepatt, and Joshi (2015) define eWOM as "Internet-mediated written communications between current or potential consumers".

Earlier studies, which follow the narrower definition of user-generated content, examine the effectiveness of online reviews, product ratings and blog entries by users. To estimate the value of user-generated content on stock market performance across six markets and 15 firms, Tirunillai and Tellis (2012) aggregate user-generated product reviews and ratings from various platforms over a four-year period. Moreover, this type of user-generated content plays an important role in the movie industry. Research examines the impact of volume and valence of movie online reviews (e.g. Yahoo, IMDb) (Bruce, Foutz, and Kolsarici 2012; Gopinath, Chintagunta, and Venkataraman 2013) or blog posts on movie or video games (Gopinath, Chintagunta, and Venkataraman 2013; Kim and Hanssens 2017; Onishi and Manchanda 2012). Furthermore, Gopinath, Thomas, and Krishnamurthi (2014) observe the influence of volume and valence of forum posts on sales of newly introduced cell phone brands.

Nam and Kannan (2014) study the informational value of users' social media bookmarks and connected social tags on the platform Delicious as a proxy to measure brand equity and predict stock market returns. These bookmarks are user-generated content, which for example connects brand-related web links to user-defined social tags. These social tags capture the users' thoughts and perceptions and are therefore associated with brand performance. In particular, the authors examine the impact of volume of bookmarks as well as social tags and the valence of social tags. Moreover, the authors capture the brands' dominance and connectedness within the product category through content analysis of social tags.

Corstjens and Umblijs (2012) extend the information from product reviews with user-generated messages from Facebook and Twitter and measure the sentiment of social media events over multiple platforms. Moreover, the authors manually determined rating of social media messages depending on the weighting of originator, reach of message, size of chain reaction and relevance of topic. Category weightings range from one (small) to three (large) and the maximum rating for a single event is 81 if the maximum weighting of three is reached in all four categories.

A more recent study by Fossen and Schweidel (2019) investigates the influence of social TV and advertising on retailer website traffic and sales. Thereby, social TV is defined as "joint viewing of television programming alongside the consumption and/or production of program-related social media chatter" (p. 274) and is measured through program and retailer mentions within Twitter tweets. Moreover, Pauwels, Aksehirli, and Lackman (2016) determine the power of user-generated messages on online and offline store traffic through the exploration of volume and valence of user-generated content from multiple platforms (Forum, Blog, Twitter, Facebook) and differentiate between WOM on a brand's advertisements, actual brand experiences and purchase process. Overall, the operationalization is manifold and needs to be considered for the following discussion of results.

## 2.4 Literature Review on Performance Measurement

Kim and Hanssens (2017) measure consumer interest for upcoming movies with online search volume and find a co-evolution between blog posts and consumer search volume. Moreover, the authors find that in the pre-launch phase of new movies and video games the elasticity of blog postings is much stronger than the elasticity of advertising. Consistent with these findings, Pauwels, Aksehirli, and Lackman (2016) find that marketing spending in TV, print, paid and search advertising have smaller elasticities on retailers' store traffic than all three types of eWOM. Whereby the elasticities for positive brand eWOM and neutral purchase eWOM are higher than the elasticity of positive eWOM on advertising for offline store traffic. For online store traffic they are about the same. Furthermore, eWOM has a long carry over effect since the long-term elasticities are even greater for offline store traffic and also the difference of effect size compared to traditional marketing is greater. However, since traditional marketing channels are more volatile than eWOM, marketing activities still have a strong impact on store traffic growth.

That the encouragement of eWOM should not replace but complement traditional marketing is also shown by the results of Fossen and Schweidel (2019) on the influence of parallel consumption of social media and TV advertising on consumer behavior. A comparison with online display spend, online search spend and online video spend shows that only retailor-related chatter on Twitter increases website traffic while watching TV. A higher consumer exchange on Twitter about the retailer, caused by social TV, therefore engages consumers into the online consumer decision journey. However, this effect is not linear since the effect diminishes at higher levels of online chatter. Moreover, the authors find that eWOM moderates the effectiveness of different TV advertising formats on online shopping behavior. When the volume of social TV is high, an increase in instant web traffic is more likely to be driven by emotional advertising rather than funny advertising.

In summary, user-generated content has a positive influence on consumer interest both online and offline. In addition, consumers have the power to influence branding to a similar extent or even more than traditional marketing activities. Furthermore, recent findings show that when traditional channels and social media are consumed in parallel, online discussions influence the effectiveness of traditional marketing activities.

Furthermore, Corstjens and Umblijs (2012) highlight the importance of management of negative eWOM. The authors find that negative user-generated content has a significant negative impact on the customer acquisition of broadband service. Moreover, the impact of negative WOM is higher than the impact of display advertising and print advertising. However, the data on broadband service adoption indicates that online affiliations and TV advertising are the most effective channels for customer acquisition. But these early studies already show that consumer opinions are becoming increasingly important for brand performance through social networks.

Trusov, Bucklin, and Pauwels (2009) show the substantial impact of WOM referrals on member growth of social media networks. They find that WOM referrals not only have larger short-term effects than advertising activities, but also longer carryover effects. Similar to this findings, Villanueva, Yoo, and Hanssens (2008) confirm that consumers of a webhosting service, that are acquired through WOM referrals, generate more short-term and long-term value.

In general, the results indicate that traditional marketing activities and user-generated messages complement each other in terms of customer acquisition. It can also be assumed that consumers who are acquired through consumer recommendations are more valuable. In addition, brands should react to negative consumer content to avoid a decline of consumers.

Most studies comparing the effects of user-generated content and traditional marketing activities on sales use data from the movie industry. Researchers agree that traditional marketing activities and user-generated content complement each other with regard to the increase of movie revenues (Bruce, Foutz, and Kolsarici 2012; Gopinath, Chintagunta, and Venkataraman 2013; Kim and Hanssens 2017; Onishi and Manchanda 2012). Both channels significantly influence movie revenues, however, the influence of channel varies depending on the release phase of the movie. Onishi and Manchanda (2012) and Gopinath, Chintagunta, and Venkataraman (2013) show a significant positive association between blog postings within the pre-release phase of a movie and movie revenue on release day or weekend and Bruce, Foutz, and Kolsarici (2012) find a marginal positive effective ($p < .1$) for online reviews. For the American market the results indicate a higher relative influence of advertising compared to user-generated content in the pre-release phase (Bruce, Foutz, and Kolsarici 2012; Gopinath, Chintagunta, and Venkataraman 2013), whereas Onishi and Manchanda (2012) find that blog posts have a higher impact than advertising on daily movie ticket sales in the Japanese market.

As described above, Kim and Hanssens (2017) find much higher elasticities for blog posts on consumer interest (i.e. search volume) than for advertising, but find a much higher correlation of opening-weekend revenue with pre-launch search volume and advertising than with blog volume. However, their findings show that blog posts have an indirect trend-setting effect on movie revenue since they significantly drive search volume.

## 2.4 Literature Review on Performance Measurement

There is evidence that although advertising has a strong influence on movie ticket sales in the pre-release phase, its impact diminishes over time and is lost in the post-release phase of a movie. However, it increases consumer engagement in eWOM (Bruce, Foutz, and Kolsarici 2012; Onishi and Manchanda 2012). In the phase after the movie launch and even in the video stage, the valence of consumer ratings and reviews drives movie revenue (Bruce, Foutz, and Kolsarici 2012; Gopinath, Chintagunta, and Venkataraman 2013). Moreover, positive blog posts from users who watched the movie are effective in driving sales (Kim and Hanssens 2017).

Gopinath, Chintagunta, and Venkataraman (2013) and Kim and Hanssens (2017) confirm their findings on movie revenue for revenues of newly launched video games and cell phones respectively. Furthermore, Corstjens and Umblijs (2012) find significant influences on flat screen TV sales for both advertising and eWOM. Positive and negative eWOM have about the same effect on sales as TV advertising and more impact than print, radio or outdoor advertising, although negative eWOM has a negative impact. Beyond that, the authors stress the risk arising from negative eWOM since 1,000 negative social media ratings have a 4.42 times as high influence as 1,000 positive social media ratings. These differences occur because the pressure of social media ratings varied over the analysis period (14.800 positive, 3.300 negative). However, display advertising and paid search as well as retailer advertising have higher impact on flat screen sales than eWOM.

Even though Fossen and Schweidel (2019) find significant positive impact of social TV on website traffic, the authors find no significant effects of Twitter mentions of retailor on retailer' online purchases. Spending on online display, online search and online video have also no significant effect on sales. However, the volume of online chatter on the program increases online purchases, even though the effect diminishes for higher levels of social TV. Moreover, high levels of online chatter moderate the effect of TV advertising. TV advertisements labelled as activating or informational have less impact on immediate online sales than funny TV advertisements when the Twitter community is actively tweeting about the program while watching TV. If the volume of online chatter suddenly raises just before the TV adverting is aired, the reverse effects occur. An increased Twitter activity one minute before the TV advertisement airs until the advertisement airs captures the attention of consumers right before the advertisement and decreases the immediate online purchases of retailers. In this case, emotional and active TV advertisements are more effective at encouraging online sales.

You, Vadakkepatt, and Joshi (2015) examine 51 studies from management and marketing science as well as from information systems research within their meta-analysis on eWOM elasticity. Overall studies, the elasticity of eWOM volume is .236 and the elasticity of eWOM valence is .417. Furthermore, the authors find that elasticity of volume and valence of eWOM are higher for low-trialability and privately consumed products since they give the consumers the possibility to compare experiences from others with own expectations. Moreover, the impact of eWOM is higher for a less competitive environment. The authors explain these effects by the delay of purchase decision within situations of choice overload. Additionally, the impact of both elasticities is influenced by the trustworthiness of the platform. Volume and valence of reviews on independent review sites have more impact on sales. In addition, the influence of eWOM volume increases for durable goods and reviews on specialized social media platforms, while the influence of eWOM valence is greater for community-based platforms. As the results on movie revenue already emphasize, the study confirms a higher elasticity of eWOM valence for products with high trialability.

Basically, research comparing user-generated content and traditional marketing activities on sales shows that both consumer messages on social media networks and traditional channels are important. Depending on the situation, the weighting of the two channels can differ. For example, traditional channels are especially important in the time before a new product is launched. They have a direct effect on sales and indirectly increase user-generated content. This in turn has a trend-setting effect through the increase in consumer interest and influences sales after the product launch significantly through consumer reviews based on consumption.

Furthermore, Tirunillai and Tellis (2012) show that the volume of consumer reviews has a positive significant impact short-term and long-term stock market returns as well as trading volume. An increase of reviews about competitors decreases stock market returns and slightly increases risk, even though it has a small significant positive influence on trading volume. Moreover, negative chatter also significantly decreases returns and increases risk, but increases trading volume. These effects could occur because the industry is growing and competitive. Within their meta-analysis on eWOM elasticity, You, Vadakkepatt, and Joshi (2015) find that within turbulent and growing markets even negative chatter increases awareness and can have positive effects. Additionally, Tirunillai and Tellis (2012) show a positive significant relationship of negative reviews on competitor and stock market returns. Overall, the impact of user-generated content is significantly larger than for TV advertising. However, the authors do not find any effects of consumer product ratings on stock market performance, even when separating for positive and negative ratings.

## 2.4 Literature Review on Performance Measurement

Besides this study, Nam and Kannan (2014) find that also social tags contain predictive value for stock market returns. The volume of popular social tags has significant positive impact on stock market performance. Positive social tags have a significant but marginal effect on returns and negative social tags have a significant negative effect. Through mapping of social tags of a brand and its competitors Nam and Kannan (2014) determine the category dominance and connectedness of a brand. Whereby category dominance measures "how strongly a brand name is connected to primary associations in the category" (p. 31) and connectedness is defined as "the mean number of competitors linked to each association of the focal brand" (p. 31). Interaction effects indicate that brands with a strong brand equity should further develop category dominance and reduce connectedness. However, the authors find no significant influence of blog posts and SG & A expenditures on stock market performance.

Both studies imply that user-generated content is a better indicator for predicting the market value of a brand than investments in traditional marketing activities.

### 2.4.2 Comparing User-generated Content and Firm-generated Content

Only two studies focus on the user-marketer interactions within customer communities and their economic impact for brands. For this purpose, research considers **user-generated content** on Facebook and Twitter from existing customers (Goh, Heng, and Lin 2013; Kumar et al. 2013). More specifically, Goh, Heng, and Lin (2013) examine user-generated content within the Facebook community of an Asian apparel retailer and qualitatively analyze the volume, valence and information richness (i.e. number of concepts extracted) of social media posts. Furthermore, the authors specify if the message is directed at one individual or the community in general. Moreover, Kumar et al. (2013) investigate the volume and valence of user-to-user messages within brand community on Twitter and Facebook.

Moreover, Kumar et al. (2013) explore if **firm-generated content** on Twitter and Facebook can impact offline sales through an increase of user-generated content. Furthermore, Goh, Heng, and Lin (2013) focus on a retailer's posts and comments on the brand-owned Facebook page. As for user-generated content, the authors specify if posts or comments are directed at a specific individual within the community. Additionally, they evaluate the informativeness and valence of firm-generated content.

Goh, Heng, and Lin (2013) find that user-generated content compared with firm-generated content on social media has a significant higher impact on retailer's sales. Undirected positive social media posts by users have the highest influence on sales, followed by undirected user posts with rich information. The smallest influence of user-generated content occurs from volume of undirected user posts on the retailer's Facebook page. However, brands can positively impact sales through posting of positive content that directly addresses individual users.

Moreover, Kumar et al. (2013) show that targeted firm-generated content on Twitter and Facebook can lead to increase of user-generated content, which, in turn leads to offline ice-crème store sales. Therefore, the authors show that owned and earned social media channels stimulate each other and build viral effects.

In summary, it can be said that social media activities have a significant impact on sales. It can be further assumed that user-generated content has a greater direct impact on sales than firm-generated content. Nevertheless, the positive effect of user-generated content can be increased by firm-generated content. To increase the direct impact of firm-generated content, brand should personalize their social media strategy.

### 2.4.3 Comparing Advertising and Firm-generated Content

Two studies compare the effectiveness of traditional advertising and firm-generated messages on sales. To compare a firm social media activities with **advertising**, Kumar et al. (2016) include TV advertising and e-mail advertising (i.e. number of opened e-mails sent by firm). Kumar, Choi, and Greene (2017) concentrate on television advertising of an American ice-crème brand.

Both studies define **firm-generated content** as content generated by marketers on the official Facebook brand pages (Kumar et al. 2016; Kumar, Choi, and Greene 2017). Kumar et al. (2016) capture the strength of a firms social media posts with three different measures. First, the valence of a post is measured by the post categories negative (-1), neutral (0) and positive (1). Second, the receptivity of a post reflects the sum of consumer engagement with this post, whereby engagement is defined as comments, likes and shares. The third measure is post susceptibility and is captured through a customer survey. Customers stated their predisposition towards social media. For example, consumers indicated if they often tweet on a scale ranging from one to five. Finally, the authors use these three dimensions to calculate the strength of firm-generated content for each customer across all firm-messages sent by the brand on Facebook within a specific

## 2.4 Literature Review on Performance Measurement

time period. However, Kumar, Choi, and Greene (2017) capture the strength of a firms Facebook posts through impressions. Impressions are defined as the number of times a firm posts is displayed on consumers' timeline on Facebook.

The studies use sales as effectiveness metric. More specifically, Kumar et al. (2016) investigate the individual purchase and cross-buying of customers in a liquor retailer's offline store. Their results show positive significant effect of firm-generated content on a retailers Facebook page on consumer spending and cross-buying overall models. Further, TV advertising and e-mail messages have a significant impact on both metrics. Within the difference-in-differences analysis the impact of firm-generated content is higher than the impact of traditional media. Moreover, the positive interaction effects between firm-generated content and TV advertisement as well as with opened e-mails sent by the brand suggest synergies between those channels.

Furthermore, Kumar, Choi, and Greene (2017) confirm a positive significant impact of firm-generated content on sales for Facebook impressions. Moreover, their findings indicate that the elasticity of social media on ice-crème brand sales is four times greater than the elasticity of TV advertising. Surprisingly the interaction effect of firm-generated content and TV advertising is not significant. However, the authors control for in-store promotion and product sampling of ice-crème. Both variables have significant impact on ice-crème sales and significantly interact with firm-generated content on Facebook. When modelling time-varying effects the authors find a nonlinear increase of firm-generated content. Over time, the relative elasticity of firm-generated content increases compared to product samples, while the elasticity of samples decreases compared to the elasticity of firm-generated content. The interaction effects of firm-generated content and in-store promotion as well as with product sampling also vary over time.

Taken together, the studies show that both firm-generated content and traditional marketing activities have an impact on sales. This research shows that a brand's social media activity has a significant impact on sales and increases over time. Moreover, it can even have a greater impact than traditional channels.

### 2.4.4 Comparing Advertising, User-generated Content and Firm-generated Content

More recent literature on channel effectiveness includes advertising activities and user-generated content as well as firm-generated content. To compare the relative impact of **advertising** on brand performance metrics, most of the papers include adverting spending across all traditional marketing activities (Colicev et al. 2018; Colicev, Kumar, and O'Connor 2019; De Vries, Gensler, and Leeflang 2017; Hewett et al. 2016; Kupfer et al. 2018). Besides that, Stephen and Galak (2012) consider the total number of brand mentions in traditional media, such as newspapers, TV or radio.

Moreover, the studies use various formats of **user-generated content**. For example, Stephen and Galak (2012) investigate the influence of blog post volume and brand community posts on sales for a microlending site. Since Kupfer et al. (2018) observe elasticities on movie revenue, they include consumer ratings to account for consumer opinion. Research investigates the volume and valence of user-generated content on Twitter (De Vries, Gensler, and Leeflang 2017; Hewett et al. 2016), Facebook (Colicev et al. 2018; Colicev, Kumar, and O'Connor 2019) and Forums (De Vries, Gensler, and Leeflang 2017). Furthermore, Colicev et al. (2018) measure the engagement volume and brand following on Facebook, Twitter and YouTube.

Brand-owned activities on social media are mainly measured through **firm-generated content** on Twitter and Facebook. Hewett et al. (2016) observe the effectiveness of volume and valence of banks' Twitter posts. To investigate the strength of firm-generated content, De Vries, Gensler, and Leeflang (2017) include the weekly number of viral impressions on brand-owned content on Facebook, whereby impressions are defined as the sum of consumer engagement through likes, comments and shares. Moreover, Stephen and Galak (2012) observe the volume of brand-owned blog posts.

Colicev et al. (2018) differentiate between brand posts and replies or retweets on Facebook and Twitter. Meanwhile, Colicev, Kumar, and O'Connor (2019) focus on the number of positive and neutral post to account for valence of brand-owned content on social media. Moreover, they add a vividness measure for a brand's social media content. Vividness is measured on a daily basis and is defined as the relative number of a brand's multimedia posts (i.e. video, image, link and music) to the total number of a brand's posts.

Kupfer et al. (2018), however, occupy a special position in this analysis. The authors examine the impact of different types of posts and comments on the Facebook page of a leading actor on the associated movie ticket sales. Since the leading actor is a dominant part of the composite product, the actor takes over the communication between brand and consumer. Actors are known for their talents outside the social media world. Moreover, actors have a certain celebrity status and share less private information on social networks, which distinguishes them from normal social media users. Compared to influencers, they build less intense relationships with their followers and their brand is not primarily characterized by presence on social media (Djafarova and Rushworth 2017). However, the ubiquity

## 2.4 Literature Review on Performance Measurement

of social media leads actors to strengthen their brand through their presence in social networks to increase their offline success (Kupfer et al. 2018). Therefore, the results of Kupfer et al. (2018) provide first indications for the effectiveness of influencer-generated messages on social media networks.

This stream of research considers different effectiveness metrics along the consumer decision journey. One focus of research is the relative channel effectiveness on brand building. More concrete, De Vries, Gensler, and Leeflang (2017) find that advertising is the only channel that significantly influences consumer awareness of a telecom firm. Moreover, the effects of traditional advertising last longer for awareness than for consideration. However, the results of Colicev et al. (2018) show positive significant effects of positive user-generated Facebook posts on consumer awareness for 45 brands in 21 different industry sectors. Together with user followings on Facebook, Twitter and YouTube, user-generated content has the greatest impact on brand awareness, followed by firm-generated content. The number of a brand's posts and replies on Facebook and Twitter and the consumer engagement with this content have both significant positive impact on brand awareness.

Colicev, Kumar, and O'Connor (2019) confirm that user-generated content on Facebook has the highest influence on brand awareness. Moreover, they specify their findings for product type. The effects of firm-generated content were also significant for durables and non-durables, which means that a brand can increase consumer recognition through communication on Facebook. Positive communication is beneficial for non-durables, while it has negative effect for durables and brands increase awareness through neutral posts. Moreover, multimedia posts on Facebook have a significant negative effect on brand awareness for services and durables. Nevertheless, vivid content has a significant positive effect for durables.

However, Colicev et al. (2018) and Colicev, Kumar, and O'Connor (2019) include traditional marketing activities as exogenous controls and do not state the relative impact of the channel. Colicev et al. (2018) assume that advertising has a stronger effect on brand awareness than on later stages of the consumer decision journey. Moreover, their sample shows that there are synergies for brands between traditional marketing activities and firm-generated content, as increased advertising expenditure is accompanied by an increased influence of firm-generated content.

Furthermore, Colicev, Kumar, and O'Connor (2019) find that firm-generated content of service brands has the strongest impact on brand consideration. Even though De Vries, Gensler, and Leeflang (2017) also find that the accumulated impressions of firm-generated content on Twitter, Facebook and YouTube significantly increases consumer consideration of a telecom service, gross media expenditures have a higher impact on consideration (De Vries, Gensler, and Leeflang 2017). Surprisingly, Colicev et al. (2018) find no significant effects of firm-generated content on purchase intention. However, the consumer engagement with this content significantly impacts consumers' purchase intentions.

According to Colicev, Kumar, and O'Connor (2019), brands should use neutral and less positive posts to increase consumer consideration and purchase intention. Otherwise, consumers could perceive the communication as to persuasive. In contrast to awareness, vivid content increases consumer consideration and purchase intention.

In general, positive user-generated content has a positive significant effect on consumer consideration and purchase intention (Colicev et al. 2018; Colicev, Kumar, and O'Connor 2019). Moreover, brand following is a good indicator for purchase intention (Colicev et al. 2018). De Vries, Gensler, and Leeflang (2017) confirm this influence of user-generated content since positive user-generated content on Twitter and Facebook is the only channel that significantly effects consumer preferences for a telecom service.

However, the results over different product types of Colicev, Kumar, and O'Connor (2019) show that the volume of user-generated content has less positive, insignificant or even negative impact on consumer consideration and purchase intentions. These effects could be explained by the results of the meta-analysis of You, Vadakkepatt, and Joshi (2015) on eWOM elasticity. The authors argue that in general valence elasticity is higher than volume elasticity. In addition, consumers in highly competitive environments need more information before making a purchase, which can translate into higher volumes of user-generated content. The higher volume of user-generated content can trigger choice overload, which can have a negative impact on purchase decisions.

Moreover, valence of user-generated content is a good indicator for customer satisfaction. Positive user-generated content has a positive significant impact on satisfaction (Colicev et al. 2018; Colicev, Kumar, and O'Connor 2019), whereas negative user-generated content has a negative significant impact (Colicev et al. 2018). On the one hand, Colicev et al. (2018) find that customer satisfaction is positively influenced by posts and replies on Facebook and Twitter. On the other hand, Colicev, Kumar, and O'Connor (2019) find different results for firm-generated content depending on the product type. Vivid content has a negative significant effect on the costumer satisfactions with durables and services, but no effect on satisfaction with non-durables. For services and products, neutral brand posts on a brand's Facebook page have a positive impact on satisfaction.

## 2.4 Literature Review on Performance Measurement

Positive brand posts have a positive effect for durables but not for services. However, positive as well as neutral firm-generated content has a negative impact on satisfaction with non-durables.

In summary, it can be said that traditional marketing activities increase consumers' brand awareness. However, consumers increasingly shape the awareness of a brand through brand-related content on social media. Therefore, firm-generated content can increase brand awareness if it enhances user-generated chatter on social media. Furthermore, positive user-generated content increases consumer consideration, preference and purchase intention. To enhance consideration and purchase intention, brands should create content that is engaging and vivid. Moreover, brands should generally use neutral statements rather than positive statements on their owned social media channels. The valence of user-generated content has a significant impact on consumer satisfaction. Furthermore, the results show that a mutual exchange between brand and consumer has a positive influence on customer satisfaction.

Besides the effects on brand building, De Vries, Gensler, and Leeflang (2017) investigate the channel effectiveness on customer acquisition of a telecom firm. Their findings indicate that all three channels have significant influence on customer acquisition. However, advertising has the strongest impact, followed by firm-generated content and volume of user-generated content. The same relative relationship exists between the channels with regard to the duration of effect.

Therefore, the findings on services indicate that owned and earned social media channels as well as advertising complement each other, though traditional marketing has the greatest impact on customer acquisition. Nevertheless, research should observe these effects for digital and non-digital products, since the relation of channel impact could differ in this context.

Another focus of this research stream is the influence of advertising and social media channels on sales. Two studies concentrate on channel effects within the financial service industry (Hewett et al. 2016; Stephen and Galak 2012) and one analyzes the impact on movie revenue (Kupfer et al. 2018). As already proposed by Corstjens and Umblijs (2012), the findings of Hewett et al. (2016) indicate a strong impact of negative WOM on brand performance. Negative user-generated WOM has a key role for customer deposits and creates a so called "echoverse". The authors define an echoverse as a system of feedback loops between channels. They find that negative WOM, whether in social media or traditional channels, spreads rapidly and spreads even across channels. Negative user-generated content significantly decreases customer deposits and sentiment. This causes banks to increase positive brand tweets, moderate press releases and spending in advertising. The brands online and offline communication activities (i.e. Twitter posts, press release and advertising spending) positively impact customer deposit. Therefore, brands can increase sales through customization of brand-owned social media content. Similar to the data of Colicev et al. (2018), Hewett et al. (2016) find that brand communication on social media networks and traditional marketing activities complement each other and unite in one communication strategy.

Furthermore, Stephen and Galak (2012) show that the number of blog posts has a positive significant impact on sales of a microlending website. Moreover, the effects of user-generated content are much higher than the effects of brand mentions within traditional media. In comparison, the community forum post (user-generated blog post) elasticity is 15.47 (1.47) for new sales and 2.68 (.37) for repeated sales, while the elasticity of is brand mentions within social media is .48 and .08, respectively. However, the authors find no significant effect for the brand-owned social media channel on sales. Therefore, it could be beneficial for brands to build alliances with social media influencers.

Initial indications of this are provided by the results of Kupfer et al. (2018). The authors find that product-related posts of the leading actor on Facebook increase movie ticket sales. Moreover, greater impact on sales is caused by leading actors that have many followers with high sharing activity. Similar, brands could leverage the social media power of influencers to increase sales. However, brands must first find the right influencers to influence brand performance. In movies, the choice of the leading actor is mainly determined by his acting talent, whereas for influencers other selection criteria should play a role. Especially, since research observes a negative association between non-product related posts and movie ticket sales (Kupfer et al. 2018).

Advertising spend has a higher impact on movie ticket sales than Facebook posts of the leading actor. However, consumer rating has the greatest influence on ticket sales and is three times greater than the influence of advertising. Since influencers are both normal users and have a special power in social media networks, it is important for brands to investigate the effectiveness of this channel (Kupfer et al. 2018).

All in all, traditional marketing activities and user-generated content have a positive impact on sales. However, due to the influence of social media, customer opinions are becoming increasingly important for brand success. Brands can use their own channels to promote positive eWOM and even more to avoid negative eWOM. In addition, recent studies have shown that brands can make use of human brands to successfully market their products.

## 2.4 Literature Review on Performance Measurement

Finally, research investigates the channel effectiveness on stock market performance (Colicev et al. 2018). The authors find that Twitter and Facebook posts and replies of a brand have marginal significant effects ($p < .1$) on stock market returns. Moreover, user engagement with firm-generated content and brand followings have positive significant impact on returns. Furthermore, the authors show that negative user-generated posts on Facebook significantly reduce abnormal returns. Colicev et al. (2018) also demonstrate that positive user-generated content marginally reduces idiosyncratic risk and negative user-generated content marginally increases risk.

Therefore, the authors show again the importance of user-generated content and prove that eWOM even has the power to influence the market value of a brand. For this reason, brands should use their own online and offline channels to positively influence eWOM.

To absorb additional influences, research includes additional **control variables**. These variables are summarized below. Besides social media channels and traditional advertisement, studies control for variables that can be influenced by the brand. For example, research controls for promotions (Corstjens and Umblijs 2012; De Vries, Gensler, and Leeflang 2017; Goh, Heng, and Lin 2013; Kumar et al. 2016; Kumar, Choi, and Greene 2017) and product sampling (Kumar, Choi, and Greene 2017) since they attract consumers. Moreover, Corstjens and Umblijs (2012) and Kumar, Choi, and Greene (2017) control for product price since it can impact sales and acquisition. Furthermore, brand performance can be influenced through special events like own press releases and announcements (Colicev et al. 2018; Colicev, Kumar, and O'Connor 2019; Hewett et al. 2016; Stephen and Galak 2012) or merger and acquisition (Colicev et al. 2018; Colicev, Kumar, and O'Connor 2019). Research also controls for the brand itself (Kumar, Choi, and Greene 2017) and the value of a brand (Colicev et al. 2018; Kupfer et al. 2018; Nam and Kannan 2014).

In context of consumer entertainment, Fossen and Schweidel (2019) control for advertisement characteristics (e.g. position of TV advertisement) and program-specific effects. Moreover, Kumar et al. (2016) control for TV channel effects. Since many studies focus performance of movies, they include movie-specific variables (e.g. genre, production budget or reviewer judgement) within their models (Bruce, Foutz, and Kolsarici 2012; Gopinath, Chintagunta, and Venkataraman 2013; Kim and Hanssens 2017; Kupfer et al. 2018). Furthermore, the results of Kupfer et al. (2018) account for several characteristics of the leading actor and cast. Moreover, they control for message type send by the leading actor.

In addition, research controls for effects that lie outside the influence of a brand. For example, research accounts for media mentions (De Vries, Gensler, and Leeflang 2017; Kupfer et al. 2018; Nam and Kannan 2014), buzz events for industry or product (Colicev et al. 2018; Colicev, Kumar, and O'Connor 2019; De Vries, Gensler, and Leeflang 2017; Tirunillai and Tellis 2012), analyst forecast (Nam and Kannan 2014; Tirunillai and Tellis 2012) or activities of the competitors (Bruce, Foutz, and Kolsarici 2012; De Vries, Gensler, and Leeflang 2017; Gopinath, Chintagunta, and Venkataraman 2013; Gopinath, Thomas, and Krishnamurthi 2014). Moreover, most research controls for time (Bruce, Foutz, and Kolsarici 2012; Corstjens and Umblijs 2012; De Vries, Gensler, and Leeflang 2017; Fossen and Schweidel 2019; Goh, Heng, and Lin 2013; Gopinath, Chintagunta, and Venkataraman 2013; Hewett et al. 2016; Kumar, Choi, and Greene 2017; Onishi and Manchanda 2012; Pauwels, Aksehirli, and Lackman 2016; Stephen and Galak 2012; Tirunillai and Tellis 2012; Trusov, Bucklin, and Pauwels 2009).

In order to control for consumer-specific effects, research includes characteristics of the total population (Corstjens and Umblijs 2012; Hewett et al. 2016; Pauwels, Aksehirli, and Lackman 2016; Stephen and Galak 2012), but also characteristics related to the customer base or individual customers (Goh, Heng, and Lin 2013; Gopinath, Chintagunta, and Venkataraman 2013; Kumar et al. 2013; Kumar et al. 2016; Kumar, Choi, and Greene 2017; Stephen and Galak 2012; Villanueva, Yoo, and Hanssens 2008).

## 2.5 Summary and Research Gaps

Several research gaps can be identified across the process of influencer marketing management. Table 1.1 illustrates the major gaps in literature.

Across all chapters, it becomes clear that the effectiveness of social media messaging can be measured by different metrics along the consumer decision journey. However, it is also evident that studies mainly examine effectiveness on individual metrics (Gap 1). Therefore, future research related to the identification of influencers, the design of viral content, or the effectiveness of channels should investigate effectiveness across different metrics along the consumer decision journey.

Based on the literature analysis regarding the identification of suitable influencers, it has been shown that there are two different streams, which have a different focus. On the one side, the advertising and endorsement literature focuses on the characteristics of the person who sends the message and the

## 2.5 Summary and Research Gaps

impact on attitudes and behavioral intentions (e.g. Breves et al. 2019; Colliander and Dahlén 2011; Kunz and Seshadri 2015; Uribe, Buzeta, and Velásquez 2016). However, this stream of research overlooks the structural resources of a message source (Gap 2). On the other side, the literature on viral marketing mainly examines the effects of the network characteristics of a message source on consumer behavior (e.g. Goldenberg et al. 2009; Katona, Zubcsek, and Sarvary 2011; Peng et al. 2018; Trusov, Bodapati, and Bucklin 2010). The studies largely neglect the personal resources of a message source (Gap 3). Research on the selection of suitable social media influencers needs a holistic approach that combines both personal and network characteristics of a message source (Gap 4).

Studies on endorser fit call for exploration of the impact of influencer brand fit (Kupfer et al. 2018). However, research lacks knowledge about the construct of influencer brand fit (Gap 5). Even though two of the studies compare influencers or bloggers with high and low influencer brand fit in terms of their impact on consumers' attitudes and purchase intentions (Breves et al. 2019; Colliander and Dahlén 2011), none of the studies goes into detail about why an influencer's brand fit is perceived high or low and what factors determine it. Moreover, there is no research on the effectiveness of influencer brand fit on consumer behavior metrics so far.

A large number of studies exist on the unitary or ego network attributes of a message source (e.g. Ansari et al. 2018; Goldenberg et al. 2009; Wang et al. 2019; Zhang, Moe, and Schweidel 2017). These show that a central position determines the diffusion of messages. Influencer marketing makes use of this effect. If several influencers are selected for the same target market, it is likely that there will be a certain overlap of followers between influencers (multiple senders). So far, no research has investigated what influence such overlap has on the diffusion of influencer campaigns or on the adoption of products (Gap 6).

The thesis addresses these research gaps through Study 1. The contribution to the research is fourfold to overcome the identified shortcomings:

(1) Investigation of consumer behavior metrics along the consumer decision journey,
(2) Application of a holistic approach combining personal and structural resources,
(3) Measurement of the influencer brand fit and its influence on consumer behavior,
(4) Investigation of influencer portfolio characteristics such as overlap and unique reach.

Based on the literature review on post design of viral social media posts, two additional research gaps can be observed. Since the virality of social media activities is an overarching goal of brands, it appears that most studies that aim to answer this research question explore the characteristics of viral brand posts (e.g. Akpinar and Berger 2017; De Vries, Gensler, and Leeflang 2012; Ordenes et al. 2019; Rietveld et al. 2020; Swani and Milne 2017). Moreover, some studies observe the characteristics of viral user-generated posts (Li and Xie 2020; Namkoong, Ro, and Henderson 2019; Rooderkerk and Pauwels 2016; Wang et al. 2019). So far, only scattered research deals with the influence of influencer message characteristics on post virality (Hughes, Swaminathan, and Brooks 2019). Therefore, the research on viral influencer content is scarce (Gap 7).

Furthermore, most studies explore the text of social media posts (e.g. Araujo, Neijens, and Vliegenthart 2015; De Vries, Gensler, and Leeflang 2012; Jalali and Papatla 2019; Meire et al. 2019; Swani and Milne 2017). However, initial studies are beginning to explore the influence of image characteristics on the virality of a post (Li and Xie 2020; Rietveld et al. 2020). This is also reflected by the social networks that are studied within research. Most research is done on Facebook and Twitter. Findings on image-based networks such as Instagram and TikTok are largely lacking and research calls for further insights into the image properties of viral posts (Gap 8).

Despite these research gaps, the thesis does not focus on the empirical analysis of design elements of viral influencer posts. On the one hand, the basic characteristics should be the same as for user-generated and firm-generated posts since the perception processes do not differ significantly. Therefore, the theoretical contribution would be rather small. On the other hand, there is also a minor contribution for marketing practice. Influencers are very independent in their role as content creators and adapt their content individually to their followers so that it goes viral. Therefore, the activity of brands is limited to monitoring this process (Leung, Gu, and Palmatier 2022). Moreover, marketers have gained a substantial knowledge through the common use of A/B testing.

The literature review of research comparing multiple channels in terms of their effectiveness has shown that most of the studies compare the effectiveness of advertising messages and user-generated content (e.g. Gopinath, Chintagunta, and Venkataraman 2013; Tirunillai and Tellis 2012; Villanueva, Yoo, and Hanssens 2008). Some studies compare user-generated content and firm-generated content (Goh, Heng, and Lin 2013; Kumar et al. 2013) or firm-generated content and advertising (Kumar et al. 2016; Kumar, Choi, and Greene 2017). Furthermore, recent literature investigates all three types of messages to evaluate the effectiveness and interaction of channels (Colicev, Kumar, and O'Connor 2019; De Vries, Gensler, and Leeflang 2017; Hewett et al. 2016; Kupfer et al. 2018). However, research lacks knowledge about the effectiveness (Gap 9) and channel interactions (Gap 10) of influencer marketing.

## 2.5 Summary and Research Gaps

The thesis addresses these research gaps through Study 2. The contribution to the research is threefold to overcome the identified shortcomings:

(1) Investigation of consumer behavior metrics along the consumer decision journey,
(2) Comparison of the effectiveness of influencer marketing and other marketing investments as well as firm-generated and consumer-generated messages on social media,
(3) Investigation of the interaction effects of the different channels and influencer marketing.

# Predicting the Influencer Value 3

Study 1 investigates the influence of both personal and structural resources of influencers on the success of influencer campaigns. The first section motivates the relevance of the topic. In the following, the objective of the first study is defined. Within Section 3.2, Study 1 is positioned within the literature on influencer selection. Based on this, the conceptual framework is formulated and the hypotheses are derived in Section 3.3. Section 3.4 outlines the data set of Study 1 and describes the operationalization of the variables. This is followed by the descriptive statistics and an illustration of the used methodology. Section 3.5 discusses the estimation results for the different phases of the consumer decision journey. The section concludes with managerial implications, limitations and future research.

## 3.1 Improving Influencer Selection through a Holistic Approach

Social media platforms offer consumers the opportunity to quickly and easily share their experiences with brands and thus play a significant role in shaping a brand's appeal (Gensler et al. 2013). For this reason, an increasing shift in consumer trust from brand-to-consumer communication to peer-to-peer communication can be observed. With influencers playing a key role in consumer communications, influencer marketing continues to gain importance as a key component of companies' digital marketing strategies (Association of National Advertisers 2018). For this reason, market analysts estimate that spending on influencer marketing will grow to as much as 15 billion USD by 2022 (Forbes 2020).

As the examples in Section 1.2 show, brands pursue different goals with their influencer strategy. Brands use influencers to create awareness and consideration for their products and services. In addition, brands can build consumer preferences and willingness to pay for their brand. Moreover, recommendations from influencers increase consumer purchase intent and purchase. Finally, brand advocacy by influencers can result in the relationship between followers and the influencer being transferred to the brand, and is reflected by consumer engagement, loyalty, and endorsement of the brand.

In preparation for Study 1, several expert interviews were conducted within the year 2018 to define relevant metrics for evaluating influencer campaigns in practice.[1] Figure 3.3 shows the guideline for these interviews and Table 3.5 gives an overview on the interview partners. The results of these interviews show that both small and medium-sized business leaders as well as those at the agency are aiming to maximize the campaign's reach to create awareness. Moreover, all the social media managers interviewed indicate that consumer engagement is the main goal of their influencer campaigns. Therefore, the interviews confirm that awareness and engagement are the current prevailing measures of success in the industry (Forbes 2019b).

However, given the recent widespread of in-platform checkout features and discussions in the field to reduce the relevance of likes on Instagram, brands are beginning to use attribution metrics tied to consumer purchase (eMarketer 2019). Through their entertaining and interactive content, influencers create a social shopping experience that transfers the concept of a shopping mall to social media platforms. This is also shown by recent studies on ecommerce behavior. According to these, more than a third of US consumers practice social commerce and consume products directly on social media sites via so-called shoppable content (Droesch 2019). Nevertheless, marketers should not rely solely on sales metrics when evaluating the success of influencer collaborations, because social commerce is still at an early stage of the adoption curve, with only 9% of consumers regularly buying products directly through social media content (Insider Intelligence 2021).

In order to comprehensively capture the effectiveness of an influencer, an influencer's impact on consumer behavior along the consumer decision journey

---

[1] The interviews were conducted between January 2018 and November 2018. Interviews were conducted with those responsible for social media activities in a small company (annual turnover below one million EUR), a medium-sized company (annual turnover between 1 and 50 million EUR) and a corporate group (annual turnover over 50 million EUR). In addition, a shadowing with the managing director of an online marketing agency was conducted in January 2018, as well as several interviews with employees of the agency.

## 3.1 Improving Influencer Selection through a Holistic Approach

should be investigated. However, the current research on message source effects on consumer behavior mainly examines effectiveness on individual metrics.

Since not every influencer is suitable for every target, a decline of average engagement rates with influencer content can be observed. Compared to 2018, the industry has seen a decrease in the average like follower ratio in important sectors of influencer marketing on Instagram: beauty, fashion, food, lifestyle, travel, sports, and fitness (InfluencerDB 2019; Rival IQ 2019). The situation is similar on Facebook and Twitter, where a drop in engagement rates can also be observed compared to 2017 (Rival IQ 2018). For an influencer, the average engagement rate per post is .19% on Facebook, .036% on Twitter and is slightly higher at 1.42% on Instagram (Rival IQ 2021). The days when brands could still achieve visible results with a "spray and pray" attitude are over (InfluencerDB 2019). Marketers need to harness the data from social platforms and implement data-driven evaluations of influencer effectiveness to create successful influencer collaborations. In doing so, they must look beyond the number of followers when selecting suitable influencers (Forbes 2019b). Managers need to have a good understanding of which influencer characteristics drive campaign results along the different phases of the consumer decision journey from the onset. However, research on the effectiveness of a message source within social media lacks a holistic approach that combines both personal and network characteristics of a message source.

Whether an influencer is considered suitable depends, among other things, on the influencer brand fit (Forbes 2019b). Within the expert interviews, this picture is confirmed as all interviewees mentioned influencer brand fit as one of their selection criteria. However, the experts could not describe exactly what constitutes this brand fit. Furthermore, also research lacks knowledge about the construct of influencer brand fit. Even though some studies consider influencer brand fit (Breves et al. 2019; Colliander and Dahlén 2011), none of the studies explain why an influencer's brand fit is perceived high or low and how consumers come to this assessment. Moreover, there is a call for research on the impact of influencer brand fit on consumer behavior (Kupfer et al. 2018).

In the expert interviews, all marketers indicated that they tend to work with a portfolio of influencers rather than selecting individual influencers for a campaign. Case studies of successful influencer campaigns also show that brands collaborate with more than one influencer for a campaign (Mediakix 2020a). Since marketers often use a portfolio of influencers, they are interested in overall campaign success rather than the effectiveness of an individual influencer. Yet, neither the industry nor research offer insights into what portfolio characteristics improve the effectiveness of an influencer campaign. Therefore, research needs to gain insights into influencer characteristics that determine an influencer's effectiveness within a portfolio.

In order to address the aforementioned research gaps the aim of the first study is to *investigate the impact of influencer characteristics on influencer campaign measures along the consumer decision journey.*

More specifically, the study examines the effects of personal and network characteristics of an influencer on (i) post reach (awareness phase), (ii) product link clicks within the influencer's story (purchase phase) and (iii) post likes and comments and story views (engagement phase). The study includes both the personal characteristics of the influencer and the characteristics of his network. Personal potential is captured through perceived expertise and influencer brand fit. In doing so, the study uses a consumer survey to measure influencer brand fit and its factors. The network potential includes the influencer network, the activity of the sender and follower activity. In particular, influencer network characteristics are considered, which are characterized by the portfolio of influencers who are involved in a campaign.

This study intends to contribute to the current research by combining and comparing several success metrics of viral campaigns, which were previously considered in isolation. Therefore, the study observes the effectiveness of an influencer across the consumer decision journey. Moreover, the study combines the perspectives of two different research streams and looks holistically at the personal and structural resources of a message source in the context of influencers. The study extends previous findings on the influence of influencer brand fit and is the first study to examine the influence of influencer brand fit on consumer behavior. Furthermore, in addition to the well-researched unitary network attributes, the study enriches the scarce research on dyadic network attributes and considers the structural resources of an influencer in relation to the influencer portfolio used for a campaign.

In addition to the theoretical contribution, the practice also gains insights into the selection of suitable influencers. By differentiating results across various measures of success, brands can optimize the effectiveness of their influencer campaigns across the entire consumer decision journey by selecting the appropriate influencers. Moreover, by taking a holistic view of message source characteristics in the context of influencer marketing, marketers gain knowledge about which characteristics to consider when selecting influencers through data-driven models. As a first step, brands can also use the study insights to better anticipate campaign results for the existing influencer metrics on platforms. Furthermore, the consumer survey to measure influencer brand fit provides valuable insights into consumer perception of influencer brand fit. Managers learn on which factors this perception is based and can transfer this knowledge for their own determination of influencer brand fit. Finally, managers gain an understanding of the impact of influencer portfolio characteristics on different campaign outcomes and can derive implications for influencer portfolio selection. All in all, the insights help managers to predict the value of an influencer depending on the campaign goal.

## 3.2 Positioning Study 1 within Literature

First, Study 1 is integrated into the existing literature and distinguished from the work that is most similar to Study 1. This is followed by a summary of the most important results of previous research on message source effects on consumer behavior in the social media context in order to prepare the derivation of the hypotheses in Section 3.3.

Based on the defined search criteria in the literature review in Chapter 2, 14 studies were identified from 2000 to 2021 that focus on the impact of message source characteristics on consumer behavior metrics (Table 3.1). The studies concentrate on different types of a message source within social media. The considered type of message source is illustrated in Column 2 of Table 3.1. The following columns summarize which message source characteristics are observed within the studies and classify them into personal and network potential of a message source. The observed consumer behavior metrics under research capture the virality of a message. As outlined before, the literature on effects of a message source on virality divides into research on message diffusion and product or service adoption. Both streams relate to different phases of the consumer decision journey. In the following and in Table 3.1, the isolated study results are assigned to the different phases of the consumer decision journey to illustrate the findings regarding the influence of message source characteristics along this decision journey. Therefore, the last three columns of Table 3.1 illustrate the specific phases of the consumer decision journey.

The studies that deal with the diffusion of a message show two perspectives of information dissemination. In order to spread a message, the message must first become visible, i.e., within social networks, many people must first see the message (awareness). Afterwards, people should ideally become advocates of the message by interacting with the message and sharing it themselves (engagement). Thus, they further enhance the virality of the message and even more people see the message. This illustrates that the phases are recurring and circular rather than acting in a specific order (Batra and Keller 2016).

Research in the context of diffusion on music-sharing platforms observe the number of songs played. The number of songs played is the equivalent to post views on other networks. Therefore, the studies capture consumer awareness in this type of network (Ansari et al. 2018; Lanz et al. 2019). Further studies on information diffusion observe consumer engagement within social media networks and investigate the impact of source characteristics on retweets and reposts (Chen et al. 2019; Namkoong, Ro, and Henderson 2019; Peng et al. 2018; Wang et al. 2019; Zhang, Moe, and Schweidel 2017), likes or favorites (Hughes, Swaminathan, and Brooks 2019; Namkoong, Ro, and Henderson 2019; Peng et al. 2018) and comments (Hughes, Swaminathan, and Brooks 2019; Rooderkerk and Pauwels 2016). In addition to studies looking at the various aspects of message diffusion, some studies focus on the influence of sender characteristics on the adoption of products and services (Goldenberg et al. 2009; Gong et al. 2017; Katona, Zubcsek, and Sarvary 2011; Kupfer et al. 2018). Thus, these studies capture consumer purchases within the consumer decision journey.

Table 3.1 further illustrates how Study 1 differs from the previous studies. As indicated in Column 2 of Table 3.1, the literature exploring source effects in the context of social media influencers is scarce (Hughes, Swaminathan, and Brooks 2019; Kupfer et al. 2018). Only two studies observe postings of social media influencers (Gong et al. 2017; Hughes, Swaminathan, and Brooks 2019). However, Hughes, Swaminathan, and Brooks (2019) focus only on blogger expertise and number of followers and neglect the campaign independent activity of influencers and followers as well as the influencer characteristics that describe their role within the campaign portfolio. Even though, Gong et al. (2017) promote TV shows with multiple influencers in their field experiment, their work also lacks the aspect of structural dependence of an influencer used in a portfolio. In addition, they refer exclusively to the structural resources of an influencer and overlook personal characteristics such as expertise and brand fit.

Although, all social media managers interviewed in preparation for Study 1 stated that an influencer's brand fit is one of the most important characteristics for selecting an influencer, and research has also shown this connection (Kupfer et al. 2018), both Gong et al. (2017) as well as Hughes, Swaminathan, and Brooks (2019) neglect this aspect in their work. Kupfer et al. (2018) are the first to study the impact of fit between an endorser and the endorsed brand on observable consumer behavior in the social media context. They transfer well-known relationships from the endorsement literature (Amos, Holmes, and Strutton 2008) to the viral marketing literature.

## 3.2 Positioning Study 1 within Literature

Kupfer et al. (2018) consider staring actors as message sources. In this context, the influence of message source characteristics on movie ticket sales is investigated. However, actors differ from social media influencers in that they are selected for their acting talent since they participate in the making of the product. Influencers, on the other hand, are characterized by their online presence on social networks and are mostly not related to the process of producing the product. In their appendix, the authors control for the influence of film mentions of other actors who were not involved in the film, and find a significant positive influence on ticket sales. The authors take these results as an indication to call for further research in the concrete context of social media influencers, as they are not necessarily related to the product created, but can still have a significant impact on the marketing of the product. For this reason, Study 1 addresses this phenomenon.

Another important point is that Study 1 looks at consumer behavior at different stages of the consumer decision journey, since almost all previous studies consider consumer behavior linked to only one stage of the journey. Just Gong et al. (2017) consider both adoption and engagement, emphasizing the impact of brand and influencer social media activities on different stages of the consumer decision journey and the interaction effects between these stages. However, even though the authors observe seeding through so called "influentials". These influentials are rather described as ordinary people with potential structural resources. Personal characteristics such as expertise and brand fit are not considered for the selection of influentials. They are randomly assigned to TV shows. Therefore, the focus does not seem to be on social media personalities, which characterize social media influencers.

To derive the framework that underlies Study 1 in the next chapter, Figure 3.1 summarizes the key findings from the defined literature. As shown in Table 3.1, consumer behavior metrics, which are examined as a dependent variables in the present studies, can be assigned to different phases of the consumer decision journey. Building on that structure, the right-hand side of Figure 3.1 is divided into the phases: awareness, purchase and engagement. The characteristics of the message source, which are organized from left to right in personal and network potential in Table 3.1, are shown from top to bottom on the left side in Figure 3.1. The characteristics and their influence are briefly explained in this order in the following.

Only few studies consider personal characteristics such as **source expertise** in the context of viral messages within social media. From the different results, it is clear that the influence of source expertise depends on the study context and

**Table 3.1** Studies considering the Effectiveness of Message Source Characteristics on Consumer Behavior Metrics

| | | Personal Potential | | Network Potential | | | Consumer Decision Journey | | |
|---|---|---|---|---|---|---|---|---|---|
| Study | Source | Expertise | Endorser Fit | Network Structure Sender | Activity of Sender | Activity of Followers | Awareness Phase | Purchase Phase | Engagement Phase |
| Ansari, et al. 2018 | UGC | | | x | x | x | x | | |
| Goldenberg et al. 2009 | UGC | | | x | | | | x | |
| Gong et al. 2017 | FGC, Influencer | | | x | x | x | | x | x |
| Hughes et al. 2019 | Influencer | x | | x | x | | | | x |
| Katona, Zubcsek, and Sarvary 2011 | UGC | | | x | | | | | |
| Kupfer et al. 2018 | FGC, Celebrity | | x | x | x | x | | x | |
| Lanz et al. 2019 | UGC | | | x | x | x | x | | |
| Namkoong, Ro, and Henderson 2019 | UGC | | | x | | | | | x |
| Peng et al. 2018 | UGC | | | x | x | x | | | x |
| Rooderkerk and Pauwels 2016 | UGC | x | | x | | | | | x |
| Trusov, Bodapati, and Bucklin 2010 | UGC | | | x | x | x | | | x |
| Valsesia, Proserpio, and Nunes 2020 | Micro Influencer | | | x | x | x | | | x |
| Wang et al. 2019 | UGC | | | x | x | x | | | x |
| Zhang, Moe, and Schweidel 2017 | FGC | | | x | x | x | | | x |
| Study 1 | Influencer | x | x | x | x | x | x | x | x |

Source: Author's own illustration. Notes: UGC = user-generated content, FGC = firm-generated content

## 3.2 Positioning Study 1 within Literature

needs further clarification. Rooderkerk and Pauwels (2016) find that in professional groups on LinkedIn, it is not the centrality of the author that influences the number of responding comments, but the expertise of an author, which is indicated by his job title. Hughes, Swaminathan, and Brooks (2019) also show that influencers with higher expertise encourage consumers to communicate more on blogs. However, influencer expertise has a negative effect on the number of Facebook likes, which can be explained by the cannibalizing effects between engagement metrics.

The direct effects of influencer expertise on blog post comments or Facebook likes become insignificant when an interaction effect with campaign target is included in the model of Hughes, Swaminathan, and Brooks (2019). Yet, this model confirms the positive effect of influencer expertise on the number of comments in the case of an awareness campaign, but not for trial campaigns. The authors explain the different importance of influencer expertise depending on the campaign goal by the fact that consumers are more or less inclined to use peripheral cues such as influencer expertise, depending on which stage of the consumer decision journey they are in. Study 1 aims to further explore these relationships by looking at the effects of influencer expertise on consumer behavior at different stages of the consumer decision journey.

As mentioned above, Kupfer et al. (2018) is the only paper in the literature to integrate the **fit between endorser and advertised brand** in their model. The actor shows a high fit if he is best known for the advertised movie genre. A high fit has a significant positive influence on the ticket sales of the movie. With their call for further research in the context of social media influencers, it remains open whether the fit between influencer and brand is equally important for every measure of success of influencer campaigns. This connection is particularly important for social media influencers because, unlike the actors in the study of Kupfer et al. (2018), influencers are usually not involved in the product creation process and are therefore not automatically associated with the brand.

According to the development of the research stream of viral marketing, the most work examines the structural resources of a message source. Most papers show that the **centrality of a message source** has a positive effect on the different phases of the consumer decision journey (Ansari et al. 2018; Goldenberg et al. 2009; Gong et al. 2017; Hughes, Swaminathan, and Brooks 2019; Kupfer et al. 2018; Namkoong, Ro, and Henderson 2019; Valsesia, Proserpio, and Nunes 2020; Wang et al. 2019). However, Figure 3.1 clarifies that there is research evidence that rules out a generalization of this positive effect.

Current research on micro influencers shows that centrality in terms of followers is beneficial for post engagement, but centrality in terms of followings has a

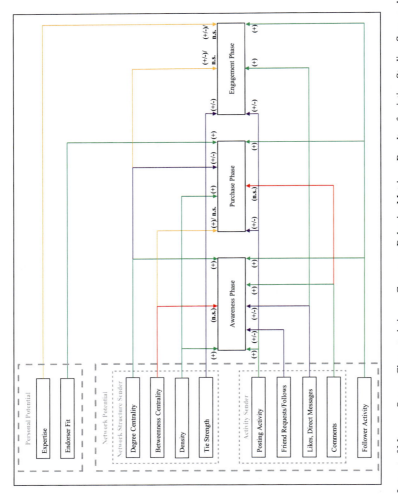

**Figure 3.1** Impact of Message Source Characteristics on Consumer Behavior Metrics – Results of existing Studies. Source: Author's own illustration. Notes: Green arrow: significant positive effect. Purple arrow: significant negative and positive effect. Red arrow: not significant effect. Yellow arrow: significant as well as not significant effect

## 3.2 Positioning Study 1 within Literature

negative impact (Valsesia, Proserpio, and Nunes 2020). Moreover, some studies show that the personal characteristics of a message source, such as expertise, may have more influence on consumer engagement than the structural position of the sender within a network (Rooderkerk and Pauwels 2016). Furthermore, in their work on the diffusion of a social network service, Katona, Zubcsek, and Sarvary (2011) shed light on the micro-perspective between message source and receiver and show that the influence of a message source on the individual receiver can decrease with the number of contacts. They find that the average number of connections of a potential influencer slightly but significantly decreases the adoption probability of the receiver. This is explained by the assumption that the intensity of communication must decrease with the number of contacts. Because an adoption of the network service could only take place by direct invitation, this assumption was confirmed in this context. Since influencers can personally reach a large number of their followers within modern networks, it seems important to prove the positive correlation between degree centrality and consumer behavior in this context.

The influence of **betweenness centrality** of an actor is based on the assumption that the actor, which connects two unrelated actors, plays a mediating role for the information process. However, previous research has not been able to demonstrate this type of influence on consumer behavior within social networks (Ansari et al. 2018; Katona, Zubcsek, and Sarvary 2011). It is up to future research to verify whether betweenness centrality has no influence in large social networks or only comes into play in contexts where independently existing groups have to be connected.

Research examining **message source network density** has shown that it has a positive influence on awareness and adoption (Ansari et al. 2018; Katona, Zubcsek, and Sarvary 2011). However, the impact of the network density of a message source on consumer engagement remains unexplored. A recent study by Chen et al. (2019) examines users' own reposting behavior in a dense network. They argue that information redundancy within a dense network increases due to the increased likelihood of repeated exposure to the same information from multiple friends. The authors classify users into creators and diffusers. A diffuser, unlike a creator, is a user who has not created any new content within the last three months. Chen et al. (2019) show that diffusers in dense networks have a higher propensity to repost popular content than creators, as they have a lower need for uniqueness in the context of information redundancy. Therefore, if increasing customer engagement is the goal of a campaign, it might be relevant to the success of influencers with a dense network what kind of users their followers are. In addition, it seems to matter what kind of engagement metrics campaigns are targeting. For example, redundancy of information in a dense network may have a negative effect on reposting behavior, but has a higher impact on metrics like likes due to multiple contact, similar to the impact on adoption.

From the micro perspective, which illuminates the **tie-strength between the sender and receiver of a message**, this relationship has already been demonstrated. Peng et al. (2018) show that the positive effect of an overlapping network between sender and receiver on the likelihood of sharing the post turns negative when the content to be shared has already been shared frequently. Wang et al. (2019) also show that a high proportion of shared followers between the sender and receiver has a negative impact on the reposting behavior of receivers. However, this negative effect becomes insignificant if the post is of high personal relevance for the receiver or highly emotional. Therefore, the influence on the receivers' reposting behavior depends strongly on the type of content if the network of a sender and a receiver overlap. This relationship should also be verified from the macro perspective, which deals with the density of the influencer network.

Unsurprisingly, the activity of a message source has a positive effect on consumer attention (Ansari et al. 2018; Trusov, Bodapati, and Bucklin 2010). The influence on later phases of the consumer decision journey, on the other side, must be viewed in a more differentiated manner. Although selected influencers for campaigns are characterized by high posting frequency, the influence of **posting behavior** within the campaign on the consumer consumption decision is strongly content-dependent (Gong et al. 2017). The results show that the number of general posts, which do not relate to the product or service, has a negative impact on the consumer consumption decision (Gong et al. 2017; Kupfer et al. 2018). Product-related posts, however, have a strong positive influence on product sales. Persuasive posts are particularly effective in this context (Kupfer et al. 2018). Similar effects are observed for the engagement phase. Non-product-related posts by influencers steer engagement away from the brand and reduce the follower growth of the brand that results from a campaign (Gong et al. 2017). However, more frequent posting of the sender itself can reduce the attention for the single post through information overload (Valsesia, Proserpio, and Nunes 2020; Zhang, Moe, and Schweidel 2017). Contrary results from Hughes, Swaminathan, and Brooks (2019) show that the number of campaign posts increases the number of likes. Because of the different effects, especially for later stages of the consumer decision journey, future research should compare the impact of influencer characteristics on different success metrics along the consumer decision journey.

Other activities of the sender that have been investigated so far, such as friend requests, follows, or likes and comments, are activities that are primarily aimed at

## 3.2 Positioning Study 1 within Literature

drawing the attention of outsiders to one's own content and thus expanding one's own network. Table 3.2 summarized the impact of activities of the sender and the followers on the network structure of the sender. The number of **friend requests or follows** sent has a direct positive effect on consumer awareness and also an indirect positive effect on awareness by increasing followers (degree centrality) (Ansari et al. 2018; Lanz et al. 2019). This means that a user of a social network can attract the attention of other users for his content in the short term by following them or sending friend requests. He can also attract the attention of other users for his content in the long term if they become followers as a result of these activities and consume his content regularly. Although increased friend requests reduce the network density of a message source, which has a positive influence on consumer awareness, this effect disappears in the long term as the new friends integrate into the network (Ansari et al. 2018). Lanz et al. (2019) include the status difference between sender and receiver and show that the positive effect on consumer awareness reduces by sending out follows to status-higher individuals. Therefore, a positive impact of network development activities seems to depend on which individuals are targeted.

The same applies for **likes**. In the context of targeting influentials for unpaid endorsements, the likes applied by an artist have an effect on the attention the artist's profile is getting, but the direction of this effect changes within the different models. However, the effects for the models show that liking posts of status-higher users outside one's own network reduces effects on awareness. In the context of micro influencer, the liking activity of micro influencers on others content increases his own likes and retweets (Valsesia, Proserpio, and Nunes 2020).

**Direct messaging** is a more private way of contacting someone via social media and should therefore be used with caution to contact users outside the own network. Sending direct messages to users outside one's network is the least successful strategy for generating awareness (Lanz et al. 2019).

The only outgoing activity that consistently had a positive direct impact on awareness and also strengthened the network of the message source is writing **comments** on postings from users outside one's own network (Ansari et al. 2018; Lanz et al. 2019). Likewise, the greater the difference in status between the actors, the less effective the comments (Lanz et al. 2019). However, Kupfer et al. (2018) cannot find significant results of responsive comments of an actor on fan comments on consumer purchase. They explain this result with the low visibility of comments on social media networks and recommend rather visible activities like product-related posts. Nevertheless, research looking at activities of the message sender that target its followers rather than users outside the network is small

**Table 3.2** Impact of Activity of Sender and Followers on Network Structure of Sender – Results of existing Studies

|  | Network Structure Sender | | | |
| --- | --- | --- | --- | --- |
|  | Degree Centrality | Betweenness Centrality | Density | Tie Strength |
| **Activity Sender** | | | | |
| Posting Activity | | | | |
| Friend Requests/Follows | + | + | − | |
| Likes, Direct Messages | +/− | | | |
| Comments | + | n.s. | | |
| **Follower Activity** | + | n.s. | + | |

Source: Author's own illustration. Notes: +/− = positive/negative effects, n.s. = not significant effects. Empty cells represent effects that have not been studied

and could benefit from further insight, since this behavior shapes the relationship between message source and followers.

The follower activity illuminates this relationship from the other side. The studies have found that the **activity of followers** of a message source has a positive influence on consumer behavior, which persists across the stages of the consumer decision journey. A message source's posts gain more attention directly through incoming friend requests and indirectly through the network growth that results from these requests (Ansari et al. 2018). Moreover, the research results suggest a positive influence of follower activity on both consumer consumption (Gong et al. 2017; Kupfer et al. 2018) and consumer engagement (Gong et al. 2017; Zhang, Moe, and Schweidel 2017). Furthermore, Wang et al. (2019) show that the likelihood that a post from a message source will increase consumer engagement increases as the number of active followers and the follower activity increases.

By summarizing the results in Figure 3.1, it becomes clear that many influences act differently depending on the context and that some are not significant or remain unexplored. In addition, the studies only cover individual characteristics of the message source or are limited to the influence on one of the phases of the consumer decision journey. In order to contribute to the existing knowledge on message source effects, the framework of Study 1 will therefore include both the personal and the structural resources of an influencer as well as their influence on different phases of the consumer decision journey. The following section derives the conceptual framework as well as the hypotheses for the first study.

## 3.3 Conceptual Framework and Hypotheses

The literature analysis has shown that the influence of a message source arises both from its personal resources and from its structural resources. Both perspectives can be aligned within power theory. The micro and macro perspectives of power determine a person's power on the one hand by his personal behavior and on the other hand by his structural position (Brass and Burkhardt 1993), thus reflecting the research.

Power theory has its origins in sociology and social psychology (French and Raven 1959). Within research on social influence, power theory has repeatedly been associated with influence and leadership and is therefore widely used in political (e.g. Dahl 1975), organizational (e.g. Mintzberg 1984) and marketing research (e.g. Gaski 1984; Homburg, Workman, and Krohmer 1999). Finally, power theory has also been applied to study influence in social networks (Kupfer et al. 2018).

To identify influencer and portfolio characteristics that affect consumer behavior along the consumer decision journey, the power theory of French and Raven (1959) is applied. The theory explains the influence of a social agent (i.e. the influencer) on a person where influence is defined as changes in attitudes and behaviors of the person (French and Raven 1959). In other words, a person has power over another person to the extent that he can make him behave in a way that he would not have behaved without him (Dahl 1975).

To describe the source of such power, French and Raven (1959) define five "bases of power": (1) reward power and (2) coercive power, which are based on a person's ability to reward or punish another person; (3) legitimate power, which is based on a person's legitimate role and gives him the right to determine the behavior of others; (4) expert power, which arises from a person's knowledge and skills; and (5) referent power, which arises from a person's identification with another person. The authors make clear that power in everyday situations is influenced by several factors and not just one power base alone. With regard to the power of social media influencers on potential consumers, both expert power and, in particular, referent power come into play.

Literature has shown that statements made by people with high expertise have a strong influence on thinking and behavior because they are considered true based on previous experience of the person and the knowledge gained through this experience (Hovland, Janis, and Kelley 1953; Ohanian 1990). Influencers characterize themselves through posts on specific topics and thus specifically target specific niches (De Veirman, Cauberghe, and Hudders 2017). To inspire their followers, they provide information on the latest trends and provide useful recommendations (Casaló, Flavián, and Ibáñez-Sánchez 2018). For example, Pamela Reif is known as a fitness influencer and shares her knowledge and experience on daily workouts and clean eating with her followers. She now sells cookbooks and products from her own food brand. In addition, Kupfer et al. (2018) have shown that the selection of an actor who has achieved a certain level of recognition for a product category through his skills positively influences the purchase decision of social media users. A similar connection can be assumed for influencers. Fitness and yoga influencer Mady Morrison, for example, promotes athletic clothing on Zalando and shows which outfits are suitable for which sports.

However, the special characteristics of social media platforms make referent power particularly relevant for social media influencers. The referent power of an influencer is high if he has a high identification potential. Social media users are attracted to an influencer with high referent power and want to build a relationship with them by following them on social media. If they are then followers, they feel the need to maintain this relationship. In order to identify with the influencer, they adopt the influencer's perceptions, values and behaviors (French and Raven 1959). Social media makes it possible to get in touch with followers anytime and anywhere through your own posts, stories, comments and likes. This persuasive communication enables influencers and brands to build up a particularly strong referent power through the interaction with their followers (Chung and Cho 2017; Kupfer et al. 2018; Lee and Jang 2013). The interaction with these posts gives followers a sense of a two-way, intimate relationship (Djafarova and Rushworth 2017; Labrecque 2014).

The conceptual model of Study 1 is shown in Figure 3.2 and includes the three concepts of power theory: (1) the personal potential of an influencer (power use), which comprises characteristics acquired through influencing behavior; (2) the network potential of an influencer (power potential), which arises from the structural position; and (3) consumer behavior along the consumer decision journey (power outcome), which results from the influence of the influencer (Brass and Burkhardt 1993). Therefore, the framework combines the results of advertising and endorsement literature as well as viral marketing literature and looks holistically at the personal and structural resources of a message source in the context of influencers.

Individuals differentiate themselves in their power over other individuals through personal abilities, skills and characteristics (Brass and Burkhardt 1993).

## 3.3 Conceptual Framework and Hypotheses

In Study 1, the personal potential of an influencer is defined by his expertise and brand fit. The posts of influencers differ in terms of their expertise. Moreover, through their behavior on social media, influencers build a certain image and fit to specific product categories. As mentioned above, Pamela Reif is a fitness influencer, who gives tips on clean eating, pays attention to sustainability and creates weekly workout plans to retrain. The quality and frequency of her training videos and posts have made her the most well-known fitness influencer in Germany. The image she has built around these videos allows her to promote products in the field of sports and sportswear, food and sustainability.

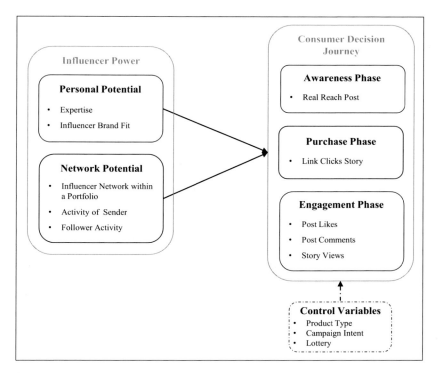

**Figure 3.2** Conceptual Framework of Study 1. Source: Author's own illustration.

The network potential of an influencer reflects the power potential. Power potential is determined by a person's position within a network. In network theory, a central position is usually assumed to have a high potential because these positions have potential control over valuable resources such as information (Brass and Burkhardt 1993). This role of influential individuals is described in the two-step flow model by Katz and Lazarsfeld (1955), and identifies the potential of these central nodes for effective information transfer. Similar to Kupfer et al. (2018), the network potential is divided into the size of the network and the activity of the network. The larger an influencer's network, the more potential customers he can reach with his message. Moreover, active followers enable an influencer to reach users outside their own network. For example, brands like Yves Saint Laurent reach about 469 thousand followers on Instagram via fashion influencer Karolina Kauer. Karolina Kauer's active follower base then in turn shares her content with its own network through shares and likes.

Another contribution from Study 1 is that the influencer's network size is determined in relation to the portfolio of influencers used in the campaign. Thus, an influencer within a campaign has a certain number of followers that only he reaches (i.e., unique follower base) and a certain number that is reached by him and other influencers in the portfolio (i.e., follower overlap). Depending on the campaign goal, one or the other can be advantageous. For example, in another campaign Yves Saint Laurent worked with the beauty influencer tamtambeauty, who at the time had a follower base of 373 thousand followers. However, 62% of her followers overlapped with the followers of other influencers who were also booked for the campaign. It is therefore essential for brands to determine for which campaign goals an overlap of the network of influencers can be advantageous and for which it is rather a drawback because brands pay twice to reach the same users.

The power of an influencer should be reflected in so-called power outcomes (Brass and Burkhardt 1993; French and Raven 1959). In the conceptual model of Study 1, the network potential and the personal potential of an influencer impact consumer behavior along the consumer decision journey. The individual characteristics of an influencer affect the awareness of customers, their purchase decision and the engagement with the content of the campaign and the brand. Therefore, the success of an influencer campaign is characterized by the post reach (awareness phase), product link clicks within the influencer's story (purchase phase) and post likes and comments and story views (engagement phase).

## 3.3.1 Impact of Personal Potential on the Consumer Decision Journey

*Effect of influencer expertise.* Influence arises, for example, from a person's reliance on information provided by another person because that person is characterized by successful behavior in a particular area or has special skills and knowledge. This influence is defined as expert power of a message source (French and Raven 1959; Hovland, Janis, and Kelley 1953). This influence can be reflected in changes in attitudes and thinking of a person, as well as in changes in behavior (Brass and Burkhardt 1993; French and Raven 1959).

A higher level of source expertise leads to a higher level of persuasion, as it induces a deeper processing of the advertising message (Homer and Kahle 1990). Several studies have already shown that the expertise of an endorser has a positive effect on consumer attitude and behavioral intentions (Amos, Holmes, and Strutton 2008; Uribe, Buzeta, and Velásquez 2016). Moreover, Hughes, Swaminathan, and Brooks (2019) and Rooderkerk and Pauwels (2016) have already been able to demonstrate these correlations for consumer engagement with social media messages. Therefore, the framework assumes the following:

*H1:   Expertise of an influencer's posts relates positively to consumer behavior along the consumer decision journey.*

*Effect of influencer brand fit.* The reference power of an influencer is based on the identification of the followers with the influencer. They identify with him because they share the same beliefs and values or because he embodies beliefs and values that they would like to hold (French and Raven 1959). In order to maintain this identification, the products that the influencer promotes should be suited to him and thus also to his followers.

The match-up hypothesis picks up this thought and assumes that the higher the congruence between the image of the celebrity endorser and the product, the more successful an advertisement will be (Forkan 1980; Kahle and Homer 1985). Colliander and Dahlén (2011) and Breves et al. (2019) also observe this relationship between influencer brand fit and brand attitudes as well as purchase intentions.

The theoretical background is, that the processing of new information is more effective and more likely to influence opinion and behavior when the information schemas about brand and message source are congruent (Misra and Beatty 1990). Moreover, it can be assumed that a higher congruence between product and message source leads to a higher credibility and thus also to higher influence (Kamins and Gupta 1994). Therefore, the framework assumes the following:

H2: *Influencer brand fit relates positively to consumer behavior along the consumer decision journey.*

### 3.3.2 Impact of Network Potential on the Consumer Decision Journey

*Effect of an influencer's network within a portfolio.* Legitimate power arises from the social structure of a group or organization. Within this group, a certain hierarchy exists, with the leaders of this hierarchy holding the power (French and Raven 1959). Influencers are defined as leaders within social network structures and can be identified through their structural links (Casaló, Flavián, and Ibáñez-Sánchez 2018; De Veirman, Cauberghe, and Hudders 2017).

The power theories draw on the social network approach and define a person with a lot of power as a person with many structural ties. These structural ties in turn represent structural dependency. Central actors have access to and control over relevant resources, such as information, and thus others are dependent on them (Emerson 1962). Within their two-step flow model, Katz and Lazarsfeld (1955) transfer this concept to the communication between media and consumers. A key role is taken by so called "influentials", who pass on the message to a broader audience. Accordingly, the audience depends on the influential, since they are searching for information and social confirmation.

The positive effect of power, which is determined by the structural position of a person, on the different phases of the consumer decision journey have already been proven in several studies on influence in social networks (Ansari et al. 2018; Goldenberg et al. 2009; Gong et al. 2017; Hughes, Swaminathan, and Brooks 2019; Kupfer et al. 2018; Namkoong, Ro, and Henderson 2019; Wang et al. 2019).

However, in practice brands do not work with an individual influencer but rather with a portfolio of influencers. Therefore, brands are not just interested how many followers the influencer has. If a brand wants to enhance the awareness for a new product launch and is aiming for an earlier stage of the consumer decision journey, it wants to know how many unique followers the influencer has that do not follow other influencers within the portfolio. Otherwise, the brand would pay to reach the same consumers twice. On the other hand, if the brand wants to drive sales, an overlap of followers should positively relate to consumer behavior in

## 3.3 Conceptual Framework and Hypotheses

later stages of the consumer decision journey. According to advertising literature, multiple exposure can enhance campaign success (Voorveld, Neijens, and Smit 2011). These findings are theoretically based on three underlying psychological processes: forward encoding (i.e., the first post primes interest in the second post) (Keller 1987), image transfer (i.e., elements in the second post may function as retrieval cues to the post memory trace from the first exposure) (Tulving and Thomson 1973), and multiple source perception (i.e., multiple sources make the message more convincing and credible) (Harkins and Petty 1987). In summary, this means that a high unique reach, as opposed to a high number of followers, always has a positive effect on the success measures of an influencer post. At the same time, a high follower overlap should have a positive impact on the purchase decision, but a negative impact on reach and engagement. Depending on the targeted stage of the consumer decision journey, brand managers should aim either for influencers with a low follower overlap and a high number of unique followers or influencers with and a high follower overlap and a high number of unique followers. Taken together, the framework assumes the following:

H3a: *An influencer's unique reach relates positively to consumer behavior along the consumer decision journey.*

H3b: *An influencer's network overlap relates (i) positively to consumer purchase decision behavior but (ii) negative to consumer awareness and engagement.*

*Effect of influencer activity.* Power theory assumes that an influencer is capable of several activities which, due to the more or less enduring relationship between him and his followers, exert influence on the followers (French and Raven 1959).

Power in a network comes from resource control. People who have valuable information thus make others dependent on them (Brass and Burkhardt 1993; Emerson 1962). In social networks, influencers have such power because their followers are interested in their content. The more frequent the degree of information transfer, the greater the dependency. Accordingly, influencers, unlike normal social media users, are characterized by a high level of posting activity and regularly produce content (Gong et al. 2017). Studies show that this activity of a message source has a positive effect on consumer behavior (Ansari et al. 2018; Trusov, Bodapati, and Bucklin 2010).

Moreover, social media activities, such as regular posting of personal content, can be used to build a personal relationship with followers (Labrecque 2014). Since influencers post frequently and often reveal private information from their daily lives, this reinforces the feeling of an intense and intimate relationship between followers and influencer and increases the potential for identification with the influencer (Djafarova and Rushworth 2017). An increased identification potential also increases the referent power of a message source (French and Raven 1959). This intense relationship can transfer to a positive attitude and purchase intention towards advertised products (Gong and Li 2017; Hung, Chan, and Tse 2011). Therefore, the framework assumes the following:

*H4a:* *An influencer's posting activity relates positively to consumer behavior along the consumer decision journey.*

Even though, followers know that influencers are getting paid for the endorsement of brands, their special relationship with their followers makes them more authentic and trustworthy than other endorsers (Djafarova and Rushworth 2017). The expert power of influencers comes from the fact that they share information with their followers and the followers trust that these information are true (French and Raven 1959). If an influencer promotes too many products, the likelihood increases that information will contradict itself and appear untrustworthy.

Moreover, the transfer of positive associations from the endorser to the advertised product creates a contextual association between the endorser and the product, which is based on attribution theory (Heider 1958). However, if an endorser promotes too many brands or products, this contextual connection is lost (Mowen and Brown 1981). Thus, the endorser can lose the trust of his followers and this leads to a negative attitude towards the endorser and the advertised brands (Tripp, Jensen, and Carlson 1994). Recent research confirms that multiple product endorsements of influencers increase consumers' expectation that their posts contain advertising and thus also increase the perception of the post as an advertisement. The perception that the post is an advertisement has a negative impact on the unobservable influencer characteristic trustworthiness and intention to engage with the post (Karagür et al. 2021). Therefore, the following relationship is assumed:

*H4b:* *The percentage of an influencer's sponsored posts relates negatively to consumer behavior along the consumer decision journey.*

Although a positive correlation between the number of product-related posts within a campaign on the purchase and engagement behavior of consumers has already been proven (Hughes, Swaminathan, and Brooks 2019; Kupfer et al. 2018), studies repeatedly show that newer posts reduce attention to and interaction with older posts (De Vries, Gensler, and Leeflang 2012; Gong et al. 2017; Zhang, Moe, and Schweidel 2017). Zhang, Moe, and Schweidel (2017)

## 3.3 Conceptual Framework and Hypotheses

explain the reduced attention and interaction with the new content by an increased information overload of the consumer. Therefore, the framework assumes the following:

H5: *The number of (a) campaign posts, (b) campaign stories, and (c) campaign story sequences by an influencer within a campaign are negatively related to consumer behavior along the consumer decision journey.*

*Effect of follower activity.* Due to the fast pace of social media networks and the displacement of older posts by newer ones, it is advantageous when content is consumed immediately. To consume content users must be active. Therefore, influential individuals in a network are characterized by the fact that their activity influences the activity of other users (Trusov, Bodapati, and Bucklin 2010). If the activity of an influencer influences the activity of its followers, this is further evidence of the power potential that emerges from the structural position of the influencer and the associated dependency of its followers (Brass and Burkhardt 1993). Empirical evidence of the power potential arising from follower activity has already been provided by some recent studies in the context of social media messages (Gong et al. 2017; Kupfer et al. 2018; Wang et al. 2019; Zhang, Moe, and Schweidel 2017).

Moreover, social media networks allow followers to interact with influencers and their content in various ways, such as comments, likes, or private messages. This two-way communication promotes the perceived intimacy of the relationship between followers and influencers (Djafarova and Rushworth 2017; Labrecque 2014). This unique relationship, in turn, increases the particularly pronounced referent power of influencers (French and Raven 1959). Therefore, the framework assumes the following:

H6: *An influencer's (a) like follower ratio and (b) comments per post relate positively to consumer behavior along the consumer decision journey.*

*Controls.* Since services are not as tangible as products, it is harder to make them visually or verbally understandable within an advertising message (Stafford 1996). Therefore, the framework controls for the type of product. Posts of products are expected to trigger more consumer behavior along the consumer decision journey than posts of services.

Furthermore, it is assumed that the campaign intent of influencer campaigns has a different impact on success metrics along the consumer decision journey, since campaign objectives such as awareness and trial also correspond to different consumer behavior along the consumer decision journey (Hughes, Swaminathan, and Brooks 2019). Therefore, the campaign goal is included in the model as a control variable.

Campaign incentives, such as lotteries, contests, or product samples, are one way to encourage targeted interactions with social media posts, such as likes, comments, or shares (Hughes, Swaminathan, and Brooks 2019; Verhoef, Reinartz, and Krafft 2010). In addition, consumers who receive free products talk more about these products, which in the ideal case leads to an increased demand for the product (Berger and Schwartz 2011). For this reason, the study controls for lotteries that are related to the campaigns.

## 3.4 Study Design

Section 3.4 includes the description of the dataset and the operationalization of the variables. The descriptive statistics are presented after the operationalization of the variables. The chapter concludes with an explanation of the methodology.

### 3.4.1 Data Set

The study examines the success of influencer campaigns on Instagram. Instagram, as one of the most popular social networks, reached one billion active monthly users worldwide in 2020 (Insider Intelligence 2020). In 2021, for 93% of marketers, Instagram was the most important channel for their influencer marketing strategy (eMarketer 2021). For this reason, the estimated global ad spend on influencer marketing was over 8 billion USD in 2020 (Statista 2021a).

The data set covers data from 13 campaigns from ten different brands, with pre- and postcampaign observations spanning from August 2018 to January 2020. Influencer campaigns of corporations for the German market are examined. The brands encompass seven different product categories: skin care, body care, makeup, accessories, web service, banking service, entertainment service. Campaign metrics and influencer characteristics were gathered for 87 influencers.

The study was conducted in collaboration with a social media agency and a company that provides an Instagram analytics tool for businesses. The precampaign data, which includes most of the influencer characteristics, such as data used to calculate influencer unique reach and overlap, was acquired through the company, which provided the Instagram analytics tool. The company's access to Instagram's official application programming interface enabled the collection of

## 3.4 Study Design

freely accessible historical data. This guarantees the completeness of the data set and excludes any bias due to unobserved social media behavior. However, in January 2020, Facebook[2] denied the company access to its application programming interface. For this reason, the data collection of the project could not be continued.

Postcampaign data was provided by the social media agency. The postcampaign data includes campaign post reach, likes and comments, as well as campaign story views and product or website link clicks within a story. Unfortunately, last-minute changes to the influencer portfolios on the agency side meant that some campaigns could not be included in the current data set, since precampaign data could not be collected for influencers added at short notice.

However, in the context of data collection, a large-scale consumer survey was conducted to define the influencers' brand fit and its determining variables. A sample of 2,152 active Instagram users was selected from Kantar's research panel (Kantar 2021). Respondents were randomly assigned to one or two of the 13 campaigns and rated several influencers on their fit to the promoting brand.

### 3.4.2 Operationalization of Variables

Table 3.3 summarizes the operationalization of the variables of Study 1. The independent variables measure the power of an influencer and are divided into personal potential and network potential. The power outcome along the consumer decision journey is described by the dependent variables, which can be assigned to the awareness, purchase and engagement phases. Table 3.4 provides the descriptive statistics of the variables.

The performance of the campaign content was recorded by the social media agency following the campaign. The consumer awareness that was achieved through the campaign is measured through the number of unique campaign post views of an influencer in proportion to the number of campaign posts of the influencer. The purchase phase of the consumer decision journey is captured by the customer's purchase intension. Clicking on a link that takes the consumer directly to the product or to the brand's website can be considered as purchase intension. Therefore, consumer purchase intension is measured through the number of link clicks within an influencer's campaign stories in proportion to the number of campaign stories of the influencer. Consumer engagement is measured through the number of likes and comments in proportion to the number of

---

[2] The company Facebook (now Meta Platforms) acquired Instagram in 2012.

**Table 3.3** Variable Operationalizations of Study 1

| Variable | Description |
|---|---|
| **Independent Variables** | |
| **Personal Potential** | |
| Expertise | Clout Summary Dimension Score (Kacewicz et al. 2014) based on the last 100 released post captions detected using LIWC, range: 0–100 |
| Influencer Brand Fit | Influencer brand fit is measured on a seven-point Likert scale (Does not fit at all / Fits very well) through a consumer survey |
| **Network Potential** | |
| **Influencer Network within a Portfolio** | |
| Unique Reach | Number of followers that are not followers of the other influencers within the portfolio |
| Overlap | Ratio of common followers of the influencer and the portfolio in proportion to his/her overall reach |
| **Activity of Sender** | |
| Postings Profile per Day | Number of posts on the influencer's profile in proportion to the number of active days on Instagram |
| Percentage of Sponsored Posts | Number of sponsored posts on the influencer's profile in proportion to the number of all posts |
| Campaign Stories | Number of the influencer's posts for the campaign |
| Campaign Posts | Number of the influencer's stories for the campaign |
| Story Sequences per Story | Number of the story sequences in proportion to the number of an influencer's stories for the campaign |
| **Follower Activity** | |
| Like Follower Ratio | The average number of likes on an influencer's profile posts in proportion to the number of followers |
| Comments per Post | Number of comments on an influencer's profile posts in proportion to the number of posts |
| **Control Variables** | |
| Product Type | Binary variable equal to 1 if the campaign promotes a product |
| Campaign Intent | Binary variable equal to 1 if the campaign is an awareness campaign |
| Lottery | Binary variable equal to 1 if the campaign post includes a lottery |

(continued)

**Table 3.3** (continued)

| Variable | Description |
| --- | --- |
| **Dependent Variables** | |
| Real Reach Post | Number of unique campaign post views of an influencer in proportion to the number of campaign posts of the influencer |
| Link Clicks Story | Number of link clicks within an influencer's campaign stories in proportion to the number of campaign stories of the influencer |
| Post Likes | Number of likes in proportion to the number of campaign posts of the influencer |
| Post Comments | Number of comments in proportion to the number of campaign posts of the influencer |
| Story Views | Number of unique campaign story views of an influencer in proportion to the number of campaign stories of the influencer |

Source: Author's own illustration.

campaign posts of the influencer. Moreover, consumer engagement is measured through the number of unique campaign story views of an influencer in proportion to the number of campaign stories of the influencer. Unlike posts, stories are not automatically displayed to the consumer, but must be actively clicked to see the story content. Although the consumer can decide to swipe the story away, a view is only recorded as completed if the consumer has followed the story to the last sequence.[3] For these reasons, story views are classified as part of the engagement phase.

Through the reporting on Instagram, it was possible for the social media agency to have all metrics indicated without, for example, story views or the reach of the post being counted twice if the same user consumed the influencer's content multiple times. However, through Instagram reporting it was not possible to determine whether consumers were reached multiple times by different influencers in the campaign. Assuming that the percentage of followers who overlap in the portfolio is the same for the followers who actually see the content, all dependent variables were corrected for this percentage.

---

[3] An Instagram Story can only be 15 sec long. If the video is longer than 15 sec, Instagram automatically cuts it into multiple 15 sec sequences.

**Table 3.4** Descriptive Statistics of the Variables of Study 1

| | Min | Max | M | SD |
|---|---|---|---|---|
| **Independent Variables** | | | | |
| **Personal Potential** | | | | |
| Expertise | 42.99 | 89.53 | 67.58 | 10.33 |
| Influencer Brand Fit | 3.51 | 5.79 | 4.69 | .41 |
| **Network Potential** | | | | |
| *Network Structure Sender* | | | | |
| Unique Reach | 4,099.00 | 1,768,699.00 | 156,563.71.00 | 262,006.50 |
| Overlap | .00% | 71.02% | 24.46% | 17.82% |
| *Activity of Sender* | | | | |
| Postings Profile per Day | .00 | 3.30 | .75 | .53 |
| Percentage of Sponsored Posts | .00% | .36% | .03% | .05% |
| Campaign Posts | .00 | 4.00 | 1.42 | .89 |
| Campaign Stories | 1.00 | 12.00 | 2.39 | 2.21 |
| Story Sequences per Story | 3.00 | 21.00 | 7.03 | 3.16 |
| *Activity of Followers* | | | | |
| Like Follower Ratio | .90% | 24.30% | 6.87% | 5.44% |
| Comments per Post | 9.40 | 1,188.40 | 148.99 | 219.21 |
| **Dependent Variables** | | | | |
| Real Reach Post | 2,249.00 | 606,224.00 | 69,115.43 | 92,173.40 |
| Link Clicks Story | 1.00 | 8,844.67 | 621.96 | 1,351.23 |
| Post Likes | 210.50 | 91,929.00 | 10,395.47 | 16,551.46 |
| Post Comments | 4.00 | 2,256.50 | 158.93 | 354.78 |
| Story Views | 304.50 | 134,567.00 | 22,748.75 | 30,340.46 |

Source: Author's own illustration.

### 3.4.2.1 Measuring Personal Potential

The expertise and the brand fit of the influencer describe the personal power potential of the influencer to act as a referent. Since the personal potential represents a starting point before the campaign, the variables are collected at the time of influencer matching. Influencer matching describes a process of the social media agency in which suitable influencers are selected for the campaign and

## 3.4 Study Design

presented to the brand. The influencer matching usually takes place in the period of one to two months before the campaign launch.

*Measuring expertise.* To measure an influencer's expertise, the influencer's last 100 posts were collected at the time of influencer matching and evaluated using the LIWC. The LIWC is a computer-based text analysis application developed as part of an exploratory study of language and disclosure. This application has been continuously developed based on further research. The most recent version of 2015 is used for the analysis (Pennebaker et al. 2015a; Pennebaker et al. 2015b). The clout dimension of the LIWC measures the social status or expertise within a group (Kacewicz et al. 2014). First, the posts were separated into German and English language, because the influencers often switched between German and English, but the analysis of the LIWC can only be done for one language at a time. Subsequently, the individual metrics were combined according to a weighting of the number of words to an overall metric of influencer expertise. In analyzing social media posts using the speech analysis software of Pennebaker et al. (2015b) to measure conceptual constructs, the study follows an established approach (Davis et al. 2019; Heimbach and Hinz 2016; Kanuri, Chen, and Sridhar 2018; Li and Xie 2020; Roorderkerk and Pauwels 2016).

*Measuring influencer brand fit.* As Section 2.2 shows, only two of the studies deal with the influence of an influencer's brand fit on consumers' attitudes and purchase intentions (Breves et al. 2019; Colliander and Dahlén 2011). Breves et al. (2019) use a short description of an influencer to manipulate a high or low brand fit of the influencer. Colliander and Dahlén (2011), however, do not call their measure brand fit, but compare bloggers to other writers in terms of their "writer-brand relationship". The authors also group blog post and article authors into authors with high or low writer-brand relationship. However, none of the studies go into detail about why an influencer's brand fit is high or low and what factors determine it.

Moreover, there are no studies that examine the effectiveness of influencer brand fit on consumer behavior so far. However, Kupfer et al. (2018) point out that an examination of brand fit seems particularly relevant for the effectiveness of influencers on social media, since influencers are not directly linked to product creation. Thus, a mismatch between influencer and brand can occur more easily.

Furthermore, several expert interviews were conducted in the preliminary stages of Study 1. These were primarily used to identify relevant metrics for evaluating influencer campaigns in practice. The experts were interviewed using semi-structured interviews. Semi-structured interviews are based on guidelines, however, they leave a certain amount of freedom to respond to the individual conversational process and to ask specific follow-up questions (Kallio et al. 2016).

The guideline for the expert interviews is shown in Figure 3.3. Table 3.5 provides a brief overview of the experts interviewed. All respondents in the expert interviews stated that influencer brand fit was one of the most important characteristics for selecting suitable influencers. Nevertheless, none of the interviewees was able to determine more precisely how this brand fit was defined overall.

---

**Guideline Expert Interview**

Introduction: Our goal is to conduct practice-oriented research and to generate solutions for relevant problems and challenges. To do this, it is important for us to learn about the perspective of companies. I am doing research on influencer marketing and would like to learn about the common practice of influencer marketing in different companies.

1. What is your company's experience with influencer marketing so far?
2. What is the internal process for running an influencer campaign, from start to finish?
    i. What is/are the goal/goals you are pursuing with your influencer campaigns? (goals in general, goals per post)
    ii. Do you have a fixed budget for your campaign or is the budget based on the set goals? If so, how do you determine the budget?
    iii. What criteria do you use to select influencers?
    iv. How is the success of the campaign determined (ROI)? (goals in general, goals per post)
3. What challenges do you see within influencer marketing for your company in the future and could research contribute in this regard, in your opinion?

---

**Figure 3.3** Guideline of Expert Interviews. Source: Author's own illustration.

Due to this gap within the literature and practice, a total of 2,152 people were interviewed in a consumer survey to measure the brand fit of influencers and determine its drivers. Respondents were selected who are social media active and have their own Instagram profile. Table 3.6 shows the demographic characteristics and variables describing social media use in the sample.

After the respondents had answered some screening questions, they were randomly assigned to one or two of the 13 campaigns. First, short quotes of the brand were shown, in which the brand briefly introduced itself. This was followed by a presentation of the website via a short video, with the help of which the subjects were able to form their own impression of the products and the image of the brand. In the next step of the survey, the subjects were told that the brand just presented was looking for cooperation partners for an influencer campaign. For this reason, they were introduced to various influencers, which they were to evaluate with regard to the specified criteria. Then an influencer was introduced with

## 3.4 Study Design

**Table 3.5** Overview of the Experts interviewed

| Company | Position |
|---|---|
| **Online Marketing Agency** | Expert 1: Managing Director<br>Expert 2: Senior Influencer Marketing Manager<br>Expert 3: Senior Account Manager |
| **Corporate Group**<br>(annual turnover over 50 million EUR) | Expert 4: Social Media Insight Manager (Cosmetic) |
| **Medium-sized Company**<br>(annual turnover between 1 and 50 million EUR) | Expert: 5: Online Marketing & Content Manager (Tourism) |
| **Small Company**<br>(annual turnover below 1 million EUR) | Expert 6: Managing Director (Sports and Entertainment)<br>Expert 7: Managing Director (Accessories) |

Source: Author's own illustration.

a snapshot of his profile and a recent post and its caption. Both were drawn from the profile at the time of the influencer matching. After the influencer post and the caption was shown, the questions followed to evaluate the influencer's brand fit. For better recall of the influencer, a small version of the influencer's post was displayed above the scales. After the evaluation of the influencer, a new influencer was introduced for whom the same procedure applied. Finally, the survey ended with some control questions.

To measure influencer brand fit and to define its drivers, the study uses established scales from the brand extension and endorsement literature to further define the concept of influencer brand fit within a social media context. Table 3.7 shows the questions that were asked of the respondents in order to assess whether the introduced influencer matches the presented brand. It also provides information about the origin of the scale. To test the transfer to the influencer context, the scales were subjected to a pre-test with 174 participants.[4]

The literature on brand extension has shown that it is crucial for the success of a brand alliance that two merging brands fit together (Völckner and Sattler 2006). Whether the brands fit together is determined by the uniform perception of the image and the similarity of the product categories (Aaker and Keller 1990;

---

[4] As a result, only respondents who were active on Instagram were selected for the main study, as some respondents stated that without this experience the evaluation was rather difficult.

**Table 3.6** Demographics and Social Media Usage of Sample

| | Items | Percentage | Frequency |
|---|---|---|---|
| Gender | Male | 45.1% | 970 |
| | Female | 54.0% | 1,163 |
| | Not given | .9% | 19 |
| Age | <18 years | .0% | 0 |
| | 18–24 years | 35.5% | 763 |
| | 25–34 years | 57.2% | 1,232 |
| | 35–44 years | 6.6% | 143 |
| | 45–54 years | .7% | 14 |
| | 55–64 years | .0% | 0 |
| | 65 + years | .0% | 0 |
| Education | No school-diploma | .6% | 12 |
| | Secondary school | 13.9% | 300 |
| | High school | 29.6% | 637 |
| | Completed training | 23.6% | 507 |
| | Bachelor | 17.8% | 383 |
| | Master | 12.0% | 258 |
| | PhD | 2.0% | 42 |
| | Other | .6% | 13 |
| Social Media Activity | Instagram | 100.0% | 2,152 |
| | Facebook | 77.2% | 1,662 |
| | TikTok | 19.8% | 426 |
| | Pinterest | 29.3 | 630 |
| | YouTube | 77.4% | 1,665 |
| | Other | .4% | 63 |
| | Not active | .0% | 1 |
| Daily Social Media Usage | <1/2 h | 7.8% | 168 |
| | 1/2–1 h | 19.0% | 409 |
| | 1–2 h | 29.8% | 640 |
| | 2–3 h | 24.8% | 533 |
| | 3 + hours | 18.6% | 401 |

(continued)

## 3.4 Study Design

**Table 3.6** (continued)

|  | Items | Percentage | Frequency |
|---|---|---|---|
| Following Influencers on Social Media | Yes | 65.9% | 1,418 |
|  | No | 34.1% | 733 |
| Following Influencers by Channel | Instagram | 93.0% | 1,319 |
|  | Facebook | 39.4% | 558 |
|  | TikTok | 16.1% | 229 |
|  | Pinterest | 11.1% | 158 |
|  | YouTube | 57.9% | 821 |
|  | Other | 1.1% | 16 |

Source: Author's own illustration.

Becker-Olsen 2003). In order to further examine to what extent the image fit and the product category fit of an influencer determine its brand fit, a factor analysis and a regression are conducted.

The aim of the factor analysis is to clarify whether the items of a construct really represent a single concept and to assess their suitability for further analysis (Hair et al. 2014, p. 89). Accordingly, the multi-item constructs image fit and product category fit were examined for their underlying structure. In the factor analysis, 11 items were included. As a rule, the sample size should be at least five times the number of variables included in the factor analysis, but a much better ratio is a 10:1 ratio (Hair et al. 2014, p. 100). The goal of the survey was to survey 150 respondents for each influencer. Respondents who did not answer the survey completely were already sorted out beforehand. In addition, 10% more respondents were surveyed in order to compensate for any data adjustments. The 2,152 respondents rated several influencers. The brand fit of 87 influencers was evaluated. This results in a total sample size of 14,417 individual influencer brand fit ratings. Thus, the sample size condition is met. Table 3.8 summarizes the criteria used to test the suitability of the data for conducting a factor analysis (here and in the following Backhaus et al. 2016, p. 397–399).

First, Bartlett's test for sphericity' checks whether the variables in the population are correlated. A significant result suggests a relationship between the variables in the population. Since the test shows a highly significant result ($p = .00$), this assumption is fulfilled. However, the test assumes a normal distribution of the variables. Although the histograms indicate a normal distribution of the variables, the Kolmogorov–Smirnov test gives a significant result for all variables ($p = .00$), indicating a non-normal distribution of the data. However,

**Table 3.7** Items of Influencer Brand Fit, Influencer Image Fit and Influencer Product Category Fit

| Variable | Source | Item |
| --- | --- | --- |
| Influencer Brand Fit | Bergkvist, Hjalmarson, and Mägi (2016) <br> – Endorsement literature; Adapted from: Lafferty (2009); Walchli (2007) <br> – Brand extension literature | How well do you think the influencer fits to the brand [brand name]? <br> Does not fit at all / Fits very well |
| Influencer Image Fit | Becker-Olsen (2003); Adapted from: Ahluwalia and Gürhan-Canli (2000); Bridges, Keller, and Sood (2000); John, Loken, and Joiner (1998) – Brand extension literature | How do you rate the image of the brand [brand name] and the image of the influencer in relation to each other with regard to the following criteria? <br> 1. Dissimilar / Similar <br> 2. Inconsistent / Consistent <br> 3. Atypical / Typical <br> 4. Not complementary / Complementary <br> 5. Low fit / High Fit <br> 6. Not meaningful / Meaningful |
| Influencer Product Category Fit | Sengupta, Goodstein, and Boninger (1997) <br> – Endorsement literature | 1. When I think of the influencer as a brand ambassador, [product category] is one of the first products I think of <br> Do not agree at all / Fully agree <br> 2. The idea that the influencer promotes [product category] represents a very good fit for me <br> Do not agree at all / Fully agree <br> 3. I think the influencer is a relevant brand ambassador for [product category] <br> Do not agree at all / Fully agree <br> 4. I think the influencer is a suitable brand ambassador for [product category] <br> Do not agree at all / Fully agree |
| | Aaker and Keller (1990) <br> – Brand extension literature | 5. To what extent are the influencer's knowledge and skills helpful in promoting the [brand name] brand <br> Not helpful at all / Very helpful |

Source: Author's own illustration. Notes: All items were measured on a seven-point Likert scale.

the assumption of normal distribution can be supported by the "central limit theorem" of statistics, which assumes a normal distribution with a sufficiently large sample (Backhaus et al. 2016, p. 99). This condition is fulfilled in the study.

Second, the anti-image covariance matrix, which indicates the proportion of unexplained variance, is tested. The variables are only suitable for factor analysis if the anti-image of the variables is as low as possible. The data is appropriate if 25% or less of the off-diagonal elements of the anti-image covariance matrix are different from zero (absolute value > .09). Since the items are theoretically based on common constructs, 0% of the off-diagonal elements are above the absolute value of .09. Moreover, the Kaiser-Meyer Olkin (KMO) criterion and measure of sampling adequacy (MSA) for all variables are above .9, which indicates that the data is "marvelous" for a factor analysis. Both criteria indicate the extent to which the variables belong together in terms of content and lie in the value range between zero and one. The former is a test variable for all variables and the latter offers a measure for each individual variable. All in all, the data is suitable for further analysis.

**Table 3.8** Data Suitability for Factor Analysis

| Criteria | Source | Fulfilled |
|---|---|---|
| Sample-size at least five times the number of variables | Hair et al. 2018, p. 100 | Fulfilled, n = 14,417 > 55 = (11*59) |
| Bartlett's test of sphericity is significant | Backhaus et al. 2016, p. 397 | Fulfilled, p = .00 |
| Anti-image covariance matrix has 25% or less off-diagonal elements that are different from zero (> .09) | Backhaus et al. 2016, pp. 398–399 | Fulfilled, 0% of the elements are > .09 |
| Kaiser-Meyer Olkin (KMO) criterion equal to or larger than .8 | Backhaus et al. 2016, pp. 398–399 | Fulfilled, KMO = .963 |
| Diagonal elements of the anti-image correlation matrix are equal to or greater than the boundary of .5 | Backhaus et al. 2016, p. 399 | Fulfilled, all elements are > .9 |

Source: Author's own illustration.

Factor analysis was performed using a varimax rotation and principal component procedure to generate independent factors and include the totality of variance in the characteristics. Based on the eigenvalues above one (Backhaus et al. 2016,

p. 415), only one factor would have to be extracted, which suggests that both dimensions measure the brand fit of an influencer. However, the scales for measuring image fit and product category fit are theoretically assigned to two different dimensions of fit (Aaker and Keller 1990; Becker-Olsen 2003). For this reason, a factor analysis with two fixed factors was conducted. Table 3.9 illustrates the rotated component matrix and shows that the items of the constructs image fit and product category fit are each assigned to one factor. Since these results reflect the scales derived from the literature, the study assumes two factors in further analysis.

**Table 3.9** Rotated Component Matrix for fixed 2-Factor Solution

|  | **Image Fit** | **Product Category Fit** |
|---|---|---|
| Image Fit 1 | .813 | .397 |
| Image Fit 2 | .832 | .371 |
| Image Fit 3 | .823 | .377 |
| Image Fit 4 | .804 | .386 |
| Image Fit 5 | .810 | .438 |
| Image Fit 6 | .797 | .439 |
| Product Category Fit 1 | .326 | .840 |
| Product Category Fit 2 | .425 | .811 |
| Product Category Fit 3 | .436 | .814 |
| Product Category Fit 4 | .449 | .806 |
| Product Category Fit 5 | .404 | .809 |

Source: Author's own illustration.

Cronbach's alpha was used to assess the internal consistency of the scales. With a value of over .9, both scales exceed the threshold value of .7, indicating a high reliability of the constructs (Hair et al. 2014, p. 123). Table 3.10 again illustrates the association of the items to the corresponding constructs and indicates the respective Cronbach's alpha.

After confirming that an influencer's image fit and product category fit are two constructs that are measured in a reliable way, the following section examines how these two dimensions affect influencer brand fit. For this purpose, an ordinary least squares (OLS) regression was run.

In order to interpret the results of the regression analysis correctly, four relevant assumptions must be met: (1) linearity of the measured phenomenon, (2) constant variance of the error terms, (3) independence of the error terms, and

## 3.4 Study Design

(4) normal distribution of errors (here and in the following Hair et al. 2014, pp. 178–181).

**Table 3.10** Cronbach's Alpha of Influencer Image Fit and Influencer Product Category Fit

| Construct | Items | Cronbach's Alpha |
| --- | --- | --- |
| Influencer Image Fit | How do you rate the image of the brand [brand name] and the image of the influencer in relation to each other with regard to the following criteria?<br>1. Dissimilar / Similar<br>2. Inconsistent / Consistent<br>3. Atypical / Typical<br>4. Not complementary / Complementary<br>5. Low Fit / High Fit<br>6. Not meaningful / Meaningful | .957 |
| Influencer Brand Fit | 1. When I think of the influencer as a brand ambassador, [product category] is one of the first products I think of<br>Do not agree at all / Fully agree<br>2. The idea that the influencer promotes [product category] represents a very good fit for me<br>Do not agree at all / Fully agree<br>3. I think the influencer is a relevant brand ambassador for [product category]<br>Do not agree at all / Fully agree<br>4. I think the influencer is a suitable brand ambassador for [product category]<br>Do not agree at all / Fully agree<br>5. To what extent are the influencer's knowledge and skills helpful in promoting the [brand name] brand<br>Not helpful at all / Very helpful | .949 |

Source: Author's own illustration.

First, the linearity of the relationship was tested. Both the dependent variable "Influencer Brand Fit" and the two independent variables "Image Fit" and "Product Category Fit" are scaled metrically. Visual inspection of the partial regression plots shows a clear positive linear relationship. Therefore, this assumption is fulfilled.

The second assumption is the constancy of the error term, which is also called homoskedasticity. Visual inspection of the residual plots indicates a constant dispersion of the residuals and does not reveal any patterns indicating heteroskedasticity. Thus, the assumption is fulfilled.

The third assumption is that the residuals in the population are uncorrelated, i.e., that there is no autocorrelation of the residuals. A violation of the assumption occurs mainly in the case of time series and a violation is not to be expected in the case of survey data. Consequently, the third assumption is also fulfilled.

Fourth, there should be a normal distribution of the residuals. If there is no normal distribution of the residuals, the significance tests (F-test and t-test) are invalid. According to the visual inspection of the normal P-P plot and the histogram of the residuals, an approximation to the normal distribution can be assumed. However, the significant result of the Kolmogorov–Smirnov test ($p = .00$) indicates that there is no normal distribution. A logistic transformation of the data could not solve the problem. However, with a large sample, it can be assumed that the significance tests are valid regardless of the distribution of the residuals and thus can be interpreted (Backhaus et al. 2016, p. 99).

The results of the regression are presented in Table 3.11. The model for the influencer brand fit is significant as a whole (F-value = 21,910.709, $p = .00$). Moreover, the independent variables explain the variance of dependent variable well ($R^2 = 75.2\%$, adj. $R^2 = 75.2\%$).

Multicollinearity, i.e., correlation among the independent variables, should not be an issue since the factors were calculated by orthogonal rotation (Hair et al. 2014, p. 196). Both the image fit ($\beta = .838$, $p = .00$) and the product category fit ($\beta = 1.219$, $p = .00$) have a significant positive influence on the overall influencer brand fit. The standardized beta coefficients are used to compare the effects (Hair et al. 2014, p. 195). These indicate that the product category fit (standardized $\beta = .715$) has a greater influence on the influencer brand fit than the image fit (standardized $\beta = .497$).

As Table 3.12 shows, these results persist even when the analysis is performed with summed scales instead of the formed factors. The model for the influencer brand fit is significant as a whole (F-value = 21,824.647, $p = .00$). Moreover, the independent variables explain the variance of dependent variable well ($R^2 = 75.2\%$, adj. $R^2 = 75.2\%$).

Both, image fit ($\beta = .223$, $p = .00$) and product category fit ($\beta = .769$, $p = .00$) have a positive significant influence on influencer brand fit, with product category (standardized $\beta = .696$) having a higher influence than image fit (standardized $\beta = .203$). Conceptually, brand fit is based only on the two dimensions, which ensures the completeness of the model. However, these effects also persist when

## 3.4 Study Design

**Table 3.11** Regression Results of Factor Solution on Influencer Brand Fit

|  | Influencer Brand Fit |
|---|---|
| Intercept | **4.687** |
| Factor 1 Image Fit | **.838** |
| Factor 2 Product Category Fit | **1.219** |
| N | 14,417 |
| F-Value | **21,910.709** |
| $R^2$ | .752 |
| Adj. $R^2$ | .752 |

Source: Author's own illustration. Notes: The table reports the unstandardized coefficients. **Bold figures**: p-value < .05

different control variables (e.g., gender or age of respondents) are included in the model.

**Table 3.12** Regression Results of Summated Scales on Influencer Brand Fit

|  | Influencer Brand Fit |
|---|---|
| Intercept | **.195** |
| Summated Image Fit | **.223** |
| Summated Product Category Fit | **.769** |
| N | 14,417 |
| F-Value | **21,824.647** |
| $R^2$ | .752 |
| Adj. $R^2$ | .752 |

Source: Author's own illustration. Notes: The table reports the unstandardized coefficients. Bold figures: p-value < .05

All in all, the result of the survey was to obtain a reliable measurement of influencer brand fit for further analysis of an influencer's power on consumer behavior along the consumer decision journey. Furthermore, insights into the drivers of influencer brand fit could already be gained, which are relevant for the interpretation of the results of the main study.

### 3.4.2.2 Measuring Network Potential

The network structure and activity of the influencer, as well as the activity of his followers, shape the influencer's network potential. Just like the personal potential of an influencer, the network potential is determined before the start of the campaign at the time of influencer matching.

*Measuring influencer network within a portfolio.* Measuring the centrality of a message source in social networks by the number of followers is a common approach (Ansari et al. 2018; Goldenberg et al. 2009; Gong et al. 2017; Hughes, Swaminathan, and Brooks 2019; Kupfer et al. 2018; Namkoong, Ro, and Henderson 2019; Wang et al. 2019). As described above, in social media campaigns with multiple influencers the network size of the influencer that is relevant for the different campaign measures depends on the network of the other influencers. Therefore, the unique reach and the overlap of an influencer within a campaign is calculated. The unique reach of an influencer within the campaign is measured through the number of followers that are not followers of the other influencers within the portfolio. The overlap reflects the reciprocal of the unique reach and is measured through the ratio of common followers of the influencer and the portfolio in proportion to his overall reach.

*Measuring activity of the sender.* The posting behavior of a message source is suitable for measuring the activity of the sender in his network and the resulting power potential. Moreover, the results of previous studies have shown that it seems useful to distinguish between brand-related content and other content, as they differ in their impact (Gong et al. 2017; Kupfer et al. 2018). The posting behavior of the influencer that is not related to the campaign is measured through the number of posts on the influencer's profile in proportion to the number of active days on Instagram. This reflects his general posting frequency. Moreover, the percentage of sponsored posts is calculated through the number of sponsored posts on the influencer's profile in proportion to the number of all his posts. Brand-related content is measured in the study by campaign-related posting behavior.

It was assumed in the hypothesis development that there is a negative association between the number of campaign contents and the attention to the individual campaign contents. Since posts and stories are displayed in different areas of the follower feed within Instagram, it cannot be assumed that these two content types compete too strongly for attention. Therefore, the number of campaign-related posts is collected separately for posts and stories. Moreover, for stories the number of the story sequences in proportion to the number of an influencer's stories for the campaign are gathered as well.

*Measuring follower activity.* In recent studies, follower activity of a social media user has been more frequently linked to the power of a social media user (Gong et al. 2017; Kupfer et al. 2018; Zhang, Moe, and Schweidel 2017). The activity of followers is measured through the average number of likes on an influencer's profile posts in proportion to the number of followers and the number of comments on an influencer's profile posts in proportion to the number of posts.

*Measuring control variables.* The control variables are captured by dummy variables. The type of product advertised in the campaign is captured, with products such as make-up coded with a one, and services such as banking service coded with a zero. The campaign objective is also recorded. Awareness campaigns are coded with a one and trial campaigns with a zero. Trial campaigns are characterized by the fact that within the posts a direct invitation to buy is given or attention is paid to certain incentives. For example, within a certain campaign period, extra samples or additional products were offered with the purchase of the product. Within the posts of awareness campaigns, the product was mentioned and its advantages were described, but there was no direct invitation to purchase. The variable "Lottery" records whether a lottery was integrated within a campaign (coded with one) or not (coded with zero). Since lotteries were only used in posts and not in stories, the variable was also only recorded for posts. Moreover, lotteries only encouraged consumers to engage in behavior such as commenting, liking, and following, and not in engagement related to stories.

### 3.4.3 Methodology

The three dependent variables for an influencer's campaign posts are $y_1$ = number of real reaches, $y_2$ = number of likes and $y_3$ = number of comments. The two dependent variables for an influencer's campaign stories are $y_4$ = number of link clicks and $y_5$ = number of views. All variables represent count data that follow a Poisson distribution. If count data contains many zero's and small discrete values, one must perform a Poisson regression (Cameron and Trivedi 2005). However, Table 3.4 clearly shows that the dependent variables are large in number. As already mentioned, the "central limit theorem" assumes a normal distribution for large counts (Backhaus et al. 2016, p. 99). Therefore, the model to explain the number of real reaches, likes and comments for an influencer's campaign post can be expressed as:

$$y_{ji} = \alpha + \beta_1 \text{EXP}_i + \beta_2 \text{IBF}_i + \beta_3 \text{UR}_i + \beta_4 \text{OL}_i + \beta_5 \text{PPD}_i + \beta_6 \text{PSP}_i \\ + \beta_7 \text{CP}_i + \beta_8 \text{LFR}_i + \beta_9 \text{CPP}_i + \beta_{10} \text{PT}_c + \beta_{11} \text{CI}_c + \beta_{12} \text{LOT}_c + \varepsilon_{ji} \quad (3.1)$$

where:

$y_{ji}$     $y_{1i}$, $y_{2i}$ or $y_{3i}$; the logged number of real reaches, likes or comments per campaign post of influencer i, respectively,

$EXP_i$     Clout Summary Dimension Score based on the last 100 released post captions of influencer i,

$IBF_i$     Influencer brand fit measured through the consumer survey on a seven-point Likert scale of influencer i (see Table 3.7),

$UR_i$     Number of unique reach of influencer i within a portfolio,

$OL_i$     Percentage of follower overlap of influencer i within a portfolio,

$PPD_i$     Number of posts in proportion to the number of active days on Instagram of influencer i,

$PSP_i$     Number of sponsored posts in proportion to the number of all posts of influencer i,

$CP_i$     Number of campaign posts of influencer i,

$LFR_i$     Like follower ratio of influencer i,

$CPP_i$     Number of comments on profile posts in proportion to the number of all profile posts of influencer i,

$PT_c$     dummy variable if campaign c promotes a product (baseline category service),

$CI_c$     dummy variable if campaign c is an awareness campaign (baseline category trial campaign),

$LOT_c$     dummy variable if campaign c includes a lottery (baseline no lottery),

$\varepsilon_{ji}$     $\varepsilon_{1i}$, $\varepsilon_{2i}$, or $\varepsilon_{3i}$, normally distributed error terms for dependent variable $y_{1i}$, $y_{2i}$ and $y_{3i}$, respectively.

The model to explain the number of link clicks and views for an influencer's campaign story considers the number of campaign stories instead of the number of campaign posts. In addition, the number of story sequences is included. The control variable "Lottery" is also omitted for the model, since lotteries are only played out via posts. The model can be expressed as:

$$y_{ji} = \alpha + \beta_1 EXP_i + \beta_2 \text{influencer brand fit}_i + \beta_3 UR_i + \beta_4 OL_i + \beta_5 PPD_i \\ + \beta_6 PSP_i + \beta_7 CS_i + \beta_8 SS_i + \beta_9 LFR_i + \beta_{10} CPP_i + \beta_{11} PT_c + \beta_{12} CI_c + \varepsilon_{ji} \quad (3.2)$$

where:

$y_{ji}$  $y_{4i}$ or $y_{5i}$; the logged number of link clicks or views per campaign story of influencer i, respectively,
$CS_i$  Number of campaign stories of influencer i,
$SS_i$  Number of the story sequences in proportion to the number of campaign stories of influencer i.

As already explained in the previous chapter, four relevant assumptions must be met to interpret the results of the OLS Regression (here and in the following Hair et al. 2014, pp. 178–181). Based on the theoretical argumentation in Section 3.3, a linear relationship of the variables is assumed. Moreover, the visual inspection of the partial regression plots also suggests a linear relationship for the metric variables. Therefore, the assumption of linearity is fulfilled.

The visual inspections of the residual plots for link clicks within the influencer's story and post likes indicate a constant dispersion of the residuals and do not reveal any patterns indicating heteroskedasticity. Thus, the assumption is fulfilled for likes and link clicks. However, the residuals for real reach and comments of an influencer's campaign post as well as the residuals of an influencer's story views show inconsistencies of dispersion and are shaped like a triangle. Despite logarithmic transformation of the data, the variance did not stabilize (Hair et al. 2014, p. 181). To reduce standard error bias, heteroskedasticity-consistent standard error estimators are used in these three OLS regressions (Hayes and Cai 2007, p. 713).

The third assumption of uncorrelated residuals is not expected to be violated in the case of survey data. Consequently, for all models the third assumption is also fulfilled.

After the logarithmic transformation of dependent variables, visual inspections of the normal P-P plot and the histogram of the residuals, as well as the Kolmogorov–Smirnov test ($p > .05$), indicate a normal distribution of errors for all models. Therefore, the fourth and last assumption is fulfilled.

## 3.5  Results of Study 1

The estimation results are presented in Table 3.13, while Table 3.14 summarizes the findings. The effects differentiate between the phases of the consumer decision journey and consumer behavior metrics.

### 3.5.1 Awareness Phase

The model for the real reach of an influencer's campaign post is significant as a whole (F-value = 15.160, p = .00). Moreover, the independent variables explain the variance of dependent variable well ($R^2$ = 71.9%, adj. $R^2$ = 67.2%).

The expertise of an influencer is significantly and positive related to the real reach per campaign post ($\beta$ = .022, p < .05), in support of *Hypothesis 1*. Furthermore, the impact of influencer brand fit on the real reach per campaign post is significant positive ($\beta$ = .482, p < .05). This is in support of *Hypothesis 2*. Therefore, an influencer's personal potential has a significant positive influence on the awareness of an influencer's campaign posts.

The unique reach of an influencer within a portfolio relates significantly and positive to the real reach per campaign post ($\beta$ = .227, p < .05), in support of *Hypothesis 3a*. Moreover, show the standardized betas that the unique reach has the highest impact on the real reach of an influencer's campaign posts. However, the overlap of an influencer's followers within a portfolio relates significantly and negatively to the real reach per campaign post ($\beta$ = −.013, p < .05). This is in support of *Hypothesis 3b*.

The number of postings per day and the percentage of sponsored posts on an influencer's profile have no significant influence on the real reach of an influencer's campaign posts. Therefore, no statistical support for *Hypothesis 4a* und *4b* is given within the model of real reach of an influencer's campaign posts. Moreover, the marginal negative effect of campaign posts on the real reach of an influencer's campaign posts disappears and is slightly above the value of .1 when the heteroskedasticity-consistent standard errors are included in the regression. Since this negative effect is confirmed for likes, it can be assumed that the effect would become significant over more observations. However, no statistical support for *Hypothesis 5a* is given within the final model.

Within the model without robust standard errors, the like follower ratio and the followers' comments per posts of an influencer have a positive significant impact on the real reach of an influencer's campaign posts. Nevertheless, the significant effect only remains for the like follower ration ($\beta$ = .083, p < .05) if heteroskedasticity-consistent standard errors are included in the model. Thus, there is support for *Hypothesis 6a* but not for *6b*.

The advertised product type has no significant impact on the reach of the campaign post. Moreover, there is no significant influence of posts including a lottery. Campaign posts of an influencer that are designed for awareness campaigns have a marginal higher real reach than posts that are designed for trial campaigns ($\beta$ = .407, p < .1).

## 3.5 Results of Study 1

**Table 3.13** Regression Results for Consumer Behavior Metrics along the Consumer Decision Journey

| | Awareness Phase | Purchase Phase | Engagement Phase | | |
|---|---|---|---|---|---|
| | Real Reach Post | Link Clicks Story | Post Likes | Post Comments | Story Views |
| Intercept | **5.678** | 3.188 | **4.609** | 2.103 | **5.829** |
| **Personal Potential** | | | | | |
| Expertise | **.022** | .028 | **.021** | .017 | **.023** |
| Influencer Brand Fit | **.482** | -0.494 | .161 | .018 | 0.010 |
| **Network Potential** | | | | | |
| **Network Structure Sender** | | | | | |
| Unique Reach[a] | **.227** | **.337** | **.238** | *.096* | **.381** |
| Overlap | **-.013** | **.024** | **-.012** | **-.015** | .005 |
| **Activity of Sender** | | | | | |
| Postings Profile per Day | .091 | *.585* | -.098 | -.246 | .329 |
| Percentage of Sponsored Posts | -.024 | -2.667 | 1.005 | .563 | -.377 |
| Campaign Posts | -0.207 | - | **-0.356** | -0.140 | - |
| Campaign Stories | - | *-.212* | - | - | -.073 |
| Story Sequences per Story | - | **.124** | - | - | .014 |
| **Activity of Followers** | | | | | |
| Like Follower Ratio | **.083** | **.151** | **.118** | .025 | **.111** |
| Comments per Post | .001 | .001 | **.001** | **.003** | .001 |
| **Control Variables** | | | | | |
| Product Type | -.155 | -.469 | -.040 | .106 | -.040 |
| Campaign Intent | *.407* | *-.979* | **.809** | .305 | -.170 |
| Lottery | .030 | - | .039 | **.748** | - |
| N | 84 | 76 | 84 | 84 | 83 |
| F-Value | **15.160** | **7.797** | **25.949** | **9.805** | **11.334** |
| $R^2$ | .719 | .598 | .814 | .624 | .660 |
| Adj. $R^2$ | .672 | .521 | .783 | .560 | .602 |

Source: Author's own illustration. Notes: The table reports the unstandardized coefficients. **Bold figures**: p-value < .05, *italic figures*: < .1, [a] = stated in 100,000's

**Table 3.14** Summary of Results

| Hypotheses | Expected | Real Reach Post (Awareness Phase) | Link Clicks Story (Purchase Phase) | Post Likes (Engagement Phase) | Post Comments (Engagement Phase) | Story Views (Engagement Phase) |
|---|---|---|---|---|---|---|
| **Personal Potential** | | | | | | |
| $H_1$: Expertise | + | ✓ | ✗ | ✓ | ✗ | ✓ |
| $H_2$: Influencer Brand Fit | + | ✓ | ✗ | ✗ | ✗ | ✗ |
| **Network Potential** | | | | | | |
| **Network Structure Sender** | | | | | | |
| $H_{3a}$: Unique Reach | + | ✓ | ✓ | ✓ | ✓ | ✓ |
| $H_{3b}$: Overlap | ± | ✓ | ✓ | ✓ | ✓ | ✗ |
| **Activity of Sender** | | | | | | |
| $H_{4a}$: Postings Profile per Day | + | ✗ | ✓ | ✗ | ✗ | ✗ |
| $H_{4b}$: Percentage of Sponsored Posts | − | ✗ | ✗ | ✗ | ✗ | ✗ |
| $H_{5a}$: Campaign Posts | − | ✗ | n.a. | ✓ | ✗ | n.a. |
| $H_{5b}$: Campaign Stories | − | n.a. | ✓ | n.a. | n.a. | ✗ |
| $H_{5c}$: Story Sequences per Story | − | n.a. | ✗ | n.a. | n.a. | ✗ |
| **Activity of Followers** | | | | | | |
| $H_{6a}$: Like Follower Ratio | + | ✓ | ✓ | ✓ | ✗ | ✓ |
| $H_{6b}$: Comments per Post | + | ✗ | ✗ | ✓ | ✓ | ✗ |

Source: Author's own illustration. Notes: ± = positive/negative hypothesis was formulated, ✓ = hypothesis has been confirmed, ✗ = hypothesis has not been confirmed, n.a. = not applicable because no hypothesis was formulated

### 3.5.2 Purchase Phase

The model for the link clicks within an influencer's campaign story is significant as a whole (F-value = 7.797, p = .00). Furthermore, the independent variables explain the variance of link clicks reasonably well ($R^2$ = 59.8%, adj. $R^2$ = 52.1%).

There is not statistical support for *Hypothesis 1* and *2*, since the expertise and the brand fit of an influencer have no significant influence on link clicks within

## 3.5 Results of Study 1

an influencer's campaign story. A possible explanation could be that the motivation and ability to process the information increase for the purchase phase of the consumer decision journey and favor central processing (Petty and Cacioppo 1986). Accordingly, it can be assumed that the effect of peripheral cues like source expertise and brand fit are less relevant for the purchase phase of the consumer decision journey compared to the awareness phase, since consumers show a higher level of involvement (Hughes, Swaminathan, and Brooks 2019).

The unique reach within a campaign portfolio has a positive significant influence on the link clicks within an influencer's campaign story ($\beta = .337$, $p < .05$). However, the overlap of the followers of an influencer with the followers of the other influencers in the portfolio has an advantage for the purchase phase in contrast to the awareness phase. The overlap of followers influences the link clicks within a campaign story positive and significant ($\beta = .024$, $p < .05$). All in all, *Hypothesis 3a* and *3b* are supported.

The general posting frequency of an influencer (postings profile per day) is marginally significant and positively related to link clicks within a campaign story ($\beta = .585$, $p < .1$). Therefore, *Hypothesis 4a* is supported. The conceptual model assumes that an influencer's posting activity on the one hand, increases his power through higher follower dependency due to valuable information (Brass and Burkhardt 1993; Emerson 1962) and that regular posting of personal content on the other hand builds a personal relationship with followers (Labrecque 2014). The fact that the effect occurs within the link click model of the purchase phase, but not in the other models, could mean that these mechanisms have a higher influence in high-involvement situations such as purchase.

The percentage of sponsored posts of an influencer has no significant impact on the link clicks of an influencer's campaign story, so the model does not support *Hypothesis 4b*. The number of campaign stories of an influencer is marginally significant and negatively related to the link clicks within an influencer's campaign stories ($\beta = -.212$, $p < .1$). This seems reasonable, since it can be assumed that clicking on a website or a product link is consciously pursued as part of the central processing of the purchase phase and is purposefully done, once at the time of purchase intension. Therefore, *Hypothesis 5b* is supported. The number of story sequences per campaign story relates significantly and positively to the link clicks of an influencer's campaign story ($\beta = .124$, $p < .05$), contrary to *Hypothesis 5c*. As already explained, consumers process information more deeply during the purchase phase and peripheral cues lose their impact. However, the impact of information that is processed centrally gains influence. This is illustrated by the positive effect of longer campaign stories by the influencer on link clicks, as it can be assumed that the value of a product or service can be better explained within a longer story than in a short story.

The like follower ratio of an influencer is significantly and positive related to the number of link clicks with an influencer's campaign story ($\beta = .151$, $p < .05$). Therefore, *Hypothesis 6a* is supported. Moreover, the standardized betas show that a follower base that frequently likes the influencer's content has the highest impact on link clicks within an influencer campaign story. However, *Hypothesis 6b* is not confirmed because the influencer's follower comments per posts are not significantly related to the link clicks within a campaign story.

There was no statistic significant difference between the link clicks within an influencer's campaign story for services and products. Awareness campaign posts have a marginally significant and negative impact on link clicks within a campaign ($\beta = -.979$, $p < .1$), which means that trial campaign posts have a marginally positive impact on link clicks. Trial campaign posts contained a direct invitation to purchase or offered free samples or goodies for immediate purchase. This highlights the importance of content for central processing in the purchase phase.

### 3.5.3 Engagement Phase

The engagement phase of the consumer decision journey is associated with three models that link consumer engagement behavior to an influencer's campaign posts and stories. First, the model for the likes of an influencer's campaign post is significant as a whole (F-value $= 25.949$, $p = .00$) and explains the variance of dependent variable well ($R^2 = 81.4\%$, adj. $R^2 = 78.3\%$). The second model is quite appropriate for explaining the variance of comments on an influencer's campaign post ($R^2 = 62.4\%$, adj. $R^2 = 56.0\%$) and is significant as a whole (F-value $= 9.805$, $p = .00$). Third, the model for an influencer's campaign story views is significant as a whole (F-value $= 11.334$, $p = .00$). Moreover, the independent variables explain the variance of the dependent variable reasonably well ($R^2 = 66.0\%$, adj. $R^2 = 60.2\%$).

The influencer's expertise is significantly positive related to campaign post likes ($\beta = .021$, $p < .05$) and campaign story views ($\beta = .023$, $p < .05$). However, the influencer's expertise is not significant related to campaign post comments. Therefore, *Hypothesis 1* is supported for post likes and story views but not for post comments. Moreover, the influencer brand fit has no significant impact on all three dependent variables of the engagement phase. It seems that influencer brand fit in particular works as a peripheral cue within the awareness phase of the

## 3.5 Results of Study 1

consumer decision journey, but loses impact in later stages of the funnel. Hence, *Hypothesis 2* is not supported for likes and comments of campaign posts as well as for campaign story views.

The influencer's unique reach within a campaign portfolio significantly increases campaign post likes ($\beta = .238$, $p < .05$) and story views ($\beta = .381$, $p < .05$). Furthermore, it is marginally significant and positive related to comments on the influencer's campaign posts ($\beta = .096$, $p < .1$). These findings are in support with *Hypothesis 3a*. *Hypothesis 3b* is supported for engagement with an influencer's campaign post because the influencer's follower overlap within a campaign portfolio has a significant negative impact on campaign post likes ($\beta = -.012$, $p < .05$) and comments ($\beta = -.015$, $p < .05$). The overlap of followers has no significant impact on engagement with an influencer's campaign stories, so there is no support of *Hypothesis 3b* for campaign story views.

The postings on an influencer's profile per day have no significant impact on the campaign post likes and comments or story views, which contradicts *Hypothesis 4a*. Moreover, the percentage of sponsored posts of an influencer also has no significant impact on the campaign post likes and comments or story views. Therefore, *Hypothesis 4b* is not supported by the data. Although followers know that influencers include advertising messages in their content, they still perceive them as a trustworthy and credible source of information due to other characteristics such as influencer brand fit. In addition, advertising through influencer posts is not perceived as intrusive as other advertising formats. This could explain the insignificant impact of the percentage of sponsored posts within the models.

The number of campaign posts is significantly and negatively related to campaign posts likes ($\beta = -.356$, $p < .05$), but is insignificant for campaign post comments. Therefore, *Hypothesis 5a* is supported for likes but not for comments. *Hypothesis 5b* and *5c* is not confirmed for campaign story view because the number of campaign stories and the number of story sequences per story have no significant association with story views.

The influencer's like follower ratio relates significantly and positively to the number of campaign post likes ($\beta = .118$, $p < .05$) and story views ($\beta = .111$, $p < .05$), in support of *Hypothesis 6a*. The effect for the influencer's like follower ratio on campaign post comments is insignificant, which contradicts *Hypothesis 6a*. However, in support of *Hypothesis 6b*, the influencer's follower comments per post associates significantly and positively to campaign post comments ($\beta = .001$, $p < .05$) and likes ($\beta = .003$, $p < .05$). The effect is insignificant for campaign story views, which is not in support of *Hypothesis 6b*. All in all, a highly active follower base has a positive impact on consumer engagement with campaign content. Looking at the standardized betas, post likes and story views are primarily increased by a high like follower ratio and a high unique reach of the influencer. Whereas the number of comments on a campaign post is best increased by influencers whose followers frequently comment on their posts.

The advertised product type has no significant impact on consumer engagement behavior. Campaign content designed for awareness campaigns is significantly related with campaign post likes ($\beta = .809$, $p < .05$), but has no significant impact on campaign post comments and story views. When a lottery is included in an influencer's campaign post, it has a positive impact on comments on campaign posts ($\beta = .748$, $p < .05$), but is insignificant for post likes. This seems plausible because followers were often directly asked to comment on posts in lotteries. This induced behavior can replace other engagements.

### 3.5.4 Managerial Implications of Study 1

The results of Study 1 show that the impact of influencer characteristics is not the same for all campaign metrics along the consumer decision journey. Therefore, the results can help the managers of social media influencer campaigns to decide which influencers they should use to drive different campaign outputs like post reach, likes and comments or story views and link clicks within those stories.

When managers aim to enhance post reach, they should select influencers who have a high unique reach and a low overlap of followers with other influencers used for the campaign. However, the implementation of such practices is still not common and the next step should be to incorporate these metrics into performance-based pricing for influencers (Influencer Marketing Hub 2020). Since social networks are funded by advertising, network operators should consider commercializing these metrics. Moreover, a high like follower ratio increases the reach of the campaign post and should be an important selection criterion for campaigns designed to increase consumer awareness. Next to this potential of an influencer based on his network, managers should use influencers with a high personal potential to increase campaign post reach. Thus, it is advantageous for the reach of a campaign post if an influencer's profile posts feature communication that demonstrates expertise and high social status. Moreover, managers should pay particular attention to ensuring that there is a high fit between the influencer and the brand. This is determined on the one hand by the image fit between the influencer and the brand and on the other hand by the product category fit of the influencer. The product category fit has a higher influence on influencer brand fit and should receive special attention from managers. Besides the characteristics of the influencer, the content of the post also

## 3.5 Results of Study 1

has an influence on its reach. The content should not be too persuasive, but rather contain a general product description to increase consumer awareness.

Managers, who explicitly want to increase website or product link clicks within campaign stories, should also use influencers with a high like follower ratio and high unique reach. However, in contrast to increasing campaign post reach, it is beneficial for increasing clicks within a campaign story if an influencer's followers overlap with the followers of the other influencers in the portfolio. For managers, this means that it is advantageous for increasing purchase intension to design the influencer portfolio of a campaign in such a way that consumers are reached multiple times by different influencers within a campaign. Furthermore, managers should choose influencers who regularly produce new content for their followers. It is assumed that influencers with a high posting frequency build a stronger relationship with their followers and thus followers are more likely to show purchase intension, as the trust in these influencers is higher. Besides these influencer characteristics, which should be considered when selecting influencers, managers should target the campaign content to consumer behavior within the purchase phase. Campaign content should be used that directly encourages the consumer to buy. In addition, managers can create incentives by offering free samples or free additional products with the purchase of a product within a certain campaign period. Within the campaign, managers should be careful not to produce too many campaign stories, but to use longer campaign stories in which the influencer has time to make the value of the product clear to his followers.

When it is the aim of the campaign to increase campaign post likes, managers should focus on influencers with a high unique reach and a highly active follower base. Similar to increasing the reach of campaign posts, influencers should be selected for the portfolio that have a low follower overlap to increase the number of likes. Moreover, likes within a campaign can be increased by selection of influencers whose communication style indicates high expertise and social status. In terms of content, managers should create campaign posts that draw attention to and describe the product or service. Managers should not use too many campaign posts within a campaign to avoid cannibalization of engagement behavior.

If managers want to increase the number of comments on campaign posts, they should pay particular attention to selecting influencers whose followers generally respond frequently with comments to their content and tend to reply to each other through comments. Furthermore, lotteries are a quick way for managers to increase the number of comments within a campaign. To get value from the comments, influencers should motivate comments that generate information for the brand or stimulate a discussion between consumers and generate attention, such as linking a friend and describing why they need that particular product.

When putting together the campaign portfolio, managers should again make sure to select influencers who have a low follower overlap and a high unique reach.

Managers who especially want to enhance the views of their campaign stories should target influencers with high unique reach and a high like follower ratio. Moreover, campaign story views are higher for influencers whose profile posts convey a high level of expertise and social status.

## 3.5.5 Limitations of Study 1 and Future Research

Study 1 is subject to some limitations that offer potential for future research. For one thing, a limited number of influencer posts was included. Although the data set is sufficient for empirical investigation of influencer characteristics driving different consumer behaviors along the consumer decision journey, a larger sample size would allow for the inclusion of additional explanatory variables.

In Study 1, the content of an influencer's campaign posts was categorized into awareness and trial campaign posts. Additionally, it was recorded whether a product or service was promoted in the posts and whether a lottery was included. Future research could further differentiate the content of campaign posts, building on the literature review on viral content design. For example, it could be investigated to what extent the posts differ in terms of their emotionality, informativeness or product centrality.

Moreover, the literature review on viral content design showed that there is little analysis of pictorial content of social media posts and its influence on consumer behavior. Especially on social networks like Instagram, where the original idea is to share visual content, the analysis of visual content is relevant. Recent studies on the analysis of visual content on Instagram call for further research in the context of influencer content (Li and Xie 2020; Rietveld et al. 2020). Furthermore, in future the consumption of content will increasingly be shaped by stories and live streams from influencers (Droesch 2021). In addition to the pictorial content of the posts, the content of the stories could also be differentiated more precisely in order to demonstrate possible influences on campaign story views or link clicks within a story.

The content of an influencer's daily stories could also be used to capture influencer characteristics such as expertise more comprehensively. It could also be used to explore how intimate the content is that the influencer shares with his followers to better characterize the relationship between influencer and followers. However, since regular Instagram stories only remain visible for 24 h and are then automatically deleted, data collection is more difficult than with saved data.

## 3.5 Results of Study 1

Study 1 has shown that it is important to consider the network size of the influencer in relation to the campaign portfolio of influencers used, as this has different effects depending on the campaign goal. Since in practice more than one influencer is used for campaigns, knowledge about portfolio characteristics should be expanded. As the costs of an influencer are largely determined by the number of his followers, future research could show to what extent optimizing the portfolio in terms of unique reach or overlap could save costs. All other things being equal, a portfolio of smaller influencers with low follower overlap, for example, could achieve the same campaign reach at a lower price than large influencers with a high overlap of followers.

In order to better illustrate the monetary value of the influencer post, it would be useful to link the available data with concrete sales data. In the data set of Study 1, the number of orders was only collected for ten of the influencers. For this reason, the variable was not included. Future research could specifically collect sales data for a larger sample. In addition, it would be of interest to managers to compare the effectiveness of influencer campaigns with other marketing activities. Study 2 will address and investigate these monetary effects of influencer marketing.

Despite its limitation, Study 1 is the first to observe the impact of an influencers personal and network potential on consumer behavior at different stages of the consumer decision journey. Furthermore, the study is the first to shed light on the influence of an influencer's brand fit and portfolio characteristics on consumer behavior. The study thus makes a significant contribution to the existent literature and offers a variety of suggestions for further research.

# 4 Investigating the Effectiveness of Influencer Marketing

Study 2 examines the impact of the interplay of consumer-generated as well as firm-generated messages on social media and other marketing activities of a brand on website visits, orders and revenue. In this context, a special interest will be placed on the investments in influencer marketing. The first section outlines the relevance of the topic and the objective of the study. Section 4.2 anchors Study 2 within the relevant literature and summarizes the scattered findings of previous research. Section 4.3 covers the study design and describes the collected data set, the operationalizations and descriptive statistics of the variables, and the methodology used. Section 4.4 presents and discusses the results of the vector autoregressive (VAR) model. Furthermore, the robustness of the results is checked by a seemingly unrelated regression (SUR) model. Implications for management as well as limitations of Study 2 and an outlook for future research complete the chapter.

## 4.1 Examine the relative Effectiveness of Influencer Marketing, Advertising, Firm-generated Messages and Consumer-generated Messages on Website Visits, Orders and Revenue

Brand management in the age of globalization and social media is characterized by a decrease in investments in traditional marketing channels and an intensive expansion of digital brand strategy (PWC 2019; Statista 2018a). The decrease of marketing budgets in advertising, such as TV advertising, and the increasing relevance of digital channels is further driven by the corona pandemic (Statista 2021c). In 2020, for the first time, the share of digital advertising in Germany exceeded the share of advertising in total advertising industry revenues (Bocksch

2020). Moreover, influencer marketing in particular continues to gain importance as a key component of companies' digital marketing strategies (Association of National Advertisers 2018). In 2018, 60% of marketers said they would increase their investment in influencer marketing compared to the previous year (Statista 2018c). Based on this trend, market analysts expect the budget for influencer marketing to double to a value of more than 15 billion USD between 2019 and 2022 (Forbes 2020).

To leverage the power of social media influencers, managers need to know how effective influencer marketing is for consumer interest and firm performance. Previous research has already demonstrated the impact of influencer messages on consumer attitude and behavioral intention (Breves et al. 2019; Colliander and Dahlén 2011; De Vries 2019; Lee and Watkins 2016; Uribe, Buzeta, and Velásquez 2016). More recent work has linked influencer activities with consumer behavior such as likes and comments (Hughes, Swaminathan, and Brooks 2019) or connected influential retweets with a boost of TV show viewing and companies' follower gain (Gong et al. 2017). Moreover, Study 1 showed that influencer messages have a positive effect on consumer behavior along the consumer decision journey. However, research and practice lack knowledge about the monetary effects of influencer marketing. Therefore, research is needed that investigates the effectiveness of influencer marketing investments on firm performance.

Furthermore, to optimize budget allocation across the marketing mix, managers need information about the relative effectiveness of their own marketing channels. Previous studies have already shown that firm-generated content on a brand's social media page can have a higher elasticity than traditional channels (Kumar et al. 2016; Kumar, Choi, and Greene 2017). Furthermore, the studies indicate that there are positive synergies between channels that lead to an increase in firm performance. These results reinforce the tendency of brands to further expand their digital presence. As Study 1 has already shown, influencer messages are an important tool for marketers to influence consumer behavior. This is also the reason why 68% of US marketers use influencer marketing in 2021, and the trend is rising (eMarketer 2021). However, managers need to know about the effectiveness of influencer marketing investments compared to the brand's other advertising investments and own social media activities. Moreover, there are missing insights on complementary effects of influencer marketing, advertising and firm-generated content on a brand's social media page.

In addition to the marketing activities of brands, the exchange of opinions and experiences between consumers on social media plays an increasingly important role in the success of brands (Gensler et al. 2013). Previous research has already extensively shown that consumer-generated messages have a significant effect on

## 4.1 Examine the relative Effectiveness of Influencer Marketing …

brand performance (e.g. Babić Rosario et al. 2016; Hennig-Thurau, Wiertz, and Feldhaus 2015; You, Vadakkepatt, and Joshi 2015). That is why it is important for brand managers to understand how they can manage consumer-generated content through their own marketing activities and what the relative effectiveness of the different channels is (De Vries, Gensler, and Leeflang 2017). Some studies have already examined the interactions between advertising and firm-generated and consumer-generated content on social media and their relative impact on brand building (Colicev, Kumar, and O'Connor 2019), brand performance (Hewett et al. 2016; Kupfer et al. 2018; Stephen and Galak 2012), or both (Colicev et al. 2018; De Vries, Gensler, and Leeflang 2017). Influencer marketing blends elements of firm-generated and consumer-generated content. Influencers are paid for the transportation of brand messages on social media, nevertheless influencers are seen as an independent part of the community. As a result, influencer messaging takes on an important leverage role between brand and consumer activities. However, there is a lack of empirical research examining the effectiveness of influencer marketing and its interaction with consumer-generated content (Leung, Gu, and Palmatier 2022).

The objective of Study 2 is to address these gaps in the literature by *investigating the relative effectiveness of influencer marketing, firm-generated as well as consumer-generated messages on social media and advertising on website visits, orders and revenue.*

The study considers orders and revenue because there is no empirical evidence on the monetary value of influencer messaging. Moreover, Table 4.1 shows that firm performance metrics are the most commonly used metrics for measuring channel effectiveness. By observing the effects on consumer interest, more precisely the effects on website visits of potential consumers, it is possible to depict the consumer decision journey and to show not only the direct effects but also the indirect effects on firm performance.

Study 2 contributes to the current research in three ways: First, it simultaneously considers and compares the effectiveness of influencer marketing, other marketing investments, and firm-generated and consumer-generated messages. Second, the interdependence of the different channels is illustrated and their complementary effects are highlighted. Third, website visits, orders and revenue are considered to capture effectiveness along the consumer decision journey.

Therefore, the findings provide the first insights for managers on the monetary value of influencer activities. Furthermore, the results help managers to evaluate the effectiveness of channel investments over time, since the study considers multiple performance metrics along the consumer decision journey. Lastly, the study's insights help managers to effectively orchestrate the various channel activities while optimizing the allocation of their marketing budget.

## 4.2 Positioning Study 2 within Literature

To answer the present research question, studies are defined as relevant literature if they consider more than one message type in their work on channel effectiveness. In this context, messages are communication activities that are directed at the consumer and are divided into consumer-generated as well as firm-generated messages on social platforms and advertising messages.

The relevant literature is based on the defined search criteria in the literature review in Chapter 2. Between 2000 and 2021, 21 studies were identified that that compare several channels in terms of their effectiveness on consumer behavior metrics. Table 4.1 classifies the relevant literature according to the examined dependent variables and places Study 2 in this context. The most important results of the studies are briefly summarized below.

Some of the studies consider **consumer interest** by observing search behavior (Kim and Hanssens 2017) or online and offline store traffic (Fossen and Schweidel 2019; Pauwels, Aksehirli, and Lackman 2016). That research demonstrates that user-generated content shows higher elasticities on consumers' online search behavior and offline as well as online store traffic than investments in advertising channels (Kim and Hanssens 2017; Pauwels, Aksehirli, and Lackman 2016). Only paid search investment has a similar elasticity on online store traffic over the long run (Pauwels, Aksehirli, and Lackman 2016). Moreover, consumers' communication on social media simultaneously with the consumption of advertising not only has a positive direct effect on website traffic, but also increases the effectiveness of the traditional channel (Fossen and Schweidel 2019).

Most of the studies observe **firm performance**. The studies consider different performance metrics. Early studies on digital services already show that customer referrals through social media have greater short-term and long-term effects on customer acquisition than traditional marketing efforts (Trusov, Bucklin, and Pauwels 2009; Villanueva, Yoo, and Hanssens 2008). Moreover, it is becoming increasingly apparent that user-generated messages on social media are gaining influence and having a significant impact on customer acquisition for services that were previously advertised using more traditional marketing measures (Corstjens and Umblijs 2012; De Vries, Gensler, and Leeflang 2017). While traditional channels often still have a stronger impact on customer acquisition, there are valuable

## 4.2 Positioning Study 2 within Literature

**Table 4.1** Studies considering the Effects of more than one Type of Message on Consumer Behavior Metrics

| Study | Compared Channels | | | | Consumer Decision Journey | |
|---|---|---|---|---|---|---|
| | Advertising | FG Messages | CG Messages | Influencer Messages | Consumer Interest | Firm Performance |
| Bruce, Foutz, and Kolsarici 2012 | x | | x | | | x |
| Corstjens and Umblijs 2012 | x | | x | | | x |
| De Vries, Gensler, and Leeflang 2017 | x | x | x | | | x |
| Fossen and Schweidel 2019 | x | | x | | x[a] | x |
| Goh, Heng, and Lin 2013 | | x | x | | | x |
| Gopinath, Chintagunta, and Venkataraman 2013 | x | | x | | | x |
| Gopinath, Thomas, and Krishnamurthi 2014 | x | | x | | | x |
| Hewett et al. 2016 | x | x | x | | | x[b] |
| Kim and Hanssens 2017 | x | | x | | x[c] | x |
| Kumar et al. 2013 | | x | x | | | x |
| Kumar et al. 2016 | x | x | | | | x |
| Kumar, Choi, and Greene 2017 | x | x | | | | x |
| Kupfer et al. 2017 | x | x | x | | | x |
| Onishi and Manchanda 2012 | x | | x | | | x |
| Pauwels, Aksehirli, and Lackman 2016 | x | | x | | x[a] | |
| Stephen and Galak 2012 | x | x | x | | | x |
| Trusov, Bucklin, and Pauwels 2009 | x | | x | | | x |
| Villanueva, Yoo, and Hanssens 2008 | x | | x | | | x |
| You, Vadakkepatt, and Joshi 2015 | x | | x | | | x |
| **Study 2** | x | x | x | x | x[a] | x |

Source: Author's own illustration. Note: FG = firm-generated, CG = consumer-generated, [a] online/offline store traffic, [b] customer deposit, [c] online search.

synergies between them and social media messages. For example, the effectiveness of advertising is increased by activating the target group with the help of firm-generated social media messages (De Vries, Gensler, and Leeflang 2017). Furthermore, several studies have shown that advertising increases the exchange of consumers on social media (Fossen and Schweidel 2019; Onishi and Manchanda 2012) and contributes to a positive customer opinion (De Vries, Gensler, and Leeflang 2017). Corstjens and Umblijs (2012) emphasize that negative user-generated content has a particularly negative impact on customer acquisition in competitive industries with low customer loyalty. Therefore, the management of user-generated messages is essential for the future success of a brand to drive customer acquisition.

Most of the research focuses on the impact of social media messaging and marketing investments on sales. Research agrees that consumer-generated messages on social media platforms and advertising complement each other in terms of increasing revenue in the movie industry (Bruce, Foutz, and Kolsarici 2012; Gopinath, Chintagunta, and Venkataraman 2013; Kim and Hanssens 2017; Onishi and Manchanda 2012). However, these effects are also confirmed for financial services (Hewett et al. 2016) or flat screens (Corstjens and Umblijs 2012) and cell phones (Gopinath, Thomas, and Krishnamurthi 2014; Onishi and Manchanda 2012).

Further, research has shown that for short life-cycle products, such as movies, advertising elasticity is very high (Gopinath, Chintagunta, and Venkataraman 2013). Therefore, it is not surprising that some studies show that traditional channels have a greater impact on firm performance than consumer-generated social media messages (Bruce, Foutz, and Kolsarici 2012; Gopinath, Chintagunta, and Venkataraman 2013; Kim and Hanssens 2017). However, Gopinath, Chintagunta, and Venkataraman (2013) emphasize that the relative effectiveness of the two channels depend on the target market and that there are, for example, target groups that respond very strongly to consumer opinions in social media. Thus, the findings of Onishi and Manchanda (2012) and Kupfer et al. (2018) indicate that consumer-generated messages have a higher elasticity than traditional channels for movie ticket sales. Stephen and Galak (2012) find similar results for microloan sales.

Taking firm-generated social media messages into account, research shows that user-generated massages evoke more firm performance than firm-generated messages (Goh, Heng, and Lin 2013; Kupfer et al. 2018). However, Kumar et al. (2016) and Kumar, Choi, and Greene (2017) show that valuable synergies develop between a firm's activities on Facebook and traditional marketing actions in terms of increasing firm performance. Moreover, firm-generated social media content increases user-generated content and thus generates a viral effect that increases firm performance (Kumar et al. 2013).

This viral effect can be created by integrating a human brand with great social media power within the company's own marketing strategy. Within the movie industry, Kupfer et al. (2018) show that the social media posting activities of actors who star in the movie have a significant positive impact on ticket sales by activating the star's social media community. It remains to be seen whether these effects are also true for social media influencers, without them being a part of the product like an actor. The authors also point out that non-product-related posts have a negative impact on revenue. Influencers often characterize themselves by documenting their lives on a daily basis, and they also promote other brands. Therefore, it is essential for managers to verify whether influencer social media messages have a positive impact on consumer interest and firm performance.

All in all, current research agrees that social media messages have a growing influence on the consumer decision journey and need to be integrated into the strategic planning of a brand's marketing activities. However, the various studies do not agree on the relative effects between channels and which activities are best suited to engage consumers at the various stages of the consumer decision journey. It is clear that more research is needed to work out the dependencies of outcomes on specific target groups, product types or industry factors.

In addition, influencers are gaining importance in the marketing mix, as they act as a targeted tool representing the brand, but at the same time have established themselves as independent users with great influence within the community. Therefore, influencers have an important mediating role on social media, which should be explored in more detail.

Because this role of influencer marketing is unexplored so far and the results of previous research on the other message types are scattered, it is difficult to formulate expectations about the relative effectiveness of the different channels beforehand. Therefore, it will be refrained from formulating individual hypotheses. Rather, empirical results are presented that show the relative effectiveness of influencer marketing, advertising and firm-generated as well as user-generated social media messages and their interdependence.

## 4.3 Study Design

The study design includes the description of the data basis and the operationalization of the variables. Moreover, the choice of method is explained and the preparation of the data for the analysis is illustrated.

## 4.3.1 Data Set

The dataset of Study 2 covers the data on website visits, orders and revenue of one of the largest specialized online retailers in Europe, resulting from the activities in one European country. Furthermore, this data is linked to the different traditional and digital channel investments of the company. Moreover, data from Instagram and a large customer review website will be added in order to explore the interrelationships between channel investments and firm-generated as well as consumer-generated social media messages. The data is reported on a weekly basis and rages from calendar week 24 in 2018 to week 23 in 2020.

According to a panel survey (n = 2,070) in the first quarter of 2021, the company achieves 68% supported brand awareness among Internet users between the ages of 18 and 69 that are in need for the product of interest. The company is characterized by a digitally anchored omnichannel concept. This means that the company's main business is anchored online. However, within the data collection, the company opened offline stores in individual cities to attract more customers through this channel. The resulting valuable synergies of this strategy are the basis of brand awareness and corporate success.

Instagram is an essential part of the company's digital presence. In 2020, Instagram was the most frequently used social network on a daily basis within the European target market (ARD/ZDF-Forschungskommission 2021). Moreover, the company's main target group, which consists of young adults between 18 and 39 years, is particularly active on social media. This age group makes up the majority of Instagram users worldwide (Statista 2021b). Due to the given relevance, the firm-generated and consumer-generated social media messages on Instagram are investigated.

## 4.3.2 Operationalization of Variables

Table 4.2 summarizes the operationalization of the variables. The variables are divided into endogenous variables and exogenous variables. The endogenous variables capture the reciprocal characteristics of marketing investments, social media messages, website visits as well as orders and revenue. The exogenous variables include environmental control variables. Furthermore, Table 4.3 illustrates the considerable value range of the metric variables over time.

*Measuring advertising.* To capture the spend on advertising, the company's actual spend on TV advertising, search engine optimization (SEO), search engine

## 4.3 Study Design

**Table 4.2** Variable Operationalizations of Study 2

| Variable | Description | Measurement Unit | Source |
|---|---|---|---|
| **Endogenous Variables** | | | |
| TV | Company's gross media expenditures on TV advertising | Gross media expenditures (EUR) | Company's database |
| Social Media Influencer | Company's gross media expenditures on influencer marketing | Gross media expenditures (EUR) | Company's database |
| SEO | Company's gross media expenditures on SEO advertising | Gross media expenditures (EUR) | Company's database |
| SEM | Company's gross media expenditures on SEM advertising | Gross media expenditures (EUR) | Company's database |
| Pricing and Shopping | Company's gross media expenditures for placement on price comparison websites and Google shopping | Gross media expenditures (EUR) | Company's database |
| Display | Company's gross media expenditures on display advertising (targeting/retargeting) on social media networks | Gross media expenditures (EUR) | Company's database |
| Affiliate | Company's gross media expenditures on affiliate marketing (mainly coupon websites) | Gross media expenditures (EUR) | Company's database |
| Offline | Company's gross media expenditures on offline advertising | Gross media expenditures (EUR) | Company's database |
| Engagement | Total engagement with company's content on Instagram based on likes, comments, and video views | Volume | Own research |
| Valence Instagram | Consumer sentiment based on Instagram comments [(positive comments - negative comments)/(all comments)] | Share | Own research |
| Volume Review | The total number of reviews (positive, neutral, and negative) on Trustpilot | Volume | Own research |
| Valence Review | Consumer sentiment based on Trustpilot reviews [(positive reviews - negative reviews)/(all reviews)] | Share | Own research |
| Visits | Number of visits on company's website | Volume | Company's database |
| Orders | Number of orders after cancelation | Volume | Company's database |
| Revenue | Company's gross revenue after returns | Gross revenues (EUR) | Company's database |

(continued)

**Table 4.2** (continued)

| Variable | Description | Measurement Unit | Source |
|---|---|---|---|
| **Control Variables (Exogenous)** | | | |
| National Holidays | National holidays | Dummy | Own research |
| School Holidays | School holidays | Dummy | Own research |
| Corona | WHO officially defines the condition as a pandemic according to the number of corona cases | Dummy | Own research |
| Season 1 | Season for product type 1 | Dummy | Company's database |
| Season 2 | Season for product type 2 | Dummy | Company's database |
| Discount Rate | Number of average discount by the company | Percentage | Company's database |
| Buzz Events | Important interventions that can create online buzz | Dummy | Company's database |
| SEO Event | Important Interventions that created an increase in SEO spendings | Dummy | Company's database |
| Store Openings | Company's store openings in the European country | Dummy | Company's database |
| Engagement Competitors | Total engagement with the content of key competitors on Instagram based on likes, comments, and video views | Volume | Own research |
| Valence Instagram Competitors | Consumer sentiment based on Instagram comments on the content of key competitors on Instagram [(positive comments - negative comments)/(all comments)] | Share | Own research |
| Volume Review Competitors | The total number of reviews (positive, neutral, and negative) on Trustpilot concerning key competitors | Volume | Own research |
| Valence Review Competitors | Consumer sentiment based on Trustpilot reviews of key competitors [(positive reviews - negative reviews)/(all reviews)] | Share | Own research |
| Nielsen Competitors | Gross media expenditures on TV advertising of key competitors | Gross media expenditures (EUR) | Nielsen |
| Influencer Measure | Investment in social media influencers is different from zero that week | Dummy | Company's database |
| Giveaway | Giveaway post on Instagram | Dummy | Own research |
| Engagement Event | Special video event on Instagram | Dummy | Own research |

Source: Author's own illustration.

## 4.3 Study Design

marketing (SEM), advertising on pricing and shopping websites, display advertising, affiliate marketing and offline advertising (e.g. offline coupons) is measured. The company provided the data on a weekly basis. Although the company focuses particularly on a younger target group and the online sale of its goods, the average expenditure on TV advertising is still the highest. Looking at the average weekly spend, SEM and advertising on pricing and shopping websites are the company's next most important channels.

*Measuring influencer marketing.* Influencer marketing follows these expenses with a similarly high average weekly expenditure. The effectiveness of this channel is of particular relevance to the company and the following study, as the company plans to increase investments in this channel in the future and to rely more heavily on it for firm performance. The investments in influencer campaigns are always recorded by the company in the first week of the campaign. For this reason, a minimum value of 0 EUR is recorded in two of the weeks, even though there are ongoing influencer campaigns. This measurement problem is addressed with the dummy variable "Influencer Measure" to catch these values.

*Measuring firm-generated messages.* To capture the impact of firm-generated messaging, weekly engagement with the company's Instagram posts is measured. The weekly engagement with the company's Instagram posts is based on the number of users' weekly likes, comments and video views. These interactions are considered as they capture the viral spread of firm-generated content across the network. Previous research has shown that this type of engagement effectively builds a brand and generates firm performance (Colicev et al. 2018; De Vries, Gensler, and Leeflang 2017).

The company posted a minimum of ten times per week and a maximum of 20 times per week. On average, the company posted 14 posts a week, including both picture posts and video posts. The company publishes more picture posts than video posts. The number of engagements with these posts is on average 5,202 (see Table 4.3). The fluctuation around the mean value of 4,949 is relatively small compared to the maximum value of 33,012. Extreme values of the number of engagements, such as 33,012, are triggered by particular video posts that are often associated with giveaways. A variable capturing high engagement video posts ("Engagement Event") and a variable capturing giveaway posts ("Giveaway") are included in the model to control for these effects.

**Table 4.3** Descriptive Statistics of Relevant Variables of Study 2

|  | M | SD | Max | Min |
|---|---|---|---|---|
| **Endogenous Variables** | | | | |
| TV (EUR) | 74,672.45 | 38,278.26 | 173,429.50 | 25.62 |
| Social Media Influencer (EUR) | 18,540.95 | 15,326.24 | 59,220.00 | .00 |
| SEO (EUR) | 1,219.51 | 1,085.11 | 11,192.42 | 48.39 |
| SEM (EUR) | 21,834.45 | 7,567.93 | 41,291.13 | 10,711.07 |
| Pricing and Shopping (EUR) | 20,315.94 | 5,067.11 | 36,096.00 | 11,184.20 |
| Display (EUR) | 13,771.13 | 7,827.79 | 46,188.58 | 3,110.80 |
| Affiliate (EUR) | 2,322.81 | 1,077.14 | 7,507.40 | 653.10 |
| Offline (EUR) | 10,695.26 | 10,618.38 | 41,376.21 | .00 |
| Engagement | 5,202.33 | 4,129.65 | 33,012.00 | 1,327.00 |
| Valence Instagram | .33 | .16 | .83 | −.10 |
| Volume Review | 116.02 | 59.28 | 461.00 | 16.00 |
| Valence Review | .71 | .05 | .84 | .56 |
| Visits | 518,198.50 | 98,437.70 | 733,966.00 | 344,605.00 |
| Orders | 31,739.97 | 5,070.90 | 45,386.52 | 20,562.74 |
| Revenue (EUR) | 1,805,598.00 | 338,596.80 | 2,748,216.00 | 1,120,456.00 |
| **Control Variables (Exogenous)** | | | | |
| Discount Rate (Share) | .10 | .02 | .16 | .07 |
| Engagement Competitors | 153,739.80 | 52,731.88 | 481,678.00 | 84,030.00 |
| Valence Instagram Competitors | .38 | .10 | .63 | .09 |
| Volume Review Competitors | 91.43 | 38.66 | 211.00 | 32.00 |
| Valence Review Competitors | .45 | .35 | 3.71 | .10 |
| Nielsen Competitors (EUR) | 1,826,396.00 | 867,991.30 | 3,775,871.00 | 322,534.60 |

Source: Author's own illustration.

## 4.3 Study Design

*Measuring consumer-generated messages.* Consumer sentiment is measured both on Instagram and on a popular consumer review platform. Previous research has shown that high user posting activity on social networks is associated with an increase of firm performance (Goh, Heng, and Lin 2013). Thus, the consumer sentiment on Instagram is captured by the valence of consumer-generated comments on the company's profile. Moreover, the volume and valence of product-related reviews or blog posts has been shown to have a significant impact on firm performance (Gopinath, Chintagunta, and Venkataraman 2013; Gopinath, Thomas, and Krishnamurthi 2014; Stephen and Galak 2012). Therefore, the volume and value of reviews on trustpilot.de is additionally measured to capture consumer opinions online.

Both the valence of the user comments on Instagram and that of the reviews are determined by the difference between the proportions of positive and negative messages (Table 4.2). The value range of the measures is between $-1$ and $+1$. If no positive (negative), but only negative (positive) messages are posted in a given week, the value is $-1$ $(+1)$. If there are as many positive messages as negative ones posted, the valence is zero.

Looking at the valence values in Table 4.3, it is clear that the comments and reviews are predominantly positive. The fact that reactions to firm-generated posts within social media networks are rather positive has already been demonstrated in earlier studies (De Vries, Gensler, and Leeflang 2012). However, the Figures 4.1 and 4.2 show a sufficient variance in the valence of comments and reviews to include the variables in the present model.

*Measuring consumer interest and firm performance.* The visits of potential customers to the brand's website were provided by the company. Website visits can accordingly be seen as a proxy for consumer interest. On average, 518,199 users visit the brand's website within a week. Around 6% of them also place an order on the website. This shows that website visits are a good measure of consumer interest, but further measures are needed to map the purchase phase of the consumer decision journey.

To capture the firm performance, the company provided data on number of orders after cancelation and revenue after return. Both measures are considered in order to check whether marketing activities have an impact not only on the number of orders, but also on successful purchase completions and thus on revenue.

*Measuring control variables.* Relating to previous research, the study includes several other factors that may have an impact on the company's website visits, orders and revenue. First of all, national holidays and school holidays are included, as many potential customers go on vacation during these periods and

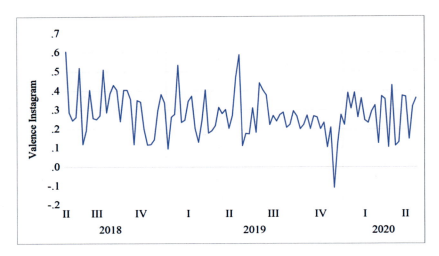

**Figure 4.1** Valence of Comments on Company's Instagram Profile over time. Source: Author's own illustration.

this can have an influence on purchasing behavior (De Vries, Gensler, and Leeflang 2012). Secondly, is controlled for the seasons, which are defined within the industry (Kumar, Choi, and Greene 2017). Within specific months, the company's products are in greater demand. Third, the weekly discount rate is included because previous research has shown that variations in discounts over time affect brand performance and product sales (Pauwels, Hanssens, and Siddarth 2002). Therefore, the weekly average discount rate is included.

The fourth group of control variables includes variables that control for special events (De Vries, Gensler, and Leeflang 2017). The company's news page was searched for potential buzz events that would bring special public attention to the brand. This category includes events such as the launch of a new designer or influencer collaboration, sponsorship of media awards, or the launch of a new service such as Apple payments.

Furthermore, one variable records special expenditures in the area of SEO. Investments in SEO are mainly caused by costs for human resources to adapt the website to the Google algorithm. Special expenditures in the area of SEO capture particularly high expenses in order to adapt the company website to a Google update, both in terms of content and technology.

## 4.3 Study Design

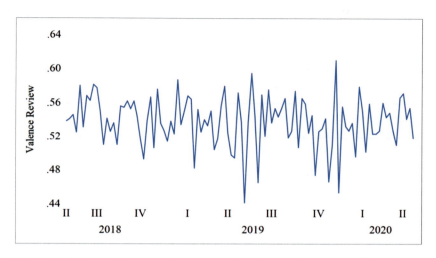

**Figure 4.2** Valence of Company Reviews over time. Source: Author's own illustration.

Due to the enormous success, the online retailer has decided to open individual offline stores in major cities. Within the data collection period, this project was still in the development phase. For this reason, a variable records the opening of additional offline stores in the country of interest. It is to be examined to what extent these have an effect on orders and revenue.

Fifth, the marketing activities and social media messages of the relevant competitors are recorded, as they can attract the attention of potential customers of the company (De Vries, Gensler, and Leeflang 2017). The gross media expenditures on TV advertising of key competitors is included. The measurement of these expenditures is provided by Nielsen[1] and was made available by the company. Further, the engagement with the firm-generated messages and the valence of user comments on Instagram is measured for the relevant competitors. Moreover, the volume and valence of competitors' reviews on trustpilot.de are observed. For all variables, an average value is calculated across all relevant competitors.

---

[1] The Nielsen Company is one of the world's leading market research companies.

### 4.3.3 Methodology

The aim of Study 2 is to investigate the reciprocal relationships between influencer marketing, firm-generated as well as consumer-generated messages on social media, advertising, consumer interest and firm performance. For this purpose, it is recommended to apply a vector autoregressive (VAR) model (Dekimpe, Hanssens, and Silva-Risso 1998; Pauwels, Hanssens, and Siddarth 2002). More precisely, a VAR model with exogenous variables (VARX) is applied which also includes the described control variables (De Vries, Gensler, and Leeflang 2017).

The VARX model is applied for three reasons: First, the response impulse functions allow to capture the relative effectiveness of influencer marketing, firm-generated as well as consumer-generated messages on social media and advertising on website visits, orders and revenue. Second, the VARX model captures the extent of the long- and short-term effects of marketing and social media activities on each other as well as on website visits, orders and revenue. Third, the response impulse functions illustrate the carryover effects over time. Fourth, the VARX model shows the interdependence of the different channels and reveals complementary effects.

In preparation for the estimation of the VAR Model, some preliminary test steps are performed:

- Stationarity of time series
- Endogeneity of variables
- Determination of lag length
- Test for autocorrelation

First, the time series are tested for **stationarity**. Nonstationary time series have an evolving mean over time (Trusov, Bucklin, and Pauwels 2009). These persistent effects can bias the results of the VAR model and should be excluded. In contrast, stationarity means that the time series have a constant mean over time and temporary effects occur, which can serve as a basis for analysis (Dekimpe and Hanssens 1999). Therefore, it is first checked whether the time series is stable in its temporary fluctuations around a fixed mean or a deterministic trend. The model includes a constant term and a deterministic time trend to control for omitted evolving variables. In this case the Phillips-Perron (PP) test is recommended to assess the stationarity of time series (Phillips and Perron 1988).

## 4.3 Study Design

**Table 4.4** Unit Root Test Results (PP Test)

| Series | Test Statistic | Prob. | Stationarity |
|---|---|---|---|
| TV | −5.73 | .00 | ✓ |
| Social Media Influencer | −8.79 | .00 | ✓ |
| SEO | −3.02 | .13 | ✗ |
| 1st Difference SEO | −17.33 | .00 | ✓ |
| SEM | −2.20 | .49 | ✗ |
| 1st Difference SEM | −9.50 | .00 | ✓ |
| Pricing and Shopping | −4.54 | .00 | ✓ |
| Display | −4.23 | .01 | ✓ |
| Affiliate | −4.49 | .00 | ✓ |
| Offline | −8.71 | .00 | ✓ |
| Engagement | −7.75 | .00 | ✓ |
| Valence Instagram | −9.60 | .00 | ✓ |
| Volume Review | −6.35 | .00 | ✓ |
| Valence Review | −12.00 | .00 | ✓ |
| Visits | −3.11 | .11 | ✗ |
| 1st Difference Visits | −14.40 | .00 | ✓ |
| Orders | −4.47 | .00 | ✓ |
| Revenue | −4.38 | .00 | ✓ |

Source: Author's own illustration. Notes: Null hypothesis: The series contains a unit root (i.e., is nonstationary). Test critical values:The critical values for PP test are −4.05 (1% level), −3.45 (5% level) and −3.15 (10% level).

Before testing for stationarity, all variables were ln-transformed to stabilize the time series (De Vries, Gensler, and Leeflang 2017). For the variables "Social Media Influencer" and "Offline", there were a few weeks with the value 0. These zeros were replaced with the value .00001 to perform the logarithmic transformation. Table 4.4 illustrates the results for the PP test. The table shows that most of the variables are stationary. The variables "SEO", "SEM" and "Visits" do not meet the requirements. In this case, it is recommended to continue with the first difference of the time series (Granger and Newbold 1986). This means that the value for each lag of the time series is subtracted from the previous one to form the difference between them. After first differencing, the variables "SEO", "SEM" and "Visits" are stationary. The model variables thus represent the change in the respective variable. Despite the transformation of the variables, they allow the same implications (Colicev et al. 2018). For example, an increase of change in visits indicates an increase in visits. When talking about visits and investments in SEO and SEM in the following, the difference of visits and the difference of investments in SEO and SEM is considered.

**Table 4.5** Results of Granger Causality Tests

| Dependent Variable Granger-caused by... | Dependent Variable | | | | | | | |
|---|---|---|---|---|---|---|---|---|
|  | [1] | [2] | [3] | [4] | [5] | [6] | [7] | [8] |
| [1] TV |  | – | – | – | – | – | .072 | .041 |
| [2] Social Media Influencer | – |  | – | – | – | – | – | – |
| [3] SEO | – | – |  | – | – | .016 | – | .073 |
| [4] SEM | – | – | – |  | – | – | .098 | – |
| [5] Pricing and Shopping | – | .031 | – | – |  | – | .031 | – |
| [6] Display | – | .001 | – | – | – |  | – | – |
| [7] Affiliate | – | – | – | – | – | – |  | – |
| [8] Offline | – | – | – | .005 | .019 | – | – |  |
| [9] Engagement | – | .039 | – | .087 | – | .027 | – | .082 |
| [10] Valence Instagram | – | .023 | – | .058 | – | – | – | .005 |
| [11] Volume Review | – | – | .068 | .015 | – | – | – | – |
| [12] Valence Review | – | – | – | – | – | – | – | .071 |
| [13] Visits | .020 | – | – | – | .092 | – | – | .001 |
| [14] Orders | – | – | – | – | – | – | .024 | .012 |
| [15] Revenue | – | – | – | – | – | .088 | .010 | .055 |

(continued)

## 4.3 Study Design

**Table 4.5** (continued)

| Dependent Variable Granger-caused by... | Dependent Variable | | | | | | |
|---|---|---|---|---|---|---|---|
| | [9] | [10] | [11] | [12] | [13] | [14] | [15] |
| [1] TV | – | – | – | – | .081 | .028 | .019 |
| [2] Social Media Influencer | .014 | – | – | .021 | – | – | – |
| [3] SEO | – | – | – | – | .055 | – | .098 |
| [4] SEM | – | – | – | – | – | .083 | .063 |
| [5] Pricing and Shopping | .066 | – | – | – | – | .002 | .003 |
| [6] Display | .010 | – | .048 | .042 | .098 | – | – |
| [7] Affiliate | – | – | – | – | – | .070 | .088 |
| [8] Offline | .081 | – | .012 | .022 | .044 | – | – |
| [9] Engagement | | – | – | .090 | .031 | .097 | – |
| [10] Valence Instagram | – | | – | – | – | – | – |
| [11] Volume Review | – | – | | – | .012 | .096 | .050 |
| [12] Valence Review | .092 | – | | | – | – | – |
| [13] Visits | – | – | .014 | .019 | | .004 | .003 |
| [14] Orders | – | – | .001 | .095 | .001 | | – |
| [15] Revenue | – | – | .001 | .061 | .003 | – | |

Source: Author's own illustration. Notes: Dashes indicate insignificant values (p > .1). Minimum p-value across four lags is displayed.

Second, the **endogeneity** of the variables is tested, as VAR models assume feedback loops between variables. For this purpose, the Granger causality test is applied following the procedure of Trusov, Bucklin, and Pauwels (2009). This procedure is based on the consideration that the causality between two variables should be representable within the period of the maximum lag length. The company's marketing activities have different impact periods. It can be assumed, for example, that expenditures for interactions with an advertisement on Google (SEM) have a direct effect on performance metrics. Expenses for influencer campaigns, however, can have an impact within a few weeks due to the campaign periods and longer validity of discount codes. The company's operational planning horizon for its marketing activities was four weeks. Therefore, the Granger causality test is applied from one to four lags, and the lowest p-values are reported. The results are shown in Table 4.5. The table shows that 67 of the 210 effects are significant at a significance level of 10%. The results clearly reveal that there are causal dependencies between the marketing activities and the social media and performance metrics. Moreover, social media and performance metrics also exhibit feedback loops. This suggests that the indirect effects between the variables as well as the feedback loops should be represented in a fully dynamic system, as a VAR model allows.

Third, the **lag length** must be defined. Different selection criteria are available for selecting the appropriate lag length. The Schwarz information criterion (SC) and the Hannan-Quinn information criterion (HQ) are strongly consistent for different conditions and therefore widely used (here and in the following Lütkepohl 2005). However, for smaller samples the Akaike information criterion (AIC) and the final prediction error (FPE) choose the correct lag order more often than the SC and the HQ. Moreover, both criteria minimize the forecast error variance for small as well large samples. Initially, models up to the fourth order were tested, as this corresponds to the maximum operational planning horizon of the company. All criteria, except for the SC (indicating 0 lags), indicate a model with four lags. However, when checking the autocorrelation of the residuals, a VAR model with four lags has to be rejected, since the results speak for residual autocorrelation. Furthermore, for a VAR model with three lags, residual autocorrelation is also observed. Table 4.6 illustrates these selection criteria and the lag order that is indicated by the respective criterion for models up to second order. The criteria do not come to the same recommendation. In the present case, observations over 104 weeks form the data basis. This is rather to be considered as a small sample. Under these conditions, the AIC and FPE are the more appropriate measures (Lütkepohl 2005). Both measures recommend a lag order of two. Furthermore, the Likelihood ratio (LR) test statistic confirms this recommendation. For this reason, a VAR model with two lags is selected.

**Table 4.6** Lag Length Criteria

| Lag | LogL | LR | FPE | AIC | SC | HQ |
| --- | --- | --- | --- | --- | --- | --- |
| 0 | 264.20 | n.a. | .00 | .41 | 7.79* | 3.40* |
| 1 | 575.31 | 412.75 | .00 | −1.29 | 11.91 | 4.05 |
| 2 | 866.82 | 300.18* | .00* | −2.61* | 16.42 | 5.09 |

Source: Author's own illustration. Notes: * indicates lag order selected by the criterion.

## 4.3 Study Design

Fourth, the assumption of white noise of residuals should be fulfilled. White noise is the absence of **autocorrelation** and means that there is no left-over information within the residuals. As recommended by Hyndman and Athanasopoulos (2018), the autocorrelation is checked up to a lag order of ten. To determine the autocorrelation of residuals the Lagrange Multiplier (LM) autocorrelation test is used. The Portmanteau tests, which can also be used to test autocorrelation, are more appropriate for larger samples and higher lag orders. Whereas the LM-test is more suitable for small samples and lower lag orders (Lütkepohl 2005). The results of the LM-test up to a lag order of ten are displayed in Table 4.7. Looking at the significance values, the results indicate that there is no autocorrelation of the residuals. Although the p-value of the Edgeworth expansion corrected likelihood ratio (LRE) statistic for Lag 8 is just below the .05 threshold, does the result of the Rao F-statistic speak for the absence of autocorrelation (.08). The simulations of Edgerton and Shukur (1999) have shown that the Rao F-statistic is superior when performing the LM test. Therefore, the assumption is fulfilled.

The **full dynamic system of the VARX model** is specified in Figure 4.3. The VAR is estimated with the stationary variables in levels and the evolving variables in differences.

**Table 4.7** Results of LM-test

| Lag | LRE stat | df  | Prob. | Rao F-stat | df           | Prob. |
|-----|----------|-----|-------|------------|--------------|-------|
| 1   | 245.59   | 225 | .17   | 1.09       | (225, 277.8) | .26   |
| 2   | 250.36   | 225 | .12   | 1.11       | (225, 277.8) | .20   |
| 3   | 205.54   | 225 | .82   | .86        | (225, 277.8) | .88   |
| 4   | 215.48   | 225 | .66   | .91        | (225, 277.8) | .76   |
| 5   | 245.06   | 225 | .17   | 1.08       | (225, 277.8) | .26   |
| 6   | 234.07   | 225 | .33   | 1.02       | (225, 277.8) | .44   |
| 7   | 258.10   | 225 | .06   | 1.16       | (225, 277.8) | .12   |
| 8   | 263.79   | 225 | .04   | 1.20       | (225, 277.8) | .08   |
| 9   | 231.57   | 225 | .37   | 1.00       | (225, 277.8) | .49   |
| 10  | 255.02   | 225 | .08   | 1.14       | (225, 277.8) | .15   |

Source: Author's own illustration. Notes: Null hypothesis: No serial correlation at lag h.

The vector of endogenous variables—logged advertising expenses for TV (TV), social media influencers (SMI), SEO, SEM, pricing and shopping websites (PRIC), display advertising (DISP), affiliate marketing (AFFIL), offline advertising (OFF) and engagement with firm-generated content on Instagram (ENG_IG), valence of consumer comments on Instagram (VAL_IG), volume (VOL_REV) and valence (VAL_REV) of consumer reviews on Trustpilot as well as website visits (VISIT), orders after cancelation (OAC) and revenue after return (RARET)—is explained by its own past values and it accounts for the dynamic relations between those endogenous variables (matrix $\Phi$). Where t indicates the week, j indicates the number of lags included in the model, and J is the maximum number of lags (here: $J = 2$). Furthermore, the exogenous dummy variables (matrix $\theta$) and exogenous metric variables (matrix $\beta$) are included. Moreover, a constant term ($\alpha$) and a deterministic trend ($\delta_t$) is included. Finally, the model contains the error terms ($\varepsilon_t$) for each endogenous variable.

As the endogenous parameters obtained by the VARX model are not directly interpretable, orthogonalized impulse response functions (IRFs) based on the VARX model are estimated and elasticities are computed to examine the impact of variables (e.g. De Vries, Gensler, and Leeflang 2017; Trusov, Bucklin, and Pauwels 2009). To estimate the IRFs a Cholesky decomposition is used (Dekimpe and Hanssens 1995). However, this decomposition method assumes a predetermined order of variables. This means that the variables must be placed in a causal order, with the upstream variables influencing the downstream variables, but not the other way around. In the present case, though, feedback loops should not be excluded. For example, increased positive consumer reviews can lead to an increase in visits and purchases, but these in turn can also lead to an additional increase in reviews. It can also be observed that investments in a TV campaign, for example, lead to an increase in performance, which in turn stimulates investments in other channels, such as an accompanying influencer campaign, which can further increase success. Therefore, the order of the endogenous variables was continuously changed and different IRFs were estimated. Following the procedure of De Vries, Gensler, and Leeflang (2017), the average was built over the different responses. A Monte Carlo bootstrapping with 1,000 runs was performed to derive the standard error estimates. Based on the IRFs, the cumulative elasticities were calculated. For the calculation of the elasticities, the significant effects with t-statistics that had an absolute value of greater than 1 were accumulated. Therefore, it is possible to compare the impact of influencer marketing, firm-generated as well as consumer-generated messages on social media, advertising on website visits, orders and revenue. The results are presented in detail in the following chapter.

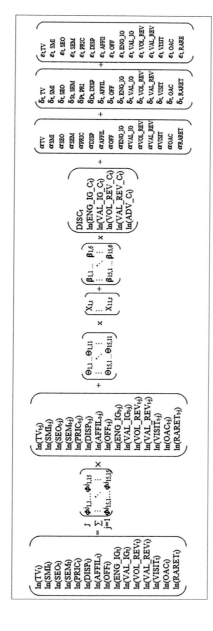

**Figure 4.3** Full Dynamic System of the VARX Model. Source: Author's own illustration.

## 4.4 Results of Study 2

The cumulative effects are shown in Table 4.8. First, the relative effectiveness of the different marketing activities and the different social media messages on website visits, orders and revenue are compared with each other. Special attention is paid to the comparison with social media influencer investments, as the effectiveness of influencer marketing is of particular interest for Study 2. This is followed by an analysis of the interrelations and feedback loops, as well as the effects of the control variables. Further, to check the robustness of the results, the VARX model is compared with a SUR model. The chapter concludes with managerial implications and limitations of the study.

### 4.4.1 Relative Effectiveness of Channels

Table 4.8 shows, investments in social media influencers are effective in building consumer interest because they significantly increase consumer visits on the company's website (.013), meaning that 1% increase in social media influencer investments leads to a .013% increase in visits. Comparing the impact of investments in social media influencers with investments in other channels, only investments in advertising on pricing and shopping websites (.024) and SEM (.022) have a higher elasticity in terms of visits. Offline advertising (.010) and affiliate marketing (.008) also effectively increase visits, however, their impact is smaller than that of social media influencer advertising.

Display advertising (.011) has a lower cumulative elasticity on visits than influencer marketing. In the short term, display advertising has the highest elasticity on visits, as in week one display advertising has an elasticity of .026. However, the impact of display advertising on visits becomes negative in week two (−.015), which in turn reduces the cumulative elasticity. The effects suggest that display advertising causes consumers to shift their consumption forward, resulting in an increase followed by a decrease in website visits.

Considering the length of effects, it can be observed that the effects of investments in advertising on pricing and shopping websites (weeks 1–3) as well as investments in display advertising (weeks 1–2) last longer than the effects of the other channels. The influence of the remaining marketing investments is limited to the first period.

The analysis of the IRFs shows no significant effect of SEO investments on visits. The missing effects for SEO investments can be explained by the fact that the investments in SEO are mainly caused by the content-related and technical

## 4.4 Results of Study 2

adjustments to the Google algorithm. Accordingly, the investments create the basic environment to be found easily, but unlike, for example, an increase in costs in SEM, they do not trigger customer needs. Moreover, the analysis of the IRFs shows no significant effect of investments in TV advertising on visits.

However, TV advertising has a significant impact on orders (.016) and revenue (.035). In this regard, the company's management emphasizes the particular relevance of TV advertising for explaining the value proposition of the company. Thus, the results could be a further indication that customers who are acquired through TV advertising order a particularly large number of products because they have a better understanding of the value proposition.

Moreover, an estimate of the influence of TV investments on online performance shows that the elasticity is somewhat the same for online orders (.015), but significantly lower for online revenue (.018). That TV advertisement explains more variance of total revenue than of online revenue can be explained by the revenue generated by offline stores. Due to the influence on customer awareness, customers are driven to the offline stores by TV investments. Consumers spend more money in offline stores because they experience the buying experience and the product itself more directly (Forbes 2019a). The data confirms that consumers spend 2.6 times more money per order in offline stores than in the online store.

Influencer marketing also offers the company the advantage to make its value proposition more comprehensible to the potential target group and create brand awareness. Due to the increasing influence of influencer marketing in the main target group, the company would like to shift budget from TV to influencer marketing in the long term. The results show that investments in social media influencers have not much lower elasticity on orders (.015) than TV advertising, but investments in social media influencers have a smaller elasticity on revenue (.018) than TV advertising. This means that a 1% increase in social media influencer investments leads to .015% increase in orders and .018% increase in revenue, respectively. However, if online revenue is considered within the estimation, influencer marketing outperforms TV advertising in terms of revenue (Elasticity influencer marketing: .022 vs. elasticity TV advertisement: .018).

The elasticities of investments in advertising on pricing and shopping websites (.032), display advertising (.019) and SEM investments (.016) on orders are higher than that of investments in social media influencers. In contrast, the elasticities of offline advertising (.013) and affiliate marketing (.010) are lower in terms of orders. With regard to revenue, investments in SEM (.021) and advertising on pricing and shopping websites (.019) have a higher influence. The elasticity of offline advertising (.018) is about the same. Moreover, the cumulative elasticities of affiliate marketing (.012) and display advertising (.008) on revenue line up

**Table 4.8** Cumulative Elasticities

| Impulse in… | Response of… | Visits | Orders | Revenue | TV | Social Media Influencer | SEO | SEM | Pricing and Shopping |
|---|---|---|---|---|---|---|---|---|---|
| TV | Elasticity | - | .016 | .035 | | .388 | - | -.015 | .043 |
|  | I/O | - | 2/2 | 2/3 | | 1/2 | - | 1/1 | 2/3 |
| Social Media Influencer | Elasticity | .013 | .015 | .018 | .309 | | .042 | - | - |
|  | I/O | 1/1 | 1/1 | 1/1 | 1/1 | | 1/1 | - | - |
| SEO | Elasticity | - | - | - | - | | | - | - |
|  | I/O | - | - | - | - | | | - | - |
| SEM | Elasticity | .022 | .016 | .021 | -.639 | | - | - | .016 |
|  | I/O | 1/1 | 1/1 | 1/1 | 1/2 | | - | - | 1/1 |
| Pricing and Shopping | Elasticity | .024 | .032 | .019 | - | .152 | - | .009 | |
|  | I/O | 1/3 | 1/3 | 1/1 | - | 1/1 | - | 1/2 | |
| Display | Elasticity | .011 | .019 | .008 | - | - | .073 | - | - |
|  | I/O | 1/2 | 1/1 | 1/3 | - | - | 3/3 | - | - |
| Affiliate | Elasticity | .008 | .010 | .012 | -.328 | .156 | - | - | -.001 |
|  | I/O | 1/1 | 1/1 | 1/1 | 1/1 | 1/1 | - | - | 1/3 |
| Offline | Elasticity | .010 | .013 | .018 | -.406 | -.126 | - | .014 | .015 |
|  | I/O | 1/1 | 1/1 | 1/1 | 1/1 | 1/1 | - | 1/1 | 1/1 |
| Engagement | Elasticity | -.004 | - | - | - | .127 | .071 | .024 | - |
|  | I/O | 2/3 | - | - | - | 1/1 | 1/1 | 1/1 | - |
| Valence Instagram | Elasticity | - | .011 | .016 | .266 | - | -.073 | .015 | .020 |
|  | I/O | - | 1/1 | 1/1 | 1/1 | - | 3/3 | 1/1 | 1/1 |
| Volume Review | Elasticity | .013 | .011 | - | - | .132 | -.008 | - | - |
|  | I/O | 1/1 | 1/1 | - | - | 1/1 | 1/3 | - | - |
| Valence Review | Elasticity | - | - | - | - | -.144 | - | - | - |
|  | I/O | - | - | - | - | 2/2 | - | - | - |
| Visits | Elasticity | | .026 | .031 | - | .283 | - | .036 | .070 |
|  | I/O | | 1/1 | 1/1 | - | 1/2 | - | 1/1 | 1/2 |
| Orders | Elasticity | .028 | | .028 | - | .105 | - | -.017 | - |
|  | I/O | 1/2 | | 1/4 | - | 1/1 | - | 3/3 | - |
| Revenue | Elasticity | .020 | .056 | | -.262 | -.101 | .050 | - | -.015 |
|  | I/O | 1/1 | 1/1 | | 1/1 | 1/1 | 1/1 | - | 1/1 |

(continued)

## 4.4 Results of Study 2

**Table 4.8** (continued)

| Impulse in... | | Display | Affiliate | Offline | Engagement | Valence Instagram | Volume Review | Valence Review |
|---|---|---|---|---|---|---|---|---|
| TV | Elasticity | - | -.050 | -.509 | - | .016 | -.055 | -.006 |
|  | I/O | - | 1/1 | 1/1 | - | 1/1 | 2/2 | 2/2 |
| Social Media Influencer | Elasticity | - | .060 | -.351 | .105 | - | .061 | - |
|  | I/O | - | 1/1 | 1/1 | 1/1 | - | 1/1 | - |
| SEO | Elasticity | -.028 | -.045 | - | .055 | - | .058 | - |
|  | I/O | - | 1/1 | - | 1/1 | - | 1/1 | - |
| SEM | Elasticity | - | - | - | .089 | .011 | - | - |
|  | I/O | - | - | - | 1/1 | 1/1 | - | - |
| Pricing and Shopping | Elasticity | .028 | .173 | - | - | .012 | - | - |
|  | I/O | 1/2 | 1/4 | - | - | 1/1 | - | - |
| Display | Elasticity | - | -.225 | - | - | -.010 | .083 | .000 |
|  | I/O | - | 1/4 | - | - | 1/1 | 3/3 | 1/1 |
| Affiliate | Elasticity | - | - | - | .096 | - | .056 | .008 |
|  | I/O | - | - | - | 1/1 | - | 1/1 | 1/2 |
| Offline | Elasticity | - | - | - | - | - | .170 | -.001 |
|  | I/O | - | - | - | - | - | 2/3 | 1/2 |
| Engagement | Elasticity | - | .071 | - | - | - | -.058 | .003 |
|  | I/O | - | 1/1 | - | - | - | 3/3 | 1/1 |
| Valence Instagram | Elasticity | - | - | .487 | - | - | - | -.004 |
|  | I/O | - | - | 2/2 | - | - | - | 2/2 |
| Volume Review | Elasticity | - | .050 | - | - | - | - | .005 |
|  | I/O | - | 1/1 | - | - | - | - | 1/1 |
| Valence Review | Elasticity | .035 | - | -.504 | .058 | -.015 | .072 | - |
|  | I/O | 1/1 | - | 1/1 | 1/1 | 2/2 | 1/1 | - |
| Visits | Elasticity | .117 | - | .442 | - | - | .139 | - |
|  | I/O | 1/1 | - | 1/1 | - | - | 1/3 | - |
| Orders | Elasticity | .032 | - | .339 | - | .014 | .059 | - |
|  | I/O | 1/1 | - | 1/1 | - | 1/1 | 3/3 | - |
| Revenue | Elasticity | - | - | - | - | - | .038 | - |
|  | I/O | - | - | - | - | - | 1/2 | - |

Source: Author's own illustration. Notes: Dashes indicate insignificant effects. Empty cells indicate own effects, which were not examined. I/O = Wear-in/Wear-out, Wear-in indicates the week in which the effect first occurs, wear-out indicates the week in which the effect dies out.

after that of influencer advertising. As for visits, the elasticity of display advertising on revenue is relatively high in week one (.023) and then becomes negative in week three (−.015), reducing the cumulative elasticity. Accordingly, targeting and retargeting by display advertising leads to a forward shift in consumption.

Again, the effects of investments in advertising on pricing and shopping websites (weeks 1–3) on orders last longer than the effects of the other channels. Further, the effect of TV advertising (week 2–3) and display advertising (week 1–3) on revenue last longer than the effects of the other channels. SEO investments has no significant effect on orders or revenue. The same explanation as for the missing effect of SEO investments on visits applies here.

Comparing the effectiveness of investments in social media influencer campaigns with the effectiveness of firm-generated social media messages shows that the engagement with firm-generated posts on Instagram (−.004) has a negative but smaller effect on visits than the investments on social media influencers. The significant effects occur at week two and three. However, these effects run in opposite directions. In week two, the elasticity of engagement with firm-generated posts on Instagram is significantly positive (.011), followed by an abrupt decline in engagement leading to a negative elasticity in week three (−.015) and thus also a negative cumulative elasticity of −.004.

These results support the Chief Executive Officer's (CEO) assumption that the current posts do not foster sustainable customer relationships. There is a high level of engagement, especially with video posts, which were also linked to giveaway campaigns. In discussions with the company's management, it became clear that one potential reason for the negative effect could be that these posts address the wrong target group. So-called "it-pieces" are used as giveaways for these posts. It could be that this type of product motivates social media users who are only looking for free products to show short-term engagement with the company. Delayed, this is then reflected in the decline of customer interest through website visits, as this does not lead to sustainable customer engagement in the long run. This conclusion is supported by the result that the positive effects for engagement with firm-generated posts on Instagram do not transfer to orders and revenue.

Comparing the effectiveness of investments in social media influencer campaigns with the effectiveness of consumer-generated social media messages shows that the volume of consumer-generated reviews (.013) has an equally strong influence on visits. However, recommendations through influencers are more manageable than consumer reviews. Moreover, the volume of consumer-generated reviews positively affects orders (.011). The elasticity of volume of consumer-generated reviews for orders is thus lower than that of social media

## 4.4 Results of Study 2

influencer investments. Further, there is no significant effect of volume of consumer-generated reviews on revenue.

Even though the valence of consumer-generated comments on Instagram has no influence on visits, it has a positive effect on orders and revenue. A 1% increase of valance of consumer-generated comments on Instagram leads to .011% increase in orders and .016% increase in revenue, respectively. Comparing the influence of social media influencer investments with the valence of consumer-generated Instagram comments on orders and revenue, the influence of social media influencer investments is higher. Further, the analysis of IRFs shows no significant influence of valence of consumer-generated reviews on visits, orders or revenue.

### 4.4.2 Interrelationships among Marketing Activities and Social Media Messages

Several significant positive as well as negative associations can be observed between channel investments. However, these associations do not reflect concrete management decisions in which investments are withdrawn from one channel and invested in another one in the short term. Rather, they illustrate the company's overall strategy.

The company pursues different goals with the individual channels and this is also reflected in the interrelationships of the variables. The company uses TV investments to increase brand awareness. Figure 4.4 clearly shows that the company invests continuously in TV, apart from the fall holidays as well as the Christmas and Easter holidays, when investments in TV are reduced.

In contrast, digital channels are used specifically to promote the later stages of the consumer decision journey. They therefore show more seasonally driven investments. Figure 4.5 illustrates these seasonal effects. As customer demand for specific products increases in these seasonal phases, higher budgets are invested in digital channels to motivate customers to buy. Therefore, the negative associations between TV advertisement and these channels should not be overestimated as they are not based on strategic budget decisions between channels.

However, social media influencer investments and TV investments are positively associated. Figure 4.6 shows the patterns of influencer marketing and TV investments. Unlike TV investments, the cuts for influencer marketing due to the holidays are not as extreme. The two lows in influencer investments towards the middle and end of 2018 are due to measurement and are caught within the control variables. The figure illustrates that influencer marketing investments are also

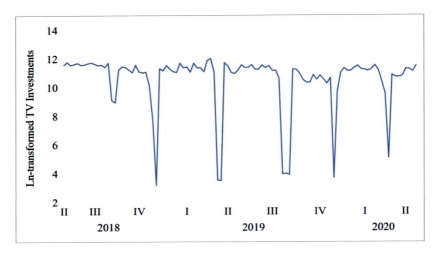

**Figure 4.4** TV Investments over time. Source: Author's own illustration.

made continuously to strengthen brand awareness. Therefore, both channels contribute to the same company goal. Due to the growing influence of influencers on brand awareness within the company's main target group, the company plans to transfer TV budget to influencer marketing in the long term.

Meanwhile, the results are an indication that the company utilizes social media influencer messages as supplement and complement of traditional channels, such as TV. Previous research has already shown that companies use social media messages to target consumers more effectively and thus increase the effectiveness of traditional channels (De Vries, Gensler, and Leeflang 2017).

Furthermore, one of the marketing managers stated that marketing tools, such as Google shopping and influencer campaigns, are used to target consumers at different stages of the decision journey. This is supported by the positive associations between influencer marketing investments and investments in other digital channels.

Only investments in offline advertising are deliberately kept low due to strategic management decisions if other campaigns are already running via salient media like TV or influencer marketing. Offline advertising includes package inserts or targeted postal mailings with discount codes. If discount codes are

## 4.4 Results of Study 2

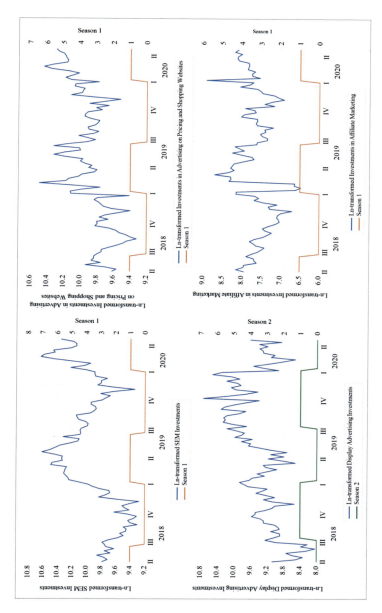

**Figure 4.5** Seasonality of Investments in SEM, Pricing and Shopping Websites, Display and Affiliate Marketing. Source: Author's own illustration.

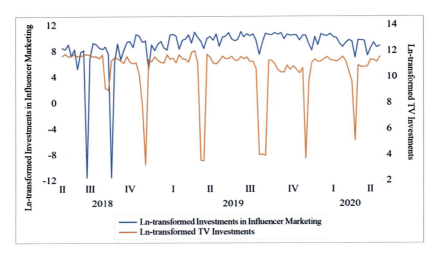

**Figure 4.6** TV and Influencer Marketing Investments over time. Source: Author's own illustration.

already very present in other advertising formats, offline advertising is deliberately scaled down by the company so that customers are not confused by different offers.

From the associations between marketing investments and firm-generated social media messages, relevant connections can be derived that can be included in future management decisions. There is a positive association of engagement with firm-generated content on Instagram and investments in social media influencers (.105), affiliate marketing (.096), SEM (.089) and SEO (.055). Therefore, the company can strategically invest in e.g. influencer marketing if it wants to increase engagement with firm-generated content. Moreover, a positive association of engagement with firm-generated content on Instagram and valence of consumer reviews (.058) suggests that firm-generated social media posting encourages interactions with consumers who have already made purchases.

Furthermore, through the observed associations of consumer-generated content and marketing investments, marketing managers gain insights into consumer response to company activities. The valence of consumer-generated comments on firm-generated Instagram posts is positively associated with TV advertising (.016), advertising on pricing and shopping websites (.012) and SEM investments (.011). However, the valence of consumer-generated Instagram comments

## 4.4 Results of Study 2

is negatively associated with display advertising (−.010). It could be that targeting as well as retargeting activities through display advertising within social media networks is perceived as intrusive by the consumer and lead to less positive comments on Instagram.

Moreover, the valence of consumer-generated Instagram comments is negatively associated with valence of consumer reviews (−.015). Consumer engagement on Instagram is positively associated with the valence of consumer-generated reviews, but valence of consumer-generated comments on Instagram is negatively related with the valence of consumer-generated reviews. This means that an increase in engagement on Instagram does not necessarily lead to an increase in valence of consumer-generated comments on Instagram. Therefore, the results indicate that users write rather neutral comments on high engagement giveaway posts. Consumers are encouraged to leave comments in this type of post, which are usually linked to a topic-specific question (e.g. "Let us know in the comments what your favorite sport is"), but do not say much about customer sentiment towards the brand. Figure 4.1 supports that a decrease in the valence of Instagram posts means that comments are becoming more neutral, but not negative. Moreover, this argumentation is in line with the negative effect of giveaways on the valence of consumer-generated Instagram comments (see Table 4.9).

The volume of consumer reviews is positively associated with various channels. The volume of consumer-generated reviews is positively connected with investments in offline advertising (.170), display advertising (.083), social media influencers (.061), SEO (.058) or affiliate marketing (.056). The volume of consumer reviews is negatively associated with TV advertising (−.055) and engagement with firm-generated social media posts (−.058). Moreover, volume of consumer reviews is positively associated with valence of consumer reviews (.072). This connection can be explained by the fact that positive reviews encourage other consumers to speak positively about the brand or to challenge this opinion.

This positive connection is also confirmed in the other direction (.005). Meaning that many positive comments in turn lead to even more consumers speaking positive about the brand. Moreover, the valence of consumer reviews is positively associated with investments in affiliate marketing (.008) and display advertising (.000) as well as with engagement with firm-generated social media posts (.003). The valence of consumer reviews is negatively connected to TV advertising (−.006) and offline advertising (−.001).

### 4.4.3 Performance Metrics and Feedback Effects

Visits positively influences the amount of orders and revenue by .026 and .031, respectively. This illustrates that customers are effectively moving along the consumer decision journey. Moreover, some feedback effects are observed. An increase of visits (1%) leads to an increase of investments in offline advertising (.442%), social media influencers (.283%), display advertising (.117%), advertising on pricing and shopping websites (.070%) and SEM (.036%). In terms of social media messages, visits are shown to have a positive impact on the volume of consumer reviews (.139).

Orders positively affect revenue (.028) from week one to four. Moreover, a 1% increase in orders leads to a .028% increase of visits in week one to two. This feedback loop shows that the performance of the company in turn also positively influences future performance. Like visits, orders also positively impact the investments in offline advertising (.339), social media influencer advertising (.105) and display advertising (.032). SEM investments, however, are negatively affected by orders ($-$.017) in week three. The consideration of feedback loops between orders and social media messages shows that orders have a positive feedback effect on the volume of consumer-generated reviews (.059, week 3) and the valence of consumer-generated comments (.012). These effects show that consumers who make an order tend to interact with the brand on social media afterwards.

The feedback loops between revenue and orders as well as visits again show that future performance is increased through past performance behavior. A 1% increase in revenue leads to a .020% increase in visits and a .056% increase in orders. Furthermore, effects from revenue on marketing activities are observed. SEO investments (.050) are positively affected by revenue. An increase in revenue of 1% leads to a decrease in investments in TV ($-$.262), social media influencers ($-$.101) and advertising on pricing and shopping websites ($-$.015). Like visits, revenue positively effects the volume of consumer-generated reviews (.038). Accordingly, increased firm performance leads to consumers increasingly talking about the brand online.

### 4.4.4 Effects of Control Variables

Table 4.9 shows the results of the VARX model and illustrates the effects of the control variables. The deterministic trend is significant and positive for investments in social media influencers ($\alpha = .017$), affiliate marketing ($\alpha = .005$) and

## 4.4 Results of Study 2

**Table 4.9** Parameter Estimates of the VARX Model

| | TV | Social Media Influencer | SEO | SEM | Pricing and Shopping | Display | Affiliate | Offline |
|---|---|---|---|---|---|---|---|---|
| TV $_{t-1}$ | **.459** | **.226** | -.038 | .005 | **.018** | **.022** | **.036** | .109 |
| TV $_{t-2}$ | **-.285** | **-.119** | .005 | .002 | -.004 | -.018 | **-.025** | **-.211** |
| Social Media Influencer $_{t-1}$ | -.026 | **.065** | -.023 | .001 | .001 | -.011 | .001 | -.062 |
| Social Media Influencer $_{t-2}$ | **-.091** | **-.056** | -.012 | .001 | .001 | -.013 | .000 | -.077 |
| SEO $_{t-1}$ | **-.746** | .097 | **-.571** | **.043** | -.018 | -.013 | .057 | .017 |
| SEO $_{t-2}$ | **-.568** | -.002 | -.265 | .017 | -.013 | **.094** | -.041 | -.256 |
| SEM $_{t-1}$ | **-6.820** | -.030 | -.207 | **.213** | .079 | **-.623** | -.229 | .682 |
| Pricing and Shopping $_{t-1}$ | -.642 | **1.318** | -.446 | **-.383** | .032 | .004 | -.348 | **-3.961** |
| Pricing and Shopping $_{t-1}$ | .054 | **1.159** | -.152 | **-.335** | **.159** | **.830** | **-.463** | .171 |
| Pricing and Shopping $_{t-2}$ | **2.234** | .348 | **-.688** | **.180** | -.014 | -.327 | **1.029** | 1.056 |
| Display $_{t-1}$ | **-1.074** | .268 | .030 | -.026 | .039 | **.478** | -.062 | -.576 |
| Display $_{t-2}$ | **1.667** | .348 | **.318** | .003 | .046 | .065 | **-.359** | **1.532** |
| Affiliate $_{t-1}$ | -.435 | .195 | -.243 | -.015 | .002 | -.007 | **.518** | -.536 |
| Affiliate $_{t-2}$ | **.810** | .074 | .069 | -.024 | **-.127** | **.171** | -.116 | -.164 |
| Offline $_{t-1}$ | -.029 | .035 | -.003 | **-.009** | -.001 | .004 | **.024** | .063 |
| Offline $_{t-2}$ | **-.122** | -.020 | **-.032** | .005 | **-.009** | -.016 | .009 | **.182** |
| Engagement $_{t-1}$ | **.718** | -.110 | **.188** | **-.033** | -.007 | **.102** | -.050 | .328 |
| Engagement $_{t-2}$ | **-.588** | **-.271** | -.088 | .021 | **-.053** | .003 | **-.111** | **-1.219** |
| Valence Instagram $_{t-1}$ | -.398 | **-1.195** | **.675** | **.228** | .057 | .134 | .173 | **7.356** |
| Valence Instagram $_{t-2}$ | **2.724** | -.258 | **-.805** | **-.183** | **-.361** | .007 | -.205 | **-2.707** |
| Volume Review $_{t-1}$ | .025 | -.009 | **.224** | -.011 | -.027 | **-.110** | **-.168** | **-.902** |
| Volume Review $_{t-2}$ | .016 | **.256** | **-.295** | .009 | .066 | **.150** | .079 | -.390 |
| Valence Review $_{t-1}$ | 1.967 | **-8.125** | .936 | -.247 | .417 | .274 | -.943 | 3.676 |
| Valence Review $_{t-2}$ | -6.051 | 3.534 | -.149 | **1.055** | .547 | **-1.977** | .885 | **25.308** |
| Visits $_{t-1}$ | **11.664** | 1.861 | .862 | -.136 | .180 | -.159 | -.238 | 3.801 |
| Visits $_{t-2}$ | **6.540** | **-1.965** | **1.144** | .349 | **.216** | -.161 | -.172 | -1.371 |
| Orders $_{t-1}$ | **-22.712** | -1.461 | .287 | **.901** | **-1.160** | -.843 | 1.287 | **17.629** |
| Orders $_{t-2}$ | **16.348** | **6.121** | .381 | **-1.505** | .148 | **2.289** | **-1.990** | -13.019 |
| Revenue $_{t-1}$ | **16.212** | .777 | .133 | **-.622** | **1.135** | .542 | -.483 | -10.196 |
| Revenue $_{t-2}$ | **-15.016** | **-2.211** | .530 | **1.091** | .015 | **-2.032** | 1.517 | **14.577** |

(continued)

**Table 4.9** (continued)

| | Engagement | Valence Instagram | Volume Review | Valence Review | Visits | Orders | Revenue |
|---|---|---|---|---|---|---|---|
| TV $_{t-1}$ | .011 | -.008 | -.039 | -.004 | .010 | .015 | .018 |
| TV $_{t-2}$ | .033 | -.001 | -.003 | -.002 | -.003 | -.001 | .001 |
| Social Media Influencer $_{t-1}$ | .034 | -.002 | -.003 | .000 | -.004 | -.002 | -.002 |
| Social Media Influencer $_{t-2}$ | .005 | -.004 | .001 | .000 | -.005 | -.001 | .000 |
| SEO $_{t-1}$ | -.075 | .019 | -.020 | -.004 | .025 | .008 | .002 |
| SEO $_{t-2}$ | -.156 | .023 | -.017 | -.007 | .006 | -.018 | -.025 |
| SEM $_{t-1}$ | .084 | .068 | .042 | -.029 | .098 | .042 | .026 |
| Pricing and Shopping $_{t-1}$ | .565 | -.212 | -.535 | .026 | -.183 | -.188 | -.224 |
| Pricing and Shopping $_{t-2}$ | .427 | .026 | .018 | .041 | -.190 | -.085 | -.105 |
| Pricing and Shopping $_{t-2}$ | -.523 | .078 | -.548 | -.035 | .310 | .247 | .260 |
| Display $_{t-1}$ | -.343 | .053 | .199 | -.007 | -.043 | -.022 | -.063 |
| Display $_{t-2}$ | -.046 | -.111 | .226 | .006 | -.052 | -.034 | -.013 |
| Affiliate $_{t-1}$ | -.326 | .052 | -.078 | .021 | -.012 | .014 | .000 |
| Affiliate $_{t-2}$ | .028 | .004 | -.248 | -.020 | .000 | .013 | .019 |
| Offline $_{t-1}$ | .029 | -.007 | .061 | .001 | .001 | .002 | .002 |
| Offline $_{t-2}$ | -.031 | -.004 | .028 | -.003 | -.008 | -.004 | -.003 |
| Engagement $_{t-1}$ | .099 | .000 | -.060 | -.010 | .045 | .029 | .034 |
| Engagement $_{t-2}$ | -.131 | -.007 | -.138 | .006 | -.049 | -.036 | -.032 |
| Valence Instagram $_{t-1}$ | -.695 | .003 | .663 | -.058 | .193 | .104 | .132 |
| Valence Intagram $_{t-2}$ | -.343 | -.152 | -.301 | -.015 | -.117 | -.068 | -.020 |
| Volume Review $_{t-1}$ | .119 | .023 | .127 | .008 | .011 | .005 | -.010 |
| Volume Review $_{t-2}$ | -.056 | -.001 | -.064 | .004 | .020 | .031 | .039 |
| Valence Review $_{t-1}$ | 1.625 | -.968 | 2.377 | -.182 | -.578 | -.319 | -.096 |
| Valence Review $_{t-2}$ | 2.522 | -.805 | -.917 | -.333 | .159 | .132 | .225 |
| Visits $_{t-1}$ | -.149 | .152 | -.474 | .056 | -.188 | .247 | .297 |
| Visits $_{t-2}$ | .535 | .187 | .599 | .036 | .192 | .255 | .224 |
| Orders $_{t-1}$ | .808 | -.077 | -3.495 | -.135 | -.199 | .069 | -.398 |
| Orders $_{t-2}$ | .937 | .200 | .928 | .238 | -.319 | -.048 | -.054 |
| Revenue $_{t-1}$ | .154 | -.141 | 3.108 | .103 | -.126 | -.100 | .376 |
| Revenue $_{t-2}$ | -1.701 | -.118 | .063 | -.185 | .066 | .032 | .043 |

(continued)

## 4.4 Results of Study 2

**Table 4.9** (continued)

| | TV | Social Media Influencer | SEO | SEM | Pricing and Shopping | Display | Affiliate |
|---|---|---|---|---|---|---|---|
| α | 28.034 | -53.810 | -11.231 | 3.087 | 3.425 | 7.986 | -.984 |
| δ₁ | -.011 | .017 | -.002 | .001 | .002 | .003 | .005 |
| National Holidays | -.111 | -.071 | -.187 | -.012 | -.019 | .106 | -.035 |
| School Holidays | .262 | -.436 | .350 | -.012 | .016 | .007 | .011 |
| Corona | -.274 | -1.210 | -.177 | -.018 | .009 | -.249 | -.433 |
| Season 1 | -.145 | -.227 | .092 | .073 | .219 | -.404 | .460 |
| Season 2 | -1.927 | .342 | -.286 | .008 | -.013 | -.008 | .696 |
| Discount Rate | -26.026 | -.252 | -.345 | .643 | 1.111 | 2.191 | .406 |
| Buzz Events | -.804 | -.002 | -.289 | .033 | .049 | .290 | -.164 |
| SEO Event | -.740 | -.250 | 2.599 | .060 | .065 | -.019 | .362 |
| Store Openings | -.587 | -.798 | .102 | -.075 | -.080 | -.154 | -.017 |
| Engagement Competitors | .125 | -.149 | .324 | -.123 | -.054 | -.230 | -.254 |
| Valence Instagram Competitors | 3.409 | 1.485 | .031 | -.294 | -.196 | -.497 | .659 |
| Volume Review Competitors | -.147 | -.603 | -.320 | -.049 | -.044 | -.030 | .068 |
| Valence Review Competitors | -3.026 | 1.344 | .270 | -.064 | -.059 | -.155 | -.274 |
| Nielsen Competitors | .401 | .008 | -.069 | -.019 | -.035 | -.043 | -.041 |
| Engagement Event | .491 | -.850 | -.187 | .108 | -.056 | -.167 | .527 |
| Influencer Measure | -1.306 | 19.410 | -.337 | .037 | .024 | .228 | .137 |
| Giveaway | -.041 | .242 | -.054 | -.034 | -.032 | -.125 | -.211 |
| R² | .603 | .963 | .682 | .568 | .860 | .832 | .733 |
| Adj. R² | .236 | .929 | .389 | .169 | .731 | .677 | .486 |

(continued)

**Table 4.9** (continued)

|  | Offline | Engagement | Valence Instagram | Volume Review | Valence Review | Visits | Orders | Revenue |
|---|---|---|---|---|---|---|---|---|
| α | **-110.405** | **19.931** | **3.342** | -10.216 | .668 | **7.921** | **9.726** | **11.730** |
| $\delta_i$ | -.025 | **.018** | -.001 | -.007 | .000 | **.001** | **.001** | **.002** |
| National Holidays | .152 | .073 | **.044** | **.161** | **-.020** | -.005 | -.028 | **-.042** |
| School Holidays | **-1.474** | .132 | -.014 | .056 | **.028** | -.026 | .006 | .003 |
| Corona | -1.016 | **-.862** | .045 | .258 | **.039** | **-.097** | -.017 | -.046 |
| Season 1 | .573 | -.095 | .025 | -.096 | **-.038** | **.117** | **.112** | **.128** |
| Season 2 | .646 | -.100 | .055 | -.126 | **-.034** | **.074** | **.059** | **.064** |
| Discount Rate | **11.046** | **-3.107** | **-1.276** | **9.531** | **-.430** | **1.210** | **2.826** | **3.053** |
| Buzz Events | -.268 | **-.314** | **.103** | -.185 | .014 | **.046** | **.070** | **.078** |
| SEO Event | .732 | **-.348** | **-.119** | -.344 | -.005 | .095 | **.168** | **.291** |
| Store Openings | .467 | **.186** | -.005 | -.021 | .006 | **-.034** | -.030 | -.032 |
| Engagement Competitors | .134 | -.161 | **-.061** | **-.323** | .011 | **-.123** | **-.093** | **-.099** |
| Valence Instagram Competitors | 2.865 | -.201 | .016 | .371 | .012 | -.065 | -.009 | .041 |
| Volume Review Competitors | **-1.624** | -.189 | **.061** | .284 | .009 | -.030 | .011 | .018 |
| Valence Review Competitors | **2.215** | .203 | **.144** | .246 | **.033** | -.061 | **-.131** | **-.143** |
| Nielsen Competitors | -.426 | -.097 | .009 | .092 | **.012** | -.025 | **.044** | **.040** |
| Engagement Event | 1.194 | **.783** | **.171** | **-.647** | **-.033** | .034 | .004 | -.006 |
| Influencer Measure | .086 | .144 | **.145** | .267 | -.007 | .030 | .012 | -.013 |
| Giveaway | **-.938** | **.449** | **-.179** | **-.248** | .004 | **-.057** | -.010 | .002 |
| R² | .457 | .724 | .680 | .697 | .580 | .685 | .866 | .880 |
| Adj. R² | -.044 | .468 | .384 | .417 | .192 | .394 | .742 | .768 |
| **Fit Statistics full VARX model** | | | | | | | | |
| Determinant resid covariance (df adj.) | | | | 2.42E-22 | | | | |
| Determinant resid covariance | | | | 1.14E-26 | | | | |
| Log likelihood | | | | 866.823 | | | | |
| Akaike information criterion | | | | -2.610 | | | | |
| Schwarz criterion | | | | 16.420 | | | | |

Source: Author's own illustration. Notes: Since the parameters of the endogenous variables of a VARX model cannot be interpreted, the IRF analyses are used for the interpretation. N = 101 after adjustments. **Bold value**: |t-statistic| > 1.

## 4.4 Results of Study 2

advertising on pricing and shopping websites ($\alpha = .002$). This indicates that these investments increase over time. Moreover, it is observed that the engagement on Instagram with firm-generated content increases over time ($\alpha = .018$). This can be explained by the increase of video and giveaway posts, which lead to higher views and thus to higher engagement. Besides, this explains that the deterministic trend of valence of consumer-generated comments is significant and negative ($\alpha = -.001$), indicating that the valence of consumer-generated comments decreases over time. Giveaway post motivate rather neutral comments. Therefore, the valence of consumer-generated comments decreases through an increase of this type of posts. The volume of consumer-generated reviews also decreases over time. Since there are already many reviews of the company on the review website and they are mostly positive, as the descriptives show, some consumers may refrain from writing reviews with similar content. Further, the deterministic trends for visits ($\alpha = .001$), orders ($\alpha = .001$) and revenue ($\alpha = .002$) are significant and positive. This speaks for a steady growth of consumer interest and firm performance.

On national holidays, SEO investments decrease ($-.187$), as these investments are mainly driven by the cost of human resources that adapt company content to the Google algorithm. Looking at the influence on social media messages, it is observed that the valence of Instagram comments increases ($.044$). Moreover, on national holidays the volume of consumer-generated reviews increases ($.161$), however, the valence of consumer reviews decreases ($-.020$). Regarding the performance metrics, it can be observed that revenue decreases on national holidays ($-.042$).

School holidays decrease investments in offline advertising ($-1.474$) and social media influencers ($-.436$). Furthermore, school holidays influence SEO investments positively ($.350$). Considering consumer-generated content, school holidays increase the valence of consumer reviews ($.028$).

Like many other companies, the company initially cut its social media spending at the onset of the corona crisis. This is reflected in a negative impact of the corona dummy variable on social media influencer spending ($-1.210$). Moreover, corona negatively affects investments in affiliate marketing ($-.433$). Looking at the impact of the corona crisis on social media messages, it is observed that the engagement with firm-generated content on social media decreases significantly ($-.862$). However, corona has a positive and significant influence on the valence of consumer-generated reviews ($.039$). The impact of corona on website visits is negative ($-.097$). However, this effect is not robust within a model considering firm performance online. In this model the effect of corona on website visits is insignificant. Within this model, the impact of corona on online revenue is significant and positive (.098). In general, this can be explained by the increase in online purchases during the corona crisis (Statista 2022b). The positive effects of online revenue during this period are also driven by the closure of the company's offline stores and those of its competitors during the lockdown. Within the full model, corona has no significant effect on orders and revenue, as the negative effect of corona on offline revenue offsets the positive effect on online revenue.

Within the season, the demand for individual products increases enormously. Therefore, during this time, additional budget is invested in the digital channels. The seasonality of product type 1 positively affects the investments in affiliate marketing (.460) and advertising on pricing and shopping websites (.219) as well as SEM marketing spending (.073). Further, it has a negative effect on investments in display advertising ($-.404$). Considering the influence of season on consumer-generated content, the valence of consumer-generated reviews is negatively affected by the season for product type 1 ($-.038$). The season for product type 1 positively impacts visits (.117), orders (.112) and revenue (.128).

The season for product type 2 has a negative impact on investments in TV advertising ($-1.927$) and SEO investments ($-.286$). As for product type 1, the season for product type 2 has a positive impact on investments in affiliate marketing (.696). Looking at the impact on consumer-generated content, the season for product type 2 negatively affects the valence of consumer-generated reviews ($-.034$). However, the season for product type 2 has a positive impact on visits (.074), orders (.059) and revenue (.064).

An increase of the company's discount rate has a negative impact on the company's investments in TV advertising ($-26.026$). An increase in the discount rate has a positive effect on visits (1.210), orders (2.826), and revenue (3.053). This increase of consumer interest and purchase behavior can also be the reason why an increase of discount has a positive influence on volume of consumer-generated reviews (9.531). However, the valence of consumer-generated reviews ($-.430$) and comments on Instagram ($-1.276$) are negatively affected by an increase of discount rate.

When a buzz event occurs than the investments in SEO investments ($-.289$) decrease. Further, buzz events have a positive effect on the investments in display advertisement (.290). Looking at the impact on social media messages, buzz events negatively impact engagement with firm-generated content ($-.314$). However, buzz events have a positive impact on the valence of consumer-generated content on Instagram (.103). The company's performance is positively influenced by buzz events. Buzz events increase visits (.046), orders (.070) and revenue (.078).

## 4.4 Results of Study 2

The dummy for SEO events has a positive impact on SEO investments (2.599). Considering the influence on consumer-generated content, the dummy for SEO events negatively affects the valence of consumer-generated comments on Instagram (−.119). The SEO event effectively increases orders (.168) and revenue (.291).

Store openings have a significant negative impact on investments in social media influencers (−.798). Moreover, store openings negatively affect SEM investments (−.075) and the investments in advertising on pricing and shopping websites (−.080) as well as display advertisement (−.154). Considering the effects on social media messages, the opening of offline stores increases the engagement with firm-generated posts on Instagram (.186).

Looking at the performance measure, it is observed that store openings have a negative impact on visits on the company's website (−.034). Therefore, the opening of offline stores leads to a decrease in online attention. An estimation on online performance shows that the store openings have a significant negative impact on online orders (−.051) and online revenue (−.068). The results suggest that the offline stores cannibalize their own online business. However, no significant effect of offline store openings occurs on total orders and revenue, since the opening of offline stores generates additional sales.

The next section of controls considers the social media messages of the relevant competitors of the brand. An increase of consumer engagement with competitors' content on Instagram positively affects SEO investments (.324). Furthermore, an increase of consumer engagement with competitors' content on Instagram negatively affects investments in affiliate marketing (−.254), display advertising (−.230) and SEM (−.123). Looking at the impact on consumer-generated social media messages, an increase of consumer engagement with competitors' content on Instagram has a negative impact on the volume of consumer reviews about the brand (−.323) and the valence of consumer-generated comments on Instagram (−.061). The results on website visits, orders and revenue illustrate the high impact of competitor-generated content on consumer interest and firm performance. An increase of consumer engagement with competitors' content on Instagram has a significant negative impact on visits (−.123), orders (−.093) and revenue (−.099).

An increase of the valence of consumer comments on the competitors' Instagram page positively affects TV advertising (3.409) and affiliate marketing (.659). Furthermore, the valence of consumer comments on the competitors' Instagram page has a positive impact on social media influencers (1.485). An increase of the valence of consumer comments on the competitors' Instagram page negatively affects SEM investments (−.294).

The results on marketing activities illustrate that consumer-generated reviews about the company's competitors negatively affect investments in offline advertising (−1.624), social media influencers (−.603) and SEO (−.320). Considering the impact on consumer-generated social media messages, the volume of consumer-generated reviews about the company's competitors positively affects the volume of reviews about the company (.284) and the valence of consumer comments on the company's Instagram page (.061).

The valence of consumer-generated reviews on the company's competitors has a positive impact on offline advertising (2.215) and advertising through social media influencers (1.344), but a negative impact on TV advertisement (- 3.026). An increase of valence of consumer-generated reviews on the company's competitors increases the valence of consumer comments on the company's Instagram page (.144) and the valence of consumer-generated reviews (.033). However, valence of consumer-generated reviews on the company's competitors has a negative impact on firm performance and reduces orders (−.131) and revenue (−.143).

Further, orders (.044) and revenue (.040) are positively influenced by competitors' advertising spend. Considering the impact on the company's social media messages, general advertising spending of competitors has a positive impact on valence of consumer generated reviews about the brand (.012). These effects are certainly due to a general increase in marketing budgets in the industry.

The last category of control variables controls for anomalies in the data. A control variable is included for particular video posts associated with giveaways since these posts have an exceptionally high engagement compared to the usual posts. These video posts have a significant positive impact on investments in affiliate marketing (.527) and SEM (.108). Moreover, these high engagement posts have a significant negative impact on investments in social media influencers (−.850). These posts drive consumer engagement (.783) and valence of consumer-generated comments on Instagram (.171). Looking at consumer-generated reviews, the volume (−.647) and valence (−.033) of reviews on the brand is negatively influenced by these special video posts.

A dummy variable is included that controls for weeks in which the company attributed no costs for influencer marketing, but actually had ongoing campaigns. The influencer dummy variable has a positive impact on investments in social media influencers (19.410). The results on the impact on social media messages show that the valence of consumer-generated comments on Instagram is positively affected by the influencer dummy (.145).

Furthermore, a giveaway dummy is included that controls for weeks with giveaway postings. Giveaway postings negatively influence investments in offline advertising (−.938), affiliate marketing (−.211) and display advertising (−.125). The giveaway posts drive consumer engagement on Instagram (.449), but negatively influence the valence of consumer-generated comments (−.179). These results can be explained by the fact that giveaway posts usually encourage consumers to like the post and shortly answer brand un-related questions that are rather neutral and do not capture the customer sentiment. Looking at the performance measures, the results show that visits are negatively influenced by giveaway posts (−.057). As stated in the discussion on engagement, it is likely that giveaways motivate the wrong target group. Further, they may even reduce genuine buying interest, as potential customers wait to see if they can win the products. Furthermore, the giveaway dummy variable has a negative impact on volume of consumer-generated reviews (−.248).

### 4.4.5 Comparison with SUR Model

A SUR model is estimated to check whether the proposed VARX model is appropriate and robust. A SUR is a system of several regression equations, which can be calculated on their own as a regression (Greene 2003). Following the approach of De Vries, Gensler, and Leeflang (2017), a restricted model is chosen that assumes a certain ordering among website visits, orders and revenue. In the special case of a SUR with identical regressors with the exclusion restriction of a small subset of the regressors the SUR model outperforms the OLS regression (Greene 2003). Therefore, a SUR is estimated for comparison.

Table 4.10 illustrates the results of the SUR model. The results and the explanatory power of the model are comparable to the VARX model. Although the effect size and direction are comparable in both models, the significance of the parameters differs slightly in some cases. However, 85% of the model parameters are consistent in both models.

As Table 4.11 shows, the $R^2$ and the adjusted $R^2$ for all equations of the VARX model are higher than for the SUR model. The root mean square errors for the equations that capture the effects on website visits, orders and revenue are lower for the VARX model than for the SUR model. Furthermore, the VARX model fits conceptually better to the assumed relationships. The significant feedback loops and interdependencies suggest a dynamic system of endogenous variables rather than exogenous relationships. Therefore, the VARX model is generalizable and seems more appropriate.

**Table 4.10** SUR Model Estimates (Restricted Model with Lagged Effects)

| | TV | Social Media Influencer | SEO | SEM | Pricing and Shopping | Display | Affiliate |
|---|---|---|---|---|---|---|---|
| TV $_{t-1}$ | **.462** | .222 | -.038 | .004 | **.017** | .019 | **.035** |
| TV $_{t-2}$ | **-.278** | **-.133** | .004 | -.001 | **-.007** | **-.026** | **-.028** |
| Social Media Influencer $_{t-1}$ | -.028 | **.070** | -.022 | .002 | .002 | -.009 | .002 |
| Social Media Influencer $_{t-2}$ | **-.093** | **-.053** | -.012 | .001 | .002 | **-.011** | .000 |
| SEO $_{t-1}$ | **-.736** | .078 | **-.573** | **.040** | -.023 | -.024 | .052 |
| SEO $_{t-2}$ | **-.559** | -.019 | **-.267** | .014 | -.018 | .084 | -.045 |
| SEM $_{t-1}$ | **-6.796** | -.074 | -.212 | **.205** | .067 | **-.649** | -.239 |
| Pricing and Shopping $_{t-1}$ | -.572 | **1.193** | **.461** | **-.408** | -.002 | -.073 | **-.377** |
| Pricing and Shopping $_{t-1}$ | .137 | **1.007** | -.169 | **-.365** | **.119** | **.738** | **-.498** |
| Pricing and Shopping $_{t-2}$ | **2.324** | .187 | **-.706** | **.148** | -.057 | **-.425** | **.992** |
| Display $_{t-1}$ | **-1.027** | .184 | .020 | **-.043** | .016 | **.428** | -.081 |
| Display $_{t-2}$ | **1.642** | **.396** | **.322** | .012 | **.059** | .093 | **-.348** |
| Affiliate $_{t-1}$ | -.389 | .112 | **-.253** | -.031 | -.020 | -.057 | **.499** |
| Affiliate $_{t-2}$ | **.827** | .043 | .065 | -.030 | **-.135** | **.152** | **-.123** |
| Offline $_{t-1}$ | -.026 | .030 | -.004 | **-.010** | -.003 | .001 | **.023** |
| Offline $_{t-2}$ | **-.120** | -.022 | **-.032** | .004 | **-.010** | **-.018** | .008 |
| Engagement $_{t-1}$ | **.720** | **-.113** | **.188** | **-.034** | -.008 | **.100** | -.051 |
| Engagement $_{t-2}$ | **-.564** | **-.315** | **-.093** | .013 | **-.065** | -.023 | **-.121** |
| Valence Instagram $_{t-1}$ | -.434 | **-1.125** | **.682** | **.241** | .075 | .174 | .189 |
| Valence Instagram $_{t-2}$ | **2.763** | -.327 | **-.813** | **-.197** | **-.379** | -.036 | -.220 |
| Volume Review $_{t-1}$ | .054 | -.063 | **.218** | -.022 | **-.041** | **-.143** | **-.180** |
| Volume Review $_{t-2}$ | .040 | **.213** | **-.300** | .000 | **.054** | .124 | .069 |
| Valence Review $_{t-1}$ | **1.895** | **-7.986** | .950 | -.221 | **.452** | .354 | -.911 |
| Valence Review $_{t-1}$ | **-6.389** | **4.150** | -.079 | **1.176** | **.711** | **-1.606** | **1.027** |
| Valence Review $_{t-2}$ | **11.676** | **1.839** | **.859** | -.141 | .174 | -.173 | -.243 |
| Visits $_{t-1}$ | **6.659** | **-2.184** | **1.119** | **.306** | **.157** | -.292 | -.223 |
| Visits $_{t-2}$ | **-22.993** | **-1.007** | .354 | **.999** | **-1.029** | -.544 | **1.386** |
| Orders $_{t-1}$ | **15.885** | **6.950** | .479 | **-1.340** | .372 | **2.795** | **-1.800** |
| Orders $_{t-2}$ | **16.019** | 1.180 | .164 | **-.551** | **1.234** | .761 | -.386 |
| Revenue $_{t-1}$ | **-14.922** | -2.370 | .508 | **1.058** | -.029 | **-2.134** | **1.481** |

(continued)

## 4.4 Results of Study 2

**Table 4.10** (continued)

| | Offline | Engagement | Valence Instagram | Volume Review | Valence Review | Visits | Orders | Revenue |
|---|---|---|---|---|---|---|---|---|
| $TV_{t-1}$ | .100 | .011 | -.008 | -.040 | -.004 | .008 | .014 | .017 |
| $TV_{t-2}$ | -.239 | .032 | -.001 | -.009 | -.002 | -.008 | -.004 | -.002 |
| Social Media Influencer$_{t-1}$ | -.051 | .034 | -.002 | -.001 | .000 | -.002 | -.001 | -.001 |
| Social Media Influencer$_{t-2}$ | -.071 | .005 | -.004 | .002 | .000 | -.004 | -.001 | .000 |
| $SEO_{t-1}$ | -.025 | -.078 | .018 | -.027 | -.004 | .018 | .004 | -.003 |
| $SEO_{t-2}$ | -.293 | -.158 | .022 | -.023 | -.007 | .000 | -.022 | -.029 |
| $SEM_{t-1}$ | .587 | .079 | .067 | .024 | -.029 | .081 | .032 | .015 |
| Pricing and Shopping$_{t-1}$ | -4.223 | .552 | -.214 | -.585 | .025 | -.231 | -.215 | -.253 |
| Pricing and Shopping$_{t-1}$ | -.152 | .410 | .023 | -.043 | .039 | -.247 | -.119 | -.141 |
| Pricing and Shopping$_{t-2}$ | .715 | -.540 | .075 | -.613 | -.037 | .248 | .212 | .222 |
| Display$_{t-1}$ | -.753 | -.352 | .051 | .166 | -.008 | -.075 | -.041 | -.082 |
| Display$_{t-2}$ | 1.637 | -.040 | -.110 | .245 | .007 | -.035 | -.023 | -.001 |
| Affiliate$_{t-1}$ | -.711 | -.335 | .050 | -.111 | .020 | -.043 | -.004 | -.019 |
| Affiliate$_{t-2}$ | -.230 | .025 | .003 | -.260 | -.020 | -.012 | .006 | .011 |
| Offline$_{t-1}$ | .054 | .029 | -.007 | .059 | .001 | -.001 | .001 | .001 |
| Offline$_{t-2}$ | .177 | -.032 | -.004 | .027 | -.003 | -.009 | -.005 | -.004 |
| Engagement$_{t-1}$ | .322 | .099 | .000 | -.061 | -.010 | .044 | .028 | .034 |
| Engagement$_{t-2}$ | -1.312 | -.136 | -.008 | -.156 | .005 | -.066 | -.046 | -.043 |
| Valence Instagram$_{t-1}$ | 7.507 | -.687 | .005 | .691 | -.057 | .218 | .120 | .149 |
| Valence Intagram$_{t-2}$ | -2.850 | -.350 | -.153 | -.329 | -.016 | -.144 | -.083 | -.036 |
| Volume Review$_{t-1}$ | -1.015 | .113 | .021 | .105 | .007 | -.009 | -.007 | -.023 |
| Volume Review$_{t-2}$ | -.481 | -.061 | -.002 | -.081 | .004 | .003 | .021 | .029 |
| Valence Review$_{t-1}$ | 3.978 | 1.642 | .964 | 2.431 | -.180 | -.529 | -.287 | -.062 |
| Valence Review$_{t-2}$ | 26.611 | 2.588 | -.792 | -.672 | -.324 | .391 | .268 | .369 |
| Visits$_{t-1}$ | 3.757 | -.151 | .151 | -.482 | .056 | -.197 | .243 | .293 |
| Visits$_{t-2}$ | -1.840 | .511 | .182 | .512 | .033 | .110 | .206 | .171 |
| Orders$_{t-1}$ | 18.525 | .847 | -.075 | -3.308 | -.128 | | .158 | -.304 |
| Orders$_{t-2}$ | -11.279 | 1.025 | .216 | 1.259 | .249 | | .133 | .137 |
| Revenue$_{t-1}$ | -9.283 | .207 | -.125 | 3.262 | .107 | | | .483 |
| Revenue$_{t-2}$ | 14.255 | -1.716 | -.120 | -.002 | -.187 | | | .008 |

(continued)

**Table 4.10** (continued)

| | TV | Social Media Influencer | SEO | SEM | Pricing and Shopping | Display | Affiliate |
|---|---|---|---|---|---|---|---|
| α | 33.938 | -64.804 | -12.410 | .973 | .531 | 1.471 | -3.546 |
| $\delta_i$ | -.011 | .016 | -.002 | .001 | .002 | .003 | .005 |
| National Holidays | -.097 | -.095 | -.190 | -.017 | -.025 | .091 | -.041 |
| School Holidays | .221 | -.363 | .358 | .002 | .036 | .051 | .028 |
| Corona | -.251 | -1.249 | -.182 | -.026 | -.001 | -.273 | -.441 |
| Season 1 | -.127 | -.260 | .088 | .067 | .210 | -.424 | .453 |
| Season 2 | -1.982 | .444 | -.275 | .028 | .014 | .053 | .720 |
| Discount Rate | -25.564 | -1.049 | -.448 | .480 | .891 | 1.691 | .226 |
| Buzz Events | -.844 | .070 | -.281 | .047 | .068 | .334 | -.147 |
| SEO Event | -.746 | -.241 | 2.600 | .062 | .068 | -.013 | .364 |
| Store Openings | -.572 | -.828 | .099 | -.080 | -.088 | -.171 | -.024 |
| Engagement Competitors | .130 | -.156 | .323 | -.124 | -.056 | -.235 | -.255 |
| Valence Instagram Competitors | 3.419 | 1.465 | .029 | -.298 | -.201 | -.508 | .654 |
| Volume Review Competitors | -.120 | -.654 | -.326 | -.059 | -.057 | -.061 | .056 |
| Valence Review Competitors | -2.999 | 1.295 | .264 | -.073 | -.071 | -.184 | -.285 |
| Nielsen Competitors | .426 | -.036 | -.075 | -.028 | -.047 | -.070 | -.051 |
| Engagement Event | .554 | -.963 | -.200 | .086 | -.086 | -.235 | .501 |
| Influencer Measure | -1.372 | 19.530 | -.324 | .061 | .056 | .300 | .165 |
| Giveaway | -.050 | .258 | -.052 | -.031 | -.028 | -.116 | -.207 |
| RMSE | 1.295 | .607 | .290 | .083 | .093 | .224 | .234 |
| $R^2$ | .602 | .963 | .682 | .555 | .854 | .826 | .732 |
| $\chi^2$ | 153.980 | 2661.140 | 218.300 | 133.540 | 636.460 | 507.560 | 278.480 |
| p-value | .000 | .000 | .000 | .000 | .000 | .000 | .000 |

(continued)

**Table 4.10** (continued)

| | Offline | Engagement | Valence Instagram | Volume Review | Valence Review | Visits | Orders | Revenue |
|---|---|---|---|---|---|---|---|---|
| α | -134.007 | 18.690 | 3.073 | -14.555 | .530 | 3.906 | 7.238 | 9.087 |
| $\delta_i$ | -.026 | .018 | -.001 | -.007 | .000 | .001 | .001 | .002 |
| National Holidays | .102 | .070 | .044 | .151 | -.021 | -.015 | -.034 | -.047 |
| School Holidays | -1.319 | .139 | -.013 | .085 | .029 | .002 | .022 | .020 |
| Corona | -1.095 | -.865 | .045 | .242 | .038 | -.113 | -.024 | -.055 |
| Season 1 | .504 | -.098 | .025 | -.109 | -.038 | .105 | .105 | .120 |
| Season 2 | .864 | -.089 | .057 | -.086 | -.032 | .112 | .082 | .088 |
| Discount Rate | 9.408 | -3.186 | -1.287 | 9.209 | -.441 | .889 | 2.659 | 2.876 |
| Buzz Events | -.113 | -.306 | .105 | -.156 | .015 | .073 | .086 | .095 |
| SEO Event | .750 | -.347 | -.119 | -.341 | -.005 | .099 | .169 | .293 |
| Store Openings | .403 | .183 | -.006 | -.032 | .005 | -.045 | -.037 | -.039 |
| Engagement Competitors | .120 | -.161 | -.061 | -.326 | .011 | -.126 | -.094 | -.101 |
| Valence Instagram Competitors | 2.823 | -.203 | .016 | .364 | .011 | -.072 | -.014 | .036 |
| Volume Review Competitors | -1.732 | -.194 | .059 | .264 | .008 | -.049 | .000 | .006 |
| Valence Review Competitors | 2.113 | .197 | .143 | .227 | .032 | -.079 | -.142 | -.154 |
| Nielsen Competitors | -.521 | -.102 | .008 | .074 | .011 | -.042 | .034 | .029 |
| Engagement Event | .954 | .771 | .169 | -.692 | -.034 | -.009 | -.021 | -.032 |
| Influencer Measure | .341 | .157 | .147 | .315 | -.005 | .075 | .039 | .016 |
| Giveaway | -.905 | .451 | -.178 | -.241 | .004 | -.051 | -.006 | .006 |
| RMSE | 1.720 | .328 | .064 | .282 | .020 | .065 | .061 | .067 |
| $R^2$ | .453 | .723 | .680 | .694 | .579 | .623 | .856 | .872 |
| $\chi^2$ | 90.060 | 264.530 | 213.850 | 237.080 | 140.380 | 166.570 | 659.590 | 786.570 |
| p-value | .000 | .000 | .000 | .000 | .000 | .000 | .000 | .000 |

Source: Author's own illustration. Notes: N = 101 after adjustments. **Bold value**: |z-statistic| > 1. The significance of the italic values is not in line with the VARX model.

**Table 4.11** Comparison of Model Fit between VARX and SUR Model

|  | SUR | | | VAR | | | Change | | |
| --- | --- | --- | --- | --- | --- | --- | --- | --- | --- |
|  | RMSE | $R^2$ | Adj. $R^2$ | RMSE | $R^2$ | Adj. $R^2$ | RMSE | $R^2$ | Adj. $R^2$ |
| TV | 1.295 | .602 | .235 | 1.308 | .603 | .236 | .012 | .000 | .001 |
| Social Media Influencer | .607 | .963 | .928 | .609 | .963 | .929 | .002 | .001 | .001 |
| SEO | .290 | .682 | .389 | .293 | .682 | .389 | .003 | .000 | .000 |
| SEM | .083 | .555 | .145 | .082 | .568 | .169 | .000 | .012 | .024 |
| Pricing and Shopping | .093 | .854 | .719 | .092 | .860 | .731 | −.001 | .006 | .011 |
| Display | .224 | .826 | .665 | .222 | .832 | .677 | −.002 | .006 | .012 |
| Affiliate | .234 | .732 | .484 | .236 | .733 | .486 | .002 | .001 | .002 |
| Offline | 1.720 | .453 | −.052 | 1.731 | .457 | −.044 | .011 | .004 | .008 |
| Engagement | .328 | .723 | .468 | .332 | .724 | .468 | .003 | .000 | .000 |
| Valence Instagram | .064 | .680 | .384 | .064 | .680 | .384 | .001 | .000 | .000 |
| Volume Review | .282 | .694 | .411 | .283 | .697 | .417 | .001 | .003 | .006 |
| Valence Review | .020 | .579 | .190 | .020 | .580 | .192 | .000 | .001 | .002 |
| Visits | .065 | .623 | .326 | .060 | .685 | .394 | −.005 | .062 | .068 |
| OAC | .061 | .856 | .734 | .059 | .866 | .742 | −.001 | .009 | .008 |
| RARET | .067 | .872 | .753 | .066 | .880 | .768 | −.001 | .008 | .015 |

Source: Author's own illustration. Notes: The differences between the models are presented in absolute values. The root mean squared errors for the VARX model are calculated RMSE = $\sqrt{SEE/(n-2)}$. The Adj. $R^2$ for the SUR model is computed as Adj. $R^2 = 1 - (1 - R^2)*(n-1)/n-p-1$.

### 4.4.6 Managerial Implications of Study 2

The company deals with the question of whether investments in influencer marketing can be economically justified. In general, the results of Study 2 indicate that influencer marketing explains a substantial amount of consumer interest and firm performance. In the following, the managerial implications for website visits, orders and revenue are specified, respectively.

For managers who want to **increase consumer interest** by increasing website visits, social media influencer marketing is an effective tool. Since website visits are a measure of consumers' digital attention, it is not surprising that especially digital channels lead to an effective increase. Investments in advertising on pricing and shopping websites and SEM have the highest impact on visits. Moreover, the effect of investments in advertising on pricing and shopping websites on website visits lasts longer than the other effects. The results further suggest that social media influencer investments can complement advertising on pricing and shopping websites. Offline advertising, affiliate marketing and display advertising also effectively increase visits, however, the cumulative elasticities are smaller than that of social media influencer advertising. SEO investments are a prerequisite for the company's content to be found quickly. However, the investments do not increase consumer interest. Furthermore, the results show that TV is not suitable for increasing consumer interest online.

The results thus confirm the company's previous strategy. Parallel to TV investments, managers should invest continuously in influencer marketing in order to strengthen brand awareness and consumer interest online, as TV has less influence on the target group with an online affinity. Furthermore, channel investments such as SEM and advertising on pricing and shopping websites should be used to target customers specifically at later stages in the buying process. The synergies between influencer marketing and other digital channels should be focused even more strongly. For example, influencers could refer specifically to advertising on pricing and shopping websites or offline coupons in their posts by moderating their own buying process.

The engagement with firm-generated content on Instagram has a negative impact on visits in the long term. As expected by the CEO, this effect is related to the negative impact of giveaway video posts. The company should avoid this type of post and use video posts that are directed to the target group and foster the consumer brand relationship. This practice would also help to better exploit the synergies between firm-generated and consumer-generated content. The results suggest that firm-generated Instagram posts motivate consumers who have already purchased the brand to also show engagement with the brand on Instagram. Video posts that specifically address the relationship with existing customers, e.g., by emphasizing shared values, could encourage consumers to engage in the long term and possibly even become brand lovers.

Moreover, the engagement with firm-generated content on Instagram is positively associated with marketing activities like investments in influencer marketing, SEM and affiliate marketing. Managers should utilize firm-generated posts more targeted as complement to build synergies with advertising investments.

Managers should use repeated reciprocal references between posts of influencers that have a long-lasting relationship with the brand and company posts to drive sustainable consumer engagement and brand loyalty. Since engagement with posts from competitors has a negative impact on visits, it is up to managers to counteract this with their own activities.

Further the results show that influencer messages have an equally strong impact on visits as consumer-generated reviews. From a management perspective, however, influencer messages are much easier to control and offer managers the opportunity to use the power of eWOM in a targeted manner. To leverage the effect of consumer-generated content even more, comments on the company's Instagram profile, for example, could be used to identify brand lovers who are suitable micro influencers.

Furthermore, the analysis of the control variables showed that the average discount rate has a positive effect on visits. Managers should consider the extent to which they can incentivize the purchase of products as part of a cost-benefit analysis. The positive effect of seasonal variables argues in favor of making more investments during this period to increase website visits. Regarding online communication, managers should communicate buzz events more present and better integrate the communication of buzz events in the communication on social media. Moreover, the company should refrain from giveaway posts to increase visits. If giveaways posts are used, the company should use products that appeal to a target group with regular consumption instead of "it-pieces" and thus activate a sustainable target group.

For managers who want to **increase orders and revenue**, the results of Study 2 are a first indication that influencer marketing not only affects website visits, but also influences actual consumer buying behavior. More specifically, influencer marketing has a similar effectiveness on orders compared to TV advertising. A 1% increase in influencer marketing (TV advertising) leads to an increase in orders by .015% (.016%). Moreover, since the percentage increase in investment depends on the absolute investment and these are significantly lower for influencer marketing than for TV advertising, a similar increase in orders can be achieved with less budget.

Both TV and influencer marketing increase revenue. Even though TV advertisements have a higher elasticity on total revenue than social media influencer investments, social media influencer investments have a higher elasticity on online revenue. Therefore, the results show that influencer marketing is an effective marketing tool if the goal is to increase revenue. Since the study considers revenue after returns, the results show that influencers not only increase orders, but consumers are also satisfied with their purchase decision and do not return the

## 4.4 Results of Study 2

products. Thus, the results show that the company should invest further budget in influencer marketing and TV advertising to increase firm performance. Especially the performance online is explained by influencer marketing investments. However, if the company continues to expand its omnichannel strategy and opens more offline stores, TV is especially important.

Moreover, the results show that digital marketing activities like investments in influencer marketing work as complements and supplements for investments in TV advertising. Thus, managers should utilize synergies between online and offline marketing. For example, influencers could be integrated into TV advertising to reach a younger audience. Influencers could also feature or reference these commercials on their own channels. Management could also further expand integrated marketing activities and strategically link content from influencer campaigns to content from TV campaigns.

Like for the increase of consumer interest, advertising on pricing and shopping websites and SEM marketing is a good investment strategy to increase orders and revenue. Except for SEO investment, the results show that all other marketing activities have a significant positive impact on orders and revenue. However, the dummy variable "SEO Event" that captures extreme increase in SEO spending has a positive impact on orders and revenue. The results support the conclusion that SEO investments are a foundation for a functioning online business. In case of a Google update, managers need to invest more in SEO to increase firm performance.

An important insight for managers is that influencer marketing has similar high elasticities on firm performance than consumer reviews and consumer-generated content on Instagram. Accordingly, managers can assume that influencers do not lose their credibility as consumers despite their employment as testimonials. Since engagement with competitors' content on Instagram and the valence of consumer reviews about competitors negatively impact orders and revenue, managers could leverage the power of influencers on consumer-generated content increase orders and revenue.

On average, consumers spend 2.6 times more per product offline than online. This confirms management's assumption that the opening of offline stores will lead to an increase in orders and revenue that will more than compensate for the negative effects on the online business. A further indication of this is provided by the significant deterministic trend for orders and revenue. These effects do not occur in the estimation of online performance. However, managers could try to transfer these effects to the online business. Managers should increase the shopping experience along the online consumer decision journey in a more targeted way to increase consumer spending per product online. For example, some influencers use live shopping experiences online with their followers to create an emotional shopping experience.

Just as for visits, buzz events and the discount rate have a positive effect on orders and revenue. Product seasons lead to an increase in firm performance, thus marketing investments are particularly recommended in this period.

### 4.4.7 Limitations of Study 2 and Future Research

This study has some limitations that provide room for future research. Compared to the other marketing investments, the company documents investments for influencer marketing differently. The investments made for an influencer campaign are always attributed to the first week of the campaign. In order to ensure a better allocation of the investments for the respective week, it would have been useful to know the actual investments per week and the number of influencer posts per week. However, this information was only partly available.

Further, firm-generated social media messages are measured through the engagement with firm-generated posts. For this reason, the metric measures the viral power of the messages sent by the company rather than the "pure" impact of the message. In the present case, a conscious decision was made to include the virality of the firm-generated messages, as this allows for a differentiated view of the type of message (Colicev et al. 2018; De Vries, Gensler, and Leeflang 2017) and is also used by the firm as a performance metric for social media messages. Future research could include the specific number of messages sent by the firm per week.

Subsequent analysis could comprise social media messages in different networks in the effectiveness assessment of the different channels. However, the company's management defines Instagram as main channel for brand communication and influencer marketing since Instagram is of particularly high relevance for the company's core target group. In this regard, the investment in influencer marketing could be broken down by social network, as the current measure includes influencer marketing on all channels, although Instagram is mainly used as a medium.

Study 2 finds that influencer marketing, firm-generated as well as consumer-generated messages on social media and advertising are complements and substitutes at the same time. To gain a more detailed insight into these relationships, further analyses could include interaction effects between these channels. However, since the VAR model already includes numerous interrelationships, including interaction effects is computationally challenging.

## 4.4 Results of Study 2

Study 2 uses website visits as a proxy for consumer interest to explore the effectiveness of marketing investments and social media messaging. However, this measure is only a representation of consumer interest online. Since this is the main channel for the company's distribution, this operationalization makes sense. However, since the variable "Store Openings" has a significant negative influence in all models, the impact on offline store visits should be considered. Due to the complexity of the measurement, this data is not available to the company and could not be included in the calculations.

Future research could incorporate brand building measures to get a more concrete idea of the effectiveness of influencer marketing and other marketing activities as well as social media messages. Customer survey data could provide insights for consumer awareness, consideration and preference (De Vries, Gensler, and Leeflang 2017)

Despite its limitation, Study 2 is the first to compare the relative effectiveness of influencer marketing, firm-generated as well as consumer-generated messages on social media and advertising on website visits, orders and revenue. Thus, the study makes a significant contribution to the existent literature and offers a variety of suggestions for further research.

# General Discussion 5

Influencer Marketing has become an integral component of brands' marketing strategies. Despite the increasing importance of influencer marketing, relatively little academic research has focused on the impact of social media influencers along the consumer decision journey. Moreover, marketers lack an adequate understanding of the effectiveness of influencer marketing, especially on the monetary value of influencer marketing. Therefore, this thesis has aimed to shed light on the impact of influencer marketing on consumer behavior and the resulting company success.

In the following, a summary of the thesis is provided and the theoretical contribution is outlined. Based on the findings of both studies, managerial implications are derived. Lastly, the thesis provides an outlook on potential future research.

## 5.1 Summary of Studies and Theoretical Contribution

To ensure the effectiveness of influencer marketing, the process of influencer marketing management must be followed. Along the process of influencer marketing management, relevant research gaps were identified.

First, it must be clear what the overarching goal of an influencer campaign is. These goals are assigned to different phases of the consumer decision journey. However, little is known about the effects of influencer marketing on consumer behavior along the different stages of the consumer decision journey (Hughes, Swaminathan, and Brooks 2019). Since all further decisions of influencer marketing management are based on this step, the overall aim of the thesis was *to investigate the potential of influencers to influence behavioral outcomes of consumers on social media.* Two empirical studies were conducted for this purpose.

© The Author(s), under exclusive license to Springer Fachmedien Wiesbaden GmbH, part of Springer Nature 2023
J. Johne, *Effectiveness of Influencer Marketing*,
https://doi.org/10.1007/978-3-658-41297-5_5

As the biggest challenges for marketers lie in identifying influencers and measuring the performance of influencer marketing, the empirical studies were linked to these phases of influencer marketing management.

The first study relates to the second step of influencer marketing management process and derives insights for the selection of suitable influencers for different campaign outputs. Study 1 is the first to observe the impact of an influencers personal and network potential on consumer behavior at different stages of the consumer decision journey.

In the preliminary stages of Study 1, expert interviews were conducted in order to derive relevant selection criteria and campaign goals from practical experience. The study focused on consumer perception of influencer marketing and empirically investigated the impact of influencer characteristics on influencer campaign measures along the consumer decision journey. Therefore, the study works with campaign data from 13 campaigns from ten different brands. Characteristics were gathered for 87 influencers, which describe their power potential to influence others. The characteristics are divided into personal resources and network resources, which result from his position within a portfolio. In order to explore the influencer brand in the respective campaigns in more detail, a consumer survey was conducted with 2,152 social media users. The survey found that influencer brand fit is determined by product category fit and image fit, with product category fit having a higher influence. This data was merged with the performance metrics of the influencers in the individual campaigns, which depict the influence on consumer awareness, purchase intention and engagement.

The findings indicate that consumers are engaged by different influencer characteristics along the consumer decision journey. The personal power potential relates positive to consumer awareness since the influencer's expertise and brand fit significantly increase the real reach of campaign posts. Within a portfolio of influencers, the unique reach of an influencer relates positive to the real reach per campaign post. However, the overlap of an influencer's followers within a portfolio relates negative to the real reach per campaign post. The general activity of followers increases consumer awareness within a campaign. If an influencer's followers frequently like his content, then the real reach of his campaign posts increases, as this triggers a viral effect. Awareness posts that describe the product rather than directly encouraging a purchase work best for consumer awareness.

The purchase intention of consumers through product link clicks within an influencer's story is enhanced both by a high unique follower count of the influencer and by a large overlap of followers within an influencer portfolio. The general posting frequency of an influencer fosters the relationship of an influencer with his followers and has a positive influence on consumers' purchase

## 5.1 Summary of Studies and Theoretical Contribution

intention. However, the product link clicks per story decreases if the number of campaign stories increases. On the contrary, the story length has a positive impact on product link clicks. Finally, the higher the like follower ratio of an influencer, the higher the purchase intention the influencer achieves within the campaign. Trial posts increase consumer purchase intention.

Influencers with higher expertise achieve higher engagement through likes and story views. Across all engagement measures, many unique followers have a positive impact on engagement with campaign posts. However, overlapping of followers within a portfolio has a negative impact on the number of likes and comments. In addition, the number of likes decreases the more campaign posts the influencer posts. Story views within the campaign are high if the influencer has a high like follower ratio. If the influencer receives a high number of comments on his posts in general, this also has a positive effect on the number of comments within the campaign. Both characteristics lead to a high level of engagement through likes within the campaign. Awareness campaigns get more likes than trial campaigns. Moreover, the number of comments increases if a lottery is included.

With these findings the theoretical contribution of Study 1 to research is fourfold. First, by simultaneously covering effects on consumer behaviour at different stages of the consumer decision journey, the study showed that different influencer characteristics matter for the different stages. Second, the first study merged the mindset of persuasion research and viral marketing literature and considered personal as well as structural resources of an influencer at once. Third, the study enriched current research on persuasion and viral marketing with insights from brand extension literature and measured influencer brand fit and its drivers. Further, the study observed the impact of this influencer brand fit measure on consumer behavior metrics. Fourth, the study included dyadic network attributes that cover the influencers network within a portfolio of influencers and showed that unique reach and overlap contribute differently to the different phases of the consumer decision journey.

The second study relates to the last step of influencer management process and derives insights for the performance measurement of influencer campaigns. Study 2 takes the company's perspective on this and is the first to compare the relative effectiveness of influencer marketing, firm-generated as well as consumer-generated messages on social media and advertising on website visits, orders and revenue. Further, it explored the interaction effects among those channels.

The study is based on data of one of the largest specialized online retailers in Europe. The data includes the company's channel investments and maps its activities on Instagram, as well as the activities of its customers on Instagram and on a large review website. This data was merged with the company's performance through website visits, orders and revenue.

The results showed that influencer marketing has a substantial influence on website visits, orders and revenue. Social media influencers explain more visits, orders and revenue than affiliate marketing and offline advertising. Display advertising has a higher short-term impact on consumer interest and firm performance. Since consumer consumption is shifted forward, the positive impact is followed by a negative impact and reduces the cumulative elasticity. Therefore, the cumulative elasticity of display advertising on website visits and revenue is lower than that of influencer marketing. However, investments in SEM and advertising on pricing and shopping websites have higher cumulative elasticities on visits, orders and revenue than influencer marketing. Even though, TV advertising is not effective to build consumer interest online, the investments in TV advertising translate to firm performance. TV advertising has the highest impact on revenue of all channels. Engagement with firm-generated social media posts has a short-term positive impact on website visits and subsequently causes an even greater drop-off in website visits. Thus, in the long term, it has a negative impact on website visits. Consumer-generated content has a positive impact on consumer interest and firm performance. Across the consumer decision journey, this impact is equal to or lower than that of influencer marketing. Finally, the results illustrated that influencer marketing works as complement and substitute for traditional and other digital channels as well as social media messages.

The theoretical contribution of the second empirical study is threefold. First, by observing the effects on website visits as well as orders and revenue, the study gained insights on how influencer marketing shapes the consumer decision journey. Further, the results show that influencer marketing translates into monetary value for the firm. Second, the study compared the effectiveness of influencer marketing, other advertising investments, and firm-generated and consumer-generated messages. Third, the study observed the interactions of the different channels and influencer marketing. Therefore, the study contributes to literature on social media effectiveness.

## 5.2 Summary of Managerial Implications

Through the results of Study 1 marketers gain an understanding which influencer characteristics engage the consumer at different points in the consumer decision journey. This allows selection criteria to be derived for the selection of suitable influencers depending on the campaign objective.

## 5.2 Summary of Managerial Implications

A holistic view of the impact of influencers' personal and structural resources on their campaign performance has shown that managers cannot rely solely on criteria that map the influencer's network. Especially for consumer awareness, personal resources act as a kind of door opener, catching consumers at the beginning of the consumer decision journey. It is particularly important to select influencers who have a high level of expertise or high social status within the target group to gain consumer awareness.

Moreover, influencers should have a high influencer brand fit to create awareness. The expert interviews have shown that marketers have problems defining exactly what constitutes this influencer brand fit. The large-scale consumer survey revealed that the perceived influencer brand fit results from both image fit and product category fit. However, the product category fit has a greater influence on influencer brand fit than the image fit. Therefore, brands should ensure that the expertise that the influencer possesses is also suitable for the product category that is to be promoted.

Further, brands should invest in tools or manpower that allow them to analyze follower overlap for eligible influencers. Although marketers agree that these metrics are important, the expert interviews confirm that overlap analysis is not yet an established selection criterion. Network operators should consider commercializing these metrics to enable brands to optimize influencer advertising. To create high consumer awareness, the influencer portfolio should be diverse. Influencers should target different customer groups and therefore have a low overlap of followers. Within this customer group they should be characterized through a high follower count, thus have a high unique reach within the portfolio. Further, to increase the viral effect of the campaign, the influencers should have a highly engaged follower base that is characterized through a high like follower ratio.

The personal resources of an influencer play a subordinate role for the purchase intention. In this phase, consumers pay less attention to peripheral cues, like influencer brand fit, and focus much more on message content, as they are already more involved within the buying process. Therefore, longer stories that can explain the value of the product increase the likelihood that consumers will follow the product link.

In all phases, a high like follower ratio has a positive effect on the purchase intention. Unlike the other phases of the consumer decision journey, it is advantageous in the case of purchase intention if the influencers' followers overlap in the portfolio. This means that if campaigns are designed to actively promote the sales of products, it makes strategic sense to work with influencers with many followers who address the same target group. This way, consumers are reached multiple times with different content, which increases the likelihood that their buying interest is activated and that they follow the product link.

However, campaign engagement is again negatively impacted by follower overlap. To increase likes, comments and story views, it is advantageous if the influencers address diverse target groups. Further, if managers want to increase engagement with their campaign posts, it is important that they rely on influencers who have high expertise or status. Moreover, engagement with branded content is more likely to be generated if the influencer's followers interact very actively with the influencer's content. To integrate potential consumers into a discussion, it makes sense for influencers to have a follower base that is also characterized by a high comment rate. Lotteries also contribute to an increase in engagement through comments. However, as the results of Study 2 showed, this type of engagement should be carefully analyzed to determine whether it has a positive impact on the company's performance.

Building on these insights, the next step for managers is to consider the findings on the effectiveness of portfolio characteristics within influencer pricing. Thus, the payment model for awareness campaigns should include the number of unique followers actually reached by an influencer. In campaigns where the focus is on product sales, influencers should act as a sales force. Since many influencers operate in groups of influencers anyway, payment models based on sales of the entire portfolio could be effective here.

In light of the discussions on virtual influencers (Cheung 2021; Leung, Gu, and Palmatier 2022), the results can also be used to design influencer avatars with respect to different campaign outputs. Since the measurement of influencer expertise or social status is based on communication content, communication patterns for virtual influencers can be derived. Moreover, the results on consumer perception of influencer brand fit make clear, which dimensions of fit are important for creating suitable avatars for brand collaborations. For example, McDonald's introduced its own virtual influencer "Happy Sister" as a brand ambassador in China in January 2021. Further, the results regarding influencer characteristics within a network are particularly relevant as brands could increase their audience with portfolios of real and virtual influencers. Moreover, collaborations with a portfolio of virtual influencers are also conceivable.

The results of Study 2 provide managers with initial insights into the impact of influencer marketing on corporate performance metrics that map the consumer decision journey. Especially, the study provides first insights into the monetary value of influencers.

First, the results show that influencer marketing is an effective way to increase website visits, orders and revenue. Due to the monetary effectiveness of influencer marketing, it therefore makes sense to increase the budget for influencer marketing. The results further show that influencer marketing acts as both a supplement and a complement for TV advertising. However, if managers consider shifting budget from TV advertising to influencer marketing, it should be kept in mind that TV advertising still has a high impact on firm performance, especially offline. Since other marketing investments, like investments in advertising on pricing and shopping websites and SEM, also have a positive impact on consumer interest and firm performance, managers should orchestrate their channels and use synergies between influencer marketing and other digital channels.

Second, the effects of engagement with firm-generated content have shown that firm posts that generate high engagement rates, such as lottery posts, cannot necessarily translate engagement into consumer interest and firm performance. Lottery posts motivate consumers to make many comments, but these do not reflect consumers' feelings toward the brand. Managers should be anxious to foster long-lasting customer relationships with their company posts, for example, by using video posts to illustrate shared values. Furthermore, influencer marketing offers valuable opportunities for managers to engage customers, promote shared values and utilize the relationship between influencers and their followers.

Third, the results demonstrate that influencer marketing has a similar and even higher impact on consumer interest and firm performance than consumer-generated messages on social media. Thus, influencers do not lose their credibility as consumers even though they act as brand ambassadors. Influencer marketing provides managers with the potential to leverage the influence of peer-to-peer communication.

In summary, Study 2 shows that it is useful for managers to track the effectiveness of their channel investments and social media activities, as well as those of their customers on consumer interest and firm performance. The insights gained from Study 2 help managers to orchestrate and optimize the various activities.

## 5.3 Outlook to the Future

This thesis provided insights into the impact of social media influencer marketing on consumers and firms. However, some questions still remain unexplored. The following highlights the most important research gaps along the process of influencer marketing management and gives an overview of which issues should be researched in the future.

The first phase of the influencer marketing management process is to define the objectives of the campaigns. In this thesis, these goals are determined by the consumer decision journey depicting the buying process of products and services. Future research could cross-check the results in other contexts by looking at campaign outputs in different areas of influencer marketing. Influencers are used in various aspects of life. It remains to be seen what role social media influencers play, for example, in a social, political or global context. In such areas, personal resources, such as expertise or brand fit, could play an even greater role. Information, personal history or involvement could have a greater influence here than structural resources.

This points to the second step of influencer management. Study 1 deals with the appropriate selection of influencers and shows that overlap and unique reach take a more differentiated look at the structural resources of influencers than just the number of followers. Depending on the goal of the campaign, the overlap of followers has advantages or disadvantages. Future research should look at optimizing pricing for influencers in a portfolio. Thereby, research should consider the structural and personal characteristics of the influencers.

Furthermore, future research should examine the role of virtual influencers more closely. This should include research on the influence of virtual influencers compared to human influencers and which characteristics are relevant for virtual influencers. It must also be critically questioned how young target groups in particular are influenced by brand-generated virtual influencers, as the independence of influencers is lost in this context.

The third phase, design of content, is predominantly in the hands of the influencer and is not determined by the brand. However, future research could take the influencer perspective. The focus should be on researching visual content, such as live streams or stories. Furthermore, platforms that have received little research attention so far, such as Instagram, TikTok, Twitch or Clubhouse, should be explored.

The fourth and final phase of the influencer marketing management process is that of performance measurement. Future research should examine the results of Study 2 in other sectors and across industries. For example, the greater impact of influencer investments on online revenue versus TV suggests that influencers may have a greater effect on sales of digital services, such as streaming services, than traditional channels.

Study 2 has shown that influencer marketing can be seen as a complement and supplement to other marketing investments and social media messages. Future research should examine the interactions of channels in more detail. For example, future research should more closely explore the synergies between influencer

## 5.3 Outlook to the Future

marketing and TV advertising before advertising budgets are diverted from traditional channels. In this context, the influence of channel investments on offline and online performance could also be differentiated, as Study 2 showed that traditional channels are still particularly relevant for offline business.

Future research could investigate the relative effectiveness of influencer marketing, firm-generated as well as consumer-generated messages on social media and advertising on brand building. The influence on customer survey data could provide insights for consumer awareness, consideration and preference and further open the black box of influencers' impact on the consumer decision journey.

The messages generated by the company in Study 2 were captured on Instagram. In a different context, other platforms may be more relevant for companies' target groups. Therefore, further studies could investigate the effectiveness of influencer marketing compared to firm-generated social media messages on other platforms.

Overall, the empirical studies provide valuable insights into how influencer marketing generates value for consumers and companies. Despite the potential limitations, the thesis demonstrates the effectiveness of influencer marketing along the consumer decision journey. It provides useful insights for academics and marketers for the selection of influencers and performance measurement of influencer marketing. The thesis offers fruitful ground for future research that aims to examine the effectiveness of influencer marketing.

# References

Aaker, David A. and Kevin L. Keller (1990), "Consumer Evaluations of Brand Extensions," *Journal of Marketing*, 54 (1), 27–41.

Ahluwalia, Rohini and Zeynep Gürhan-Canli (2000), "The Effects of Extensions on the Family Brand Name: An Accessibility-Diagnosticity Perspective," *Journal of Consumer Research*, 27 (3), 371–81.

Akpinar, Ezgi and Jonah Berger (2017), "Valuable Virality," *Journal of Marketing Research*, 54 (2), 318–30.

Amos, Clinton, Gary Holmes, and David Strutton (2008), "Exploring the relationship between celebrity endorser effects and advertising effectiveness," *International Journal of Advertising*, 27 (2), 209–34.

Ansari, Asim, Florian Stahl, Mark Heitmann, and Lucas Bremer (2018), "Building a Social Network for Success," *Journal of Marketing Research*, 55 (3), 321–38.

Araujo, Theo, Peter Neijens, and Rens Vliegenthart (2015), "What Motivates Consumers To Re-Tweet Brand Content?," *Journal of Advertising Research*, 55 (3), 284–95.

ARD/ZDF-Forschungskommission (2021), "Ergebnispräsentation | ARD/ZDF-Forschungskommission," (accessed August 19, 2021), [available at https://www.ard-zdf-onlinestudie.de/ardzdf-onlinestudie/ergebnispraesentation/].

Association of National Advertisers (2018), "Advertisers Love Influencer Marketing: ANA Study," (accessed July 18, 2020), [available at https://www.ana.net/content/show/id/48437].

Audrezet, Alice, Gwarlann de Kerviler, and Julie Guidry Moulard (2018), "Authenticity under threat: When social media influencers need to go beyond self-presentation," *Journal of Business Research*, 117, 557–69.

Babić Rosario, Ana, Francesca Sotgiu, Kristine de Valck, and Tammo H. Bijmolt (2016), "The Effect of Electronic Word of Mouth on Sales: A Meta-Analytic Review of Platform, Product, and Metric Factors," *Journal of Marketing Research*, 53 (3), 297–318.

Backhaus, Klaus, Bernd Erichson, Wulff Plinke, and Rolf Weiber (2016), *Multivariate Analysemethoden. Eine anwendungsorientierte Einführung*, 14., überarbeitete und aktualisierte Auflage. Berlin, Heidelberg: Springer Gabler.

Batra, Rajeev and Kevin L. Keller (2016), "Integrating Marketing Communications: New Findings, New Lessons, and New Ideas," *Journal of Marketing*, 80 (6), 122–45.

Becker-Olsen, Karen L. (2003), "And Now, A Word from Our Sponsor—A Look at the Effects of Sponsored Content and Banner Advertising," *Journal of Advertising*, 32 (2), 17–32.

Beckers, Sander F. M., Jenny van Doorn, and Peter C. Verhoef (2018), "Good, better, engaged? The effect of company-initiated customer engagement behavior on shareholder value," *Journal of the Academy of Marketing Science*, 46 (3), 366–83.

Berger, Jonah (2014), "Word of mouth and interpersonal communication: A review and directions for future research," *Journal of Consumer Psychology*, 24 (4), 586–607.

Berger, Jonah and Katherine L. Milkman (2012), "What Makes Online Content Viral?," *Journal of Marketing Research*, 49 (2), 192–205.

Berger, Jonah and Eric M. Schwartz (2011), "What Drives Immediate and Ongoing Word of Mouth?," *Journal of Marketing Research*, 48 (5), 869–80.

Bergkvist, Lars, Hanna Hjalmarson, and Anne W. Mägi (2016), "A new model of how celebrity endorsements work: attitude toward the endorsement as a mediator of celebrity source and endorsement effects," *International Journal of Advertising*, 35 (2), 171–84.

Bocksch, René (2020), "Digitale Werbung auf dem Vormarsch," (accessed May 16, 2021), [available at https://de.statista.com/infografik/22257/anteil-digitaler-und-traditioneller-werbung-am-marktvolumen/].

Boerman, Sophie C., Lotte M. Willemsen, and Eva P. van der Aa (2017), "This Post Is Sponsored," *Journal of Interactive Marketing*, 38, 82–92.

Borah, Abhishek, Sourindra Banerjee, Yu-Ting Lin, Apurv Jain, and Andreas B. Eisingerich (2020), "Improvised Marketing Interventions in Social Media," *Journal of Marketing*, 84 (2), 69–91.

Brass, D. J. and M. E. Burkhardt (1993), "Potential Power and Power Use: An Investigation of Structure and Behavior," *The Academy of Management Journal*, 36 (3), 441–70.

Breves, Priska L., Nicole Liebers, Marina Abt, and Annika Kunze (2019), "The Perceived Fit between Instagram Influencers and the Endorsed Brand," *Journal of Advertising Research*, 59 (4), 440–54.

Bridges, Sheri, Kevin L. Keller, and Sanjay Sood (2000), "Communication Strategies for Brand Extensions: Enhancing Perceived Fit by Establishing Explanatory Links," *Journal of Advertising*, 29 (4), 1–11.

Briner, Rob B. and David Denyer, eds. (2012), *Systematic Review and Evidence Synthesis as a Practice and Scholarship Tool*: Oxford University Press.

Bruce, Norris I., Natasha Z. Foutz, and Ceren Kolsarici (2012), "Dynamic Effectiveness of Advertising and Word of Mouth in Sequential Distribution of New Products," *Journal of Marketing Research*, 49 (4), 469–86.

Business Insider (2021), "The 24-year-old and the 40-year-old are driving the economy right now," (accessed January 29, 2022), [available at https://www.businessinsider.com/24-gen-z-trends-40-millennial-spending-changing-economy-2021-9?amp].

Cameron, A. C. and P. K. Trivedi (2005), *Microeconometrics. Methods and Applications*. New York: Cambridge University Press.

Casaló, Luis V., Carlos Flavián, and Sergio Ibáñez-Sánchez (2018), "Influencers on Instagram: Antecedents and consequences of opinion leadership," *Journal of Business Research*, 117, 510–19.

Chen, Xingyu, Xing Li, Dai Yao, and Zhimin Zhou (2019), "Seeking the support of the silent majority: are lurking users valuable to UGC platforms?," *Journal of the Academy of Marketing Science*, 47 (6), 986–1004.

Cheung, Christy M., Pui-Yee Chiu, and Matthew K. Lee (2011), "Online social networks: Why do students use facebook?," *Computers in Human Behavior*, 27 (4), 1337–43.

Cheung, Man-chung (2021), "In China, virtual influencers are taking on media roles traditionally held by humans," (accessed March 6, 2022), [available at https://www.emarketer.com/content/china-virtual-influencers-taking-on-media-roles-traditionally-held-by-humans?ecid=NL1001].

Chung, Siyoung and Hichang Cho (2017), "Fostering Parasocial Relationships with Celebrities on Social Media: Implications for Celebrity Endorsement," *Psychology & Marketing*, 34 (4), 481–95.

Coleman, James S. (1988), "Social Capital in the Creation of Human Capital," *American Journal of Sociology* (94), 95–120.

Colicev, Anatoli, Ashish Kumar, and Peter O'Connor (2019), "Modeling the relationship between firm and user generated content and the stages of the marketing funnel," *International Journal of Research in Marketing*, 36 (1), 100–16.

Colicev, Anatoli, Ashwin Malshe, Koen Pauwels, and Peter O'Connor (2018), "Improving Consumer Mindset Metrics and Shareholder Value through Social Media: The Different Roles of Owned and Earned Media," *Journal of Marketing*, 82 (1), 37–56.

Colliander, Jonas and Micael Dahlén (2011), "Following the Fashionable Friend: The Power of Social Media," *Journal of Advertising Research*, 51 (1), 313–20.

Corstjens, Marcel and Andris Umblijs (2012), "The Power of Evil," *Journal of Advertising Research*, 52 (4), 433–49.

Dahl, Robert A. (1975), "The Concept of Power," *Behavioral Science*, 2 (3), 201–15.

Davis, Scott W., Csilla Horváth, Anaïs Gretry, and Nina Belei (2019), "Say what? How the interplay of tweet readability and brand hedonism affects consumer engagement," *Journal of Business Research*, 100, 150–64.

De Veirman, Marijke, Veroline Cauberghe, and Liselot Hudders (2017), "Marketing through Instagram influencers: the impact of number of followers and product divergence on brand attitude," *International Journal of Advertising*, 36 (5), 798–828.

De Vries, Eline L. E. (2019), "When more likes is not better: the consequences of high and low likes-to-followers ratios for perceived account credibility and social media marketing effectiveness," *Marketing Letters*, 30 (3–4), 275–91.

De Vries, Lisette (2015), *Impact of social media on consumers and firms*. Groningen.

De Vries, Lisette, Sonja Gensler, and Peter S. Leeflang (2012), "Popularity of Brand Posts on Brand Fan Pages: An Investigation of the Effects of Social Media Marketing," *Journal of Interactive Marketing*, 26 (2), 83–91.

De Vries, Lisette, Sonja Gensler, and Peter S. Leeflang (2017), "Effects of Traditional Advertising and Social Messages on Brand-Building Metrics and Customer Acquisition," *Journal of Marketing*, 81 (5), 1–15.

Dekimpe, Marnik G. and Dominique M. Hanssens (1995), "The Persistence of Marketing Effects on Sales," *Marketing Science*, 14 (1), 1–21.

Dekimpe, Marnik G. and Dominique M. Hanssens (1999), "Sustained Spending and Persistent Response: A New Look at Long-Term Marketing Profitability," *Journal of Marketing Research*, 36 (4), 397.

Dekimpe, Marnik G., Dominique M. Hanssens, and Jorge M. Silva-Risso (1998), "Long-run effects of price promotions in scanner markets," *Journal of Econometrics*, 89 (1–2), 269–91.

Dholakia, Utpal M., Richard P. Bagozzi, and Lisa K. Pearo (2004), "A social influence model of consumer participation in network- and small-group-based virtual communities," *International Journal of Research in Marketing*, 21 (3), 241–63.

Djafarova, Elmira and Chloe Rushworth (2017), "Exploring the credibility of online celebrities' Instagram profiles in influencing the purchase decisions of young female users," *Computers in Human Behavior*, 68, 1–7.

Droesch, Blake (2019), "Social Commerce Leads Consumer Adoption of New Retail Technology," (accessed March 29, 2021), [available at https://www.emarketer.com/content/social-commerce-leads-consumer-adoption-of-new-retail-technology].

Droesch, Blake (2021), "Livestreaming finds a home among influencers," (accessed May 11, 2021), [available at https://www.emarketer.com/content/livestreaming-finds-home-among-influencers?ecid=NL1016].

Du, Rex Y. and Wagner A. Kamakura (2011), "Measuring Contagion in the Diffusion of Consumer Packaged Goods," *Journal of Marketing Research*, 48 (1), 28–47.

Edgerton, David and Ghazi Shukur (1999), "Testing autocorrelation in a system perspective testing autocorrelation," *Econometric Reviews*, 18 (4), 343–86.

eMarketer (2017), "Social Network Users and Penetration Worldwide, 2016–2021 (billions, % change and % of internet users)," (accessed July 17, 2020), [available at https://www.emarketer.com/chart/214528/social-network-users-penetration-worldwide-2016-2021-billions-change-of-internet-users].

eMarketer (2019), "Instagram Removing Likes Could Boost Social Commerce and Retail Measurement," (accessed March 25, 2021), [available at https://www.emarketer.com/content/instagram-removing-likes-could-boost-social-commerce-and-retail-measurement?ecid=NL1016].

eMarketer (2021), "Creators are becoming a serious business for brands," (accessed May 18, 2021), [available at https://www.emarketer.com/content/creators-becoming-serious-business-brands?ecid=NL1014].

Emerson, Richard M. (1962), "Power-Dependence Relations," *American Sociological Review*, 27 (1), 31–41.

Erdogan, B. Z. (1999), "Celebrity Endorsement: A Literature Review," *Journal of Marketing Management*, 15 (4), 291–314.

Evans, Nathaniel J., Joe Phua, Jay Lim, and Hyoyeun Jun (2017), "Disclosing Instagram Influencer Advertising: The Effects of Disclosure Language on Advertising Recognition, Attitudes, and Behavioral Intent," *Journal of Interactive Advertising*, 17(2), 138–49.

Faltl, M. and J. Freese (2017), "Influencer Marketing Evolution, Chancen und Herausforderungen der neuen Komponente im Kommunikationsmix," (accessed June 19, 2020), [available at https://docplayer.org/57261245-Forschungsreihe-04-2017-influencer-marketing-evolution-chancen-und-herausforderungen-der-neuen-komponente-im-kommunikationsmix.html].

Festinger, Leon (1957), *A Theory of Cognitive Dissonance*. Stanford: Stanford University Press.

Forbes (2019a), "Consumers Are Spending More Per Visit In-Store than Online. What Does This Mean for Retailers?," (accessed January 21, 2022), [available at https://www.forbes.com/sites/gregpetro/2019/03/29/consumers-are-spending-more-per-visit-in-store-than-online-what-does-this-man-for-retailers/].

Forbes (2019b), "Reflections On Influencer Marketing Measurement: KPIs For 2019b And Beyond," (accessed March 25, 2021), [available at https://www.forbes.com/sites/forbes communicationscouncil/2019/09/12/reflections-on-influencer-marketing-measurement-kpis-for-2019-and-beyond/].

Forbes (2020), "Is Influencer Marketing Worth It In 2020?," (accessed May 16, 2021), [available at https://www.forbes.com/sites/theyec/2020/01/10/is-influencer-marketing-worth-it-in-2020/].

Forbes (2021), "The Five Greatest Challenges Facing Instagram Influencer Marketing," (accessed January 27, 2022), [available at https://www.forbes.com/sites/theyec/2021/11/08/the-five-greatest-challenges-facing-instagram-influencer-marketing/].

Forkan, J. (1980), "Product Matchup Key to Effective Star Presentations," *Advertising Age*, 42 (51), 117–32.

Fossen, Beth L. and David A. Schweidel (2019), "Social TV, Advertising, and Sales: Are Social Shows Good for Advertisers?," *Marketing Science*, 38 (2), 274–95.

Freberg, Karen, Kristin Graham, Karen McGaughey, and Laura A. Freberg (2011), "Who are the social media influencers? A study of public perceptions of personality," *Public Relations Review*, 37 (1), 90–92.

French, John R. P. and Bertram Raven (1959), "The Bases of Social Power," in *Studies in social power*, Dorwin Cartwright, ed. Oxford: The Univ. of Michigan, 150–67.

Gaski, John F. (1984), "The Theory of Power and Conflict in Channels of Distribution," *Journal of Marketing*, 48 (3), 9–29.

Gensler, Sonja, Franziska Völckner, Yuping Liu-Thompkins, and Caroline Wiertz (2013), "Managing Brands in the Social Media Environment," *Journal of Interactive Marketing*, 27 (4), 242–56.

Gholston, Kira, Matthew Kuofie, and Amy Cooper Hakin (2016), "Social Media for Marketing by Small Businesses," *Journal of Marketing and Management*, 7 (1), 24–39.

Goh, Khim Y., Cheng S. Heng, and Zhijie Lin (2013), "Social Media Brand Community and Consumer Behavior: Quantifying the Relative Impact of User- and Marketer-Generated Content," *Information Systems Research*, 24 (1), 88–107.

Goldenberg, Jacob, Sangman Han, Donald R. Lehmann, and Jae W. Hong (2009), "The Role of Hubs in the Adoption Process," *Journal of Marketing*, 73 (2), 1–13.

Gong, Shiyang, Juanjuan Zhang, Ping Zhao, and Xuping Jiang (2017), "Tweeting as a Marketing Tool: A Field Experiment in the TV Industry," *Journal of Marketing Research*, 54 (6), 833–50.

Gong, Wanqi and Xigen Li (2017), "Engaging fans on microblog: the synthetic influence of parasocial interaction and source characteristics on celebrity endorsement," *Psychology & Marketing*, 34 (7), 720–32.

Gopinath, Shyam, Pradeep K. Chintagunta, and Sriram Venkataraman (2013), "Blogs, Advertising, and Local-Market Movie Box Office Performance," *Management Science*, 59 (12), 2635–54.

Gopinath, Shyam, Jacquelyn S. Thomas, and Lakshman Krishnamurthi (2014), "Investigating the Relationship Between the Content of Online Word of Mouth, Advertising, and Brand Performance," *Marketing Science*, 33 (2), 241–58.

Granger, Clive W. J. and Paul Newbold (1986), *Forecasting Economic Time Series,* 2nd ed. San Francisco, CA: Academic Press.

Granovetter, Mark S. (1973), "The Strength of Weak Ties," *American Journal of Sociology*, 78 (6), 1360–80.

Gräve, Jan-Frederik (2017), "Exploring the Perception of Influencers Vs. Traditional Celebrities," in *SMSociety' 17*, 1–5.

Greene, William H. (2003), *Econometric analysis*, 5. ed. Upper Saddle River, NJ: Prentice-Hall.

Hair, Joseph F., William C. Black, Barry J. Babin, and Rolph E. Anderson (2014), *Multivariate Data Analysis. Pearson New International Edition*, 7th ed. Harlow: Pearson Education Limited.

Harkins, Stephen G. and Richard E. Petty (1987), "Information utility and the multiple source effect," *Journal of Personality and Social Psychology*, 52 (2), 260–68.

Hautz, Julia, Johann Füller, Katja Hutter, and Carina Thürridl (2014), "Let Users Generate Your Video Ads? The Impact of Video Source and Quality on Consumers' Perceptions and Intended Behaviors," *Journal of Interactive Marketing*, 28 (1), 1–15.

Hayes, Andrew F. and Li Cai (2007), "Using heteroskedasticity-consistent standard error estimators in OLS regression: an introduction and software implementation," *Behavior Research Methods*, 39 (4), 709–22.

Heider, F. (1958), *The Psychology of Interpersonal Relations*. New York: John Wiley and Sons, Inc.

Heimbach, Irina and Oliver Hinz (2016), "The impact of content sentiment and emotionality on content virality," *International Journal of Research in Marketing*, 33 (3), 695–701.

Hennig-Thurau, Thorsten, Kevin P. Gwinner, Gianfranco Walsh, and Dwayne D. Gremler (2004), "Electronic word-of-mouth via consumer-opinion platforms: What motivates consumers to articulate themselves on the Internet?," *Journal of Interactive Marketing*, 18 (1), 38–52.

Hennig-Thurau, Caroline Wiertz, and Fabian Feldhaus (2015), "Does Twitter matter? The impact of microblogging word of mouth on consumers' adoption of new movies," *Journal of the Academy of Marketing Science*, 43 (3), 375–94.

Hewett, Kelly, William Rand, Roland T. Rust, and Harald J. van Heerde (2016), "Brand Buzz in the Echoverse," *Journal of Marketing*, 80 (3), 1–24.

Hinz, Oliver, Bernd Skiera, Christian Barrot, and Jan U. Becker (2011), "Seeding Strategies for Viral Marketing: An Empirical Comparison," *Journal of Marketing*, 75 (6), 55–71.

Homburg, Christian, John P. Workman, and Harley Krohmer (1999), "Marketing's Influence within the Firm," *Journal of Marketing*, 63 (2), 1–17.

Homer, Pamela M. and Lynn R. Kahle (1990), "Source Expertise, Time of Source Identification, and Involvement in Persuasion: An Elaborative Processing Perspective," *Journal of Advertising*, 19 (1), 30–39.

Horizont (2016), "#Schachtelglück: So souverän beherrscht DM das Spiel mit dem Influencer Marketing," (accessed June 19, 2020), [available at https://www.horizont.net/marketing/nachrichten/Schachtelglueck-So-souveraen-beherrscht-DM-das-Spiel-mit-dem-Influencer-Marketing-144330].

Horizont (2018), "Gewinnerin des #bestjobever: Das ist die neue Influencerin von About You," (accessed June 19, 2020), [available at https://www.horizont.net/marketing/nachrichten/gewinnerin-des-bestjobever-das-ist-die-neue-influencerin-von-about-you-169179].

# References

Horizont (2019), "Wavemaker-Studie: Die Glaubwürdigkeit von Influencern bröckelt," (accessed January 9, 2022), [available at https://www.horizont.net/marketing/nachrichten/wavemaker-studie-die-glaubwuerdigkeit-von-influencern-broeckelt-178308].

Horton, D. and R. R. Wohl (1956), "Mass communication and para-social interaction," *Psychiatry: Journal for the Study of Interpersonal Processes* (19), 215–29.

Hovland, Carl I., Irving L. Janis, and Harold H. Kelley (1953), *Communication and Persuasion. Psychological Studies of Opinion Change.* New Haven: Yale University Press.

Hovland, Carl I., Arthur A. Lumsdaine, and Fred D. Sheffield (1949), *Experiments on mass communication. Studies in social psychology in World War II:* Princeton University Press.

Hu, Yansong and Christophe van den Bulte (2014), "Nonmonotonic Status Effects in New Product Adoption," *Marketing Science*, 33 (4), 509–33.

Hughes, Christian, Vanitha Swaminathan, and Gillian Brooks (2019), "Driving Brand Engagement Through Online Social Influencers: An Empirical Investigation of Sponsored Blogging Campaigns," *Journal of Marketing*, 83 (5), 78–96.

Hung, Kineta, Kimmy W. Chan, and Caleb H. Tse (2011), "Assessing Celebrity Endorsement Effects in China," *Journal of Advertising Research*, 51 (4), 608–23.

Hyndman, Rob. J. and George Athanasopoulos (2018), *Forecasting Principles and Practice. A comprehensive introduction to the latest forecasting methods using R. Learn to improve your forecast accuracy using dozens of real data examples.*, 2nd Edition. Melbourne: OTexts.

Influencer Marketing Hub (2020), "Why the black box of pricing in Influencer Marketing will be changing," (accessed February 22, 2022), [available at https://influencermarketinghub.com/why-the-black-box-of-pricing-in-influencer-marketing-will-be-changing/].

Influencer Marketing Hub (2021), "The State of Influencer Marketing 2021: Benchmark Report," (accessed January 27, 2022), [available at https://influencermarketinghub.com/influencer-marketing-benchmark-report-2021/].

InfluencerDB (2019), "Influencer Marketing Benchmarks Report 2019. Engagement Metrics For Influencer Marketing Success," (accessed July 17, 2020), [available at https://influencerdb.com/blog/influencer-marketing-benchmarks-2019/].

Insider Intelligence (2020), "Global Instagram Users 2020. The Pandemic Propels Worldwide User Base to 1.00 Billion for the First Time," (accessed May 4, 2021), [available at https://www.emarketer.com/content/global-instagram-users-2020].

Insider Intelligence (2021), "Social commerce offers the promise of discovery—but not without challenges," (accessed March 29, 2021), [available at https://www.emarketer.com/content/social-commerce-offers-promise-of-discovery-but-not-without-challenges?ecid=NL1014].

Iyengar, Raghuram, Christophe van den Bulte, and Thomas W. Valente (2011), "Opinion Leadership and Social Contagion in New Product Diffusion," *Marketing Science*, 30 (2), 195–212.

Jalali, Nima Y. and Purushottam Papatla (2019), "Composing tweets to increase retweets," *International Journal of Research in Marketing*, 36 (4), 647–68.

John, Deborah R., Barbara Loken, and Christopher Joiner (1998), "The Negative Impact of Extensions: Can Flagship Products be Diluted?," *Journal of Marketing*, 62 (1), 19–32.

Kacewicz, Ewa, James W. Pennebaker, Matthew Davis, Moongee Jeon, and Arthur C. Graesser (2014), "Pronoun Use Reflects Standings in Social Hierarchies," *Journal of Language and Social Psychology*, 33 (2), 125–43.

Kahle, Lynn R. and Pamela M. Homer (1985), "Physical Attractiveness of the Celebrity Endorser: A Social Adaptation Perspective," *Journal of Consumer Research*, 11 (4), 954–61.

Kallio, Hanna, Anna-Maija Pietilä, Martin Johnson, and Mari Kangasniemi (2016), "Systematic methodological review: developing a framework for a qualitative semi-structured interview guide," *Journal of advanced nursing*, 72 (12), 2954–65.

Kamins, Michael A. and Kamal Gupta (1994), "Congruence between spokesperson and product type: A matchup hypothesis perspective," *Psychology & Marketing*, 11 (6), 569–86.

Kantar (2021), "Research Services from Kantar," (accessed May 4, 2021), [available at https://www.kantar.com/expertise/research-services].

Kanuri, Vamsi K., Yixing Chen, and Shrihari Sridhar (2018), "Scheduling Content on Social Media: Theory, Evidence, and Application," *Journal of Marketing*, 82 (6), 89–108.

Karagür, Zeynep, Jan-Michael Becker, Kristina Klein, and Alexander Edeling (2021), "How, why, and when disclosure type matters for influencer marketing," *International Journal of Research in Marketing*.

Katona, Zsolt, Peter P. Zubcsek, and Miklos Sarvary (2011), "Network Effects and Personal Influences: The Diffusion of an Online Social Network," *Journal of Marketing Research*, 48 (3), 425–43.

Katz, Elihu and Paul Lazarsfeld (1955), *Personal Influence. The Part Played by People in the Flow of Mass Communication*. Illinois: The Free Press.

Keller, Kevin L. (1987), "Memory Factors in Advertising: The Effect of Advertising Retrieval Cues on Brand Evaluations," *Journal of Consumer Research*, 14 (3), 316.

Keller, Kevin L. (2009), "Building strong brands in a modern marketing communications environment," *Journal of Marketing Communications*, 15 (2–3), 139–55.

Kim, Ho and Dominique M. Hanssens (2017), "Advertising and Word-of-Mouth Effects on Pre-launch Consumer Interest and Initial Sales of Experience Products," *Journal of Interactive Marketing*, 37, 57–74.

Kumar, Ashish, Ram Bezawada, Rishika Rishika, Ramkumar Janakiraman, and P. K. Kannan (2016), "From Social to Sale: The Effects of Firm-Generated Content in Social Media on Customer Behavior," *Journal of Marketing*, 80 (1), 7–25.

Kumar, V., Vikram Bhaskaran, Rohan Mirchandani, and Milap Shah (2013), "Practice Prize Winner —Creating a Measurable Social Media Marketing Strategy: Increasing the Value and ROI of Intangibles and Tangibles for Hokey Pokey," *Marketing Science*, 32 (2), 194–212.

Kumar, V., JeeWon B. Choi, and Mallik Greene (2017), "Synergistic effects of social media and traditional marketing on brand sales: capturing the time-varying effects," *Journal of the Academy of Marketing Science*, 45 (2), 268–88.

Kunath, G., Manon Pico, and Reto Hofstetter (2018), "Erfolgreiches Influencer Marketing-Management," *Marketing Review St. Gallen*, 2, 14–21.

Kunz, Werner and Sukanya Seshadri (2015), "From virtual travelers to real friends: Relationship-building insights from an online travel community," *Journal of Business Research*, 68 (9), 1822–28.

Kupfer, Ann-Kristin, Nora Pähler vor der Holte, Raoul V. Kübler, and Thorsten Hennig-Thurau (2018), "The Role of the Partner Brand's Social Media Power in Brand Alliances," *Journal of Marketing*, 82 (3), 25–44.

Labrecque, Lauren I. (2014), "Fostering Consumer–Brand Relationships in Social Media Environments: The Role of Parasocial Interaction," *Journal of Interactive Marketing*, 28 (2), 134–48.

Lafferty, Barbara A. (2009), "Selecting the right cause partners for the right reasons: The role of importance and fit in cause-brand alliances," *Psychology & Marketing*, 26 (4), 359–82.

Lamberton, Cait and Andrew T. Stephen (2016), "A Thematic Exploration of Digital, Social Media, and Mobile Marketing: Research Evolution from 2000 to 2015 and an Agenda for Future Inquiry," *Journal of Marketing*, 80 (6), 146–72.

Lanz, Andreas, Jacob Goldenberg, Daniel Shapira, and Florian Stahl (2019), "Climb or Jump: Status-Based Seeding in User-Generated Content Networks," *Journal of Marketing Research*, 56 (3), 361–78.

Lee, Eun-Ju and Jeong-woo Jang (2013), "Not So Imaginary Interpersonal Contact With Public Figures on Social Network Sites," *Communication Research*, 40 (1), 27–51.

Lee, Jung E. and Brandi Watkins (2016), "YouTube vloggers' influence on consumer luxury brand perceptions and intentions," *Journal of Business Research*, 69 (12), 5753–60.

Leung, Fine F., Flora F. Gu, and Robert W. Palmatier (2022), "Online influencer marketing," *Journal of the Academy of Marketing Science*, 50 (2), 226–51.

Li, Yiyi and Ying Xie (2020), "Is a Picture Worth a Thousand Words? An Empirical Study of Image Content and Social Media Engagement," *Journal of Marketing Research*, 57 (1), 1–19.

Lin, Hsin-Chen, Patrick F. Bruning, and Hepsi Swarna (2018), "Using online opinion leaders to promote the hedonic and utilitarian value of products and services," *Business Horizons*, 61 (3), 431–42.

Lin, Kuan-Yu and Hsi-Peng Lu (2011), "Why people use social networking sites: An empirical study integrating network externalities and motivation theory," *Computers in Human Behavior*, 27 (3), 1152–61.

Linqia (2021), "The State of Influencer Marketing 2021," (accessed January 27, 2022), [available at https://www.linqia.com/wp-content/uploads/2021/04/Linqia-The-State-of-Influencer-Marketing-2021.pdf].

Liu, Yuping and L. J. Shrum (2002), "What is Interactivity and is it Always Such a Good Thing? Implications of Definition, Person, and Situation for the Influence of Interactivity on Advertising Effectiveness," *Journal of Advertising*, 31 (4), 53–64.

Lütkepohl, Helmut (2005), *New introduction to multiple time series analysis. With 49 Figures and 36 Tables,* 1st ed., corr. 2nd printing. Berlin, Heidelberg, New York: Springer.

McGuire, William J. (1985), "Attitudes and Attitude Change," in *Handbook of Social Psychology*, Vol. 2, Gardner Lindzey and Elliot Aronson, eds. New York: Random House, 233–346.

Mediakix (2018), "6 Influencer Marketing Challenges That'll Make Or Break A Campaign," (accessed June 5, 2020), [available at https://mediakix.com/blog/influencer-marketing-challenges-campaign-problems/].

Mediakix (2019), "Case Study: Gillette Marketing Earns Respect With Instagram Influencers," (accessed June 19, 2020), [available at https://mediakix.com/blog/gillette-influencer-marketing-case-study-instagram/].

Mediakix (2020a), "The Best Influencer Marketing Case Studies: Campaigns From Top Brands, Influencers, & More," (accessed March 31, 2021), [available at https://mediakix.com/blog/influencer-marketing-case-studies-top-brands-campaigns-influencers/].

Mediakix (2020b), "8 Brands Doing Coronavirus Influencer Marketing Right on Instagram and TikTok," (accessed June 19, 2020b), [available at https://mediakix.com/blog/coronavirus-influencer-marketing-case-studies/].

Meire, Matthijs, Kelly Hewett, Michel Ballings, V. Kumar, and Dirk van den Poel (2019), "The Role of Marketer-Generated Content in Customer Engagement Marketing," *Journal of Marketing*, 83 (6), 21–42.

Mintzberg, Henry (1984), "Power and Organization Life Cycles," *Academy of Management Review*, 9 (2), 207–24.

Misra, Shekhar and Sharon E. Beatty (1990), "Celebrity spokesperson and brand congruence," *Journal of Business Research*, 21 (2), 159–73.

Moro, Sérgio, Paulo Rita, and Bernardo Vala (2016), "Predicting social media performance metrics and evaluation of the impact on brand building: A data mining approach," *Journal of Business Research*, 69 (9), 3341–51.

Mowen, John C. and Stephen W. Brown (1981), "On Explaining and Predicting the Effectiveness of Celebrity Endorsers," *NA – Advances in Consumer Research Volume*, 8, 437–41.

Myers, David G. (2009), *Social psychology*, 10. ed. New York: McGraw-Hill.

Nam, Hyoryung and P. K. Kannan (2014), "The Informational Value of Social Tagging Networks," *Journal of Marketing*, 78 (4), 21–40.

Namkoong, Jae-Eun, Joon H. Ro, and Marlone D. Henderson (2019), "Responding to Causal Uncertainty in the Twitterverse: When Abstract Language and Social Prominence Increase Message Engagement," *Journal of Interactive Marketing*, 45, 81–98.

Ohanian, Roobina (1990), "Construction and Validation of a Scale to Measure Celebrity Endorsers' Perceived Expertise, Trustworthiness, and Attractiveness," *Journal of Advertising*, 19 (3), 39–52.

Omnicore (2022), "Instagram by the Numbers (2022): Stats, Demographics & Fun Facts," (accessed January 23, 2022), [available at https://www.omnicoreagency.com/instagram-statistics/].

Onishi, Hiroshi and Puneet Manchanda (2012), "Marketing activity, blogging and sales," *International Journal of Research in Marketing*, 29 (3), 221–34.

Ordenes, Francisco, Dhruv Grewal, Stephan Ludwig, Ko de Ruyter, Dominik Mahr, and Martin Wetzels (2019), "Cutting through Content Clutter: How Speech and Image Acts Drive Consumer Sharing of Social Media Brand Messages," *Journal of Consumer Research*, 45 (5), 988–1012.

Pauwels, Koen, Zeynep Aksehirli, and Andrew Lackman (2016), "Like the ad or the brand? Marketing stimulates different electronic word-of-mouth content to drive online and offline performance," *International Journal of Research in Marketing*, 33 (3), 639–55.

Pauwels, Koen, Dominique M. Hanssens, and S. Siddarth (2002), "The Long-Term Effects of Price Promotions on Category Incidence, Brand Choice, and Purchase Quantity," *Journal of Marketing Research*, 39 (4), 421–39.

Peng, Jing, Ashish Agarwal, Kartik Hosanagar, and Raghuram Iyengar (2018), "Network Overlap and Content Sharing on Social Media Platforms," *Journal of Marketing Research*, 55 (4), 571–85.

# References

Pennebaker, J. W., R. J. Booth, R. L. Boyd, and M. E. Francis (2015a), *Linguistic Inquiry and Word Count: LIWC2015*. Austin, TX: Pennebaker Conglomerates (www.LIWC.net).

Pennebaker, J. W., R. L. Boyd, K. Jordan, and K. Blackburn (2015b), *The development and Psychometric properties of LIWC2015*. Austin, TX: University of Texas at Austin

Petty, Richard E. and John T. Cacioppo (1986), "The Elaboration Likelihood Model of Persuasion," in *Advances in Experimental Social Psychology. Advances in Experimental Social Psychology*, L. Berkowitz, ed., Vol. 19. New York: Academic Press, 123–205.

Phillips, Peter C. B. and Pierre Perron (1988), "Testing for a Unit Root in Time Series Regression," *Biometrika*, 75 (2), 335–46.

PWC (2019), "PwC Markenstudie 2019," (accessed May 16, 2021), [available at https://www.pwc.de/de/consulting/markenstudie-2019-pwc.pdf].

Rietveld, Robert, Willemijn van Dolen, Masoud Mazloom, and Marcel Worring (2020), "What You Feel, Is What You Like Influence of Message Appeals on Customer Engagement on Instagram," *Journal of Interactive Marketing*, 49, 20–53.

Rival IQ (2018), "2018 Social Media Industry Benchmark Report," (accessed March 31, 2021), [available at https://www.rivaliq.com/blog/2018-social-media-industry-benchmark-report/#influencers_title].

Rival IQ (2019), "2019 Social Media Industry Benchmark Report," (accessed March 31, 2021), [available at https://www.rivaliq.com/blog/2019-social-media-benchmark-report/#title-influencers].

Rival IQ (2021), "2021 Social Media Industry Benchmark Report | Rival IQ," (accessed March 25, 2021), [available at https://www.rivaliq.com/blog/social-media-industry-benchmark-report/].

Rogers, Everett M. and David G. Cartano (1962), "Methods of Measuring Opinion Leadership," *The Public Opinion Quarterly* (26 (3)), 435–41.

Rooderkerk, Robert P. and Koen H. Pauwels (2016), "No Comment?! The Drivers of Reactions to Online Posts in Professional Groups," *Journal of Interactive Marketing*, 35, 1–15.

Rubin, Rebecca B. and Michael P. McHugh (1987), "Development of parasocial interaction relationships," *Journal of Broadcasting & Electronic Media*, 31 (3), 279–92.

Sengupta, Jaideep, Ronald C. Goodstein, and David S. Boninger (1997), "All Cues are not Created Equal: Obtaining Attitude Persistence under Low- Involvement Conditions," *Journal of Consumer Research*, 23 (4), 351–61.

Smith, Andrew N., Eileen Fischer, and Chen Yongjian (2012), "How Does Brand-related User-generated Content Differ across YouTube, Facebook, and Twitter?," *Journal of Interactive Marketing*, 26 (2), 102–13.

Stafford, Marla R. (1996), "Tangibility in Services Advertising: An Investigation of Verbal versus Visual Cues," *Journal of Advertising*, 25 (3), 13–28.

Statista (2018a), "Marketing – Budgetentwicklung nach Marketingformen in Deutschland 2018a | Statista," (accessed May 16, 2021), [available at https://de.statista.com/statistik/daten/studie/613110/umfrage/umfrage-zur-entwicklung-des-marketingbudgets-in-deutschland/].

Statista (2018b), "Return on Investment von Social Media – Messungen durch Unternehmen weltweit 2018b | Statista," (accessed June 19, 2020), [available at https://de.statista.com/statistik/daten/studie/917032/umfrage/messung-des-return-on-investment-von-social-media-aktivitaeten-durch-unternehmen-weltweit/].

Statista (2018c), "Werbetreibende – Werbevolumens für digitale Werbung 2019 | Statista," (accessed May 16, 2021), [available at https://de.statista.com/statistik/daten/studie/207300/umfrage/umfrage-unter-werbungtreibenden-zur-entwicklung-der-werbeausgaben/].

Statista (2019a), "Ad blocker usage in U.S. | Statista," (accessed July 17, 2020), [available at https://www.statista.com/statistics/804008/ad-blocking-reach-usage-us/].

Statista (2019b), "Influencer marketing market size worldwide from 2016 to 2019," (accessed July 17, 2020), [available at https://www.statista.com/statistics/1092819/global-influencer-market-size/].

Statista (2019c), "Share of online users in the United States who say they pay attention to recommendations from social media influencers as of April 2019c, by age group," (accessed July 17, 2020), [available at https://www.statista.com/statistics/1081751/attention-towards-influencer-recommendations-age-us/].

Statista (2019d), "Worldwide daily social media usage by region 2019 | Statista," (accessed June 19, 2020), [available at https://www.statista.com/statistics/1031948/global-usage-duration-of-social-networks-by-region/].

Statista (2020), "Social Media Advertising – worldwide | Statista Market Forecast," (accessed July 17, 2020), [available at https://www.statista.com/outlook/220/100/social-media-advertising/worldwide/].

Statista (2021a), "Global Instagram influencer marketing spending 2020 | Statista," (accessed May 4, 2021a), [available at https://www.statista.com/statistics/950920/global-instagram-influencer-marketing-spending/].

Statista (2021b), "Instagram: age distribution of global audiences 2021 | Statista," (accessed August 19, 2021), [available at https://www.statista.com/statistics/325587/instagram-global-age-group/].

Statista (2021c), "TV- & Video Werbung – Weltweit | Statista Marktprognose," (accessed May 16, 2021c), [available at https://de.statista.com/outlook/amo/werbung/tv-video-werbung/weltweit#werbeausgaben].

Statista (2022a), "Influencer share of marketing budgets 2021 | Statista," (accessed January 11, 2022), [available at https://www.statista.com/statistics/268641/share-of-marketing-budgets-spent-on-digital-worldwide/].

Statista (2022b), "Increase in online shopping since COVID-19 in Germany 2020, by category | Statista," (accessed January 16, 2022), [available at https://www.statista.com/statistics/1139044/increase-in-online-shopping-since-covid-19-in-germany/].

Stephen, Andrew T. and Jeff Galak (2012), "The Effects of Traditional and Social Earned Media on Sales: A Study of a Microlending Marketplace," *Journal of Marketing Research*, 49 (5), 624–39.

Swani, Kunal and George R. Milne (2017), "Evaluating Facebook brand content popularity for service versus goods offerings," *Journal of Business Research*, 79, 123–33.

Tellis, Gerard J., Deborah J. MacInnis, Seshadri Tirunillai, and Yanwei Zhang (2019), "What Drives Virality (Sharing) of Online Digital Content? The Critical Role of Information, Emotion, and Brand Prominence," *Journal of Marketing*, 83 (4), 1–20.

Thompson, Debora V. and Prashant Malaviya (2013), "Consumer-Generated Ads: Does Awareness of Advertising Co-Creation Help or Hurt Persuasion?," *Journal of Marketing*, 77 (3), 33–47.

TikTok (2020), "#distancedance Hashtag Videos on TikTok," (accessed June 19, 2020), [available at https://www.tiktok.com/tag/distancedance?lang=de].

# References

Tirunillai, Seshadri and Gerard J. Tellis (2012), "Does Chatter Really Matter? Dynamics of User-Generated Content and Stock Performance," *Marketing Science*, 31 (2), 198–215.

Tripp, Carolyn, Thomas D. Jensen, and Les Carlson (1994), "The Effects of Multiple Product Endorsements by Celebrities on Consumers' Attitudes and Intentions," *Journal of Consumer Research*, 20 (4), 535–47.

Trusov, Michael, Anand V. Bodapati, and Randolph E. Bucklin (2010), "Determining Influential Users in Internet Social Networks," *Journal of Marketing Research*, 47 (4), 643–58.

Trusov, Michael, Randolph E. Bucklin, and Koen Pauwels (2009), "Effects of Word-of-Mouth versus Traditional Marketing: Findings from an Internet Social Networking Site," *Journal of Marketing*, 73 (5), 90–102.

Tucker, Catherine E. (2014), "Social Networks, Personalized Advertising, and Privacy Controls," *Journal of Marketing Research*, 51 (5), 546–62.

Tulving, Endel and Donald M. Thomson (1973), "Encoding specificity and retrieval processes in episodic memory," *Psychological Review*, 80 (5), 352–73.

Uribe, Rodrigo, Cristian Buzeta, and Milenka Velásquez (2016), "Sidedness, commercial intent and expertise in blog advertising," *Journal of Business Research*, 69 (10), 4403–10.

Valsesia, Francesca, Davide Proserpio, and Joseph C. Nunes (2020), "The Positive Effect of Not Following Others on Social Media," *Journal of Marketing Research*, 57 (6), 1152–68.

van den Bulte, Christophe and Yogesh V. Joshi (2007), "New Product Diffusion with Influentials and Imitators," *Marketing Science*, 26 (3), 400–21.

van Doorn, Jenny, Katherine N. Lemon, Vikas Mittal, Stephan Nass, Doreén Pick, Peter Pirner, and Peter C. Verhoef (2010), "Customer Engagement Behavior: Theoretical Foundations and Research Directions," *Journal of Service Research*, 13 (3), 253–66.

Verhoef, Peter C., Werner J. Reinartz, and Manfred Krafft (2010), "Customer Engagement as a New Perspective in Customer Management," *Journal of Service Research*, 13 (3), 247–52.

Villanueva, Julian, Shijin Yoo, and Dominique M. Hanssens (2008), "The Impact of Marketing-Induced Versus Word-of-Mouth Customer Acquisition on Customer Equity Growth," *Journal of Marketing Research*, 45 (1), 48–59.

Völckner, Franziska and Henrik Sattler (2006), "Drivers of Brand Extension Success," *Journal of Marketing*, 70 (2), 18–34.

Voorveld, Hilde A., Peter C. Neijens, and Edith G. Smit (2011), "Opening the black box: Understanding cross-media effects," *Journal of Marketing Communications*, 17 (2), 69–85.

Walchli, Suzanne B. (2007), "The effects of between-partner congruity on consumer evaluation of co-branded products," *Psychology & Marketing*, 24 (11), 947–73.

Wang, Qingliang, Fred Miao, Giri K. Tayi, and En Xie (2019), "What makes online content viral? The contingent effects of hub users versus non–hub users on social media platforms," *Journal of the Academy of Marketing Science*, 47 (6), 1005–26.

Wasserman, Stanley and Katherine Faust (1999), *Social network analysis. Methods and applications. Structural analysis in the social sciences*, Vol. 8, Reprinted. Cambridge: Cambridge Univ. Press.

Webster, Jane and Richard T. Watson (2002), "Analyzing the Past to Prepare for the Future: Writing a Literature Review," *MIS Quarterly*, 26 (2), pp. xiii–xxiii.

Wergen, Sandra (2019), "11 erfolgreiche Influencer-Kampagnen, von denen Sie sich inspirieren lassen können," (accessed June 19, 2020), [available at https://blog.hubspot.de/marketing/influencer-kampagnen].

Wiesel, Thorsten, Koen Pauwels, and Joep Arts (2011), "Practice Prize Paper —Marketing's Profit Impact: Quantifying Online and Off-line Funnel Progression," *Marketing Science*, 30 (4), 604–11.

Williams, Kipling D., Martin J. Bourgeois, and Robert T. Croyle (1993), "The effects of stealing thunder in criminal and civil trials," *Law and Human Behavior*, 17 (6), 597–609.

You, Ya, Gautham G. Vadakkepatt, and Amit M. Joshi (2015), "A Meta-Analysis of Electronic Word-of-Mouth Elasticity," *Journal of Marketing*, 79 (2), 19–39.

Yuan, Chun L., Juran Kim, and Sang J. Kim (2016), "Parasocial relationship effects on customer equity in the social media context," *Journal of Business Research*, 69 (9), 3795–803.

Zhang, Yuchi, Wendy W. Moe, and David A. Schweidel (2017), "Modeling the role of message content and influencers in social media rebroadcasting," *International Journal of Research in Marketing*, 34 (1), 100–19.

Printed in the United States
by Baker & Taylor Publisher Services